OUR GERMAN COUSINS

BOOKS BY JOHN MANDER

Berlin: The Eagle and the Bear. 1959.
The Writer and Commitment. 1961.
Berlin: Hostage for the West. 1962.
Great Britain or Little England? 1963.
Static Society: The Paradox of Latin America. 1969.
Elegiacs. 1972.

TRANSLATIONS

Klaus Roehler: *The Dignity of Night.* 1960.
Carl Zuckmayer: *Carnival Confession.* 1961.
Georg Lukacs: *The Meaning of Contemporary Realism.* 1963.

OUR GERMAN COUSINS

*Anglo-German Relations
in the 19th and 20th Centuries*

John Mander

JOHN MURRAY

Printed in Great Britain by
Butler and Tanner Ltd,
Frome and London

0 7195 2894 1

FOR

MICHAEL HAMBURGER

POET, CRITIC

TRANSLATOR EXTRAORDINARY

GERMAN. adj. of or pertaining to Germany and its inhabitants. 1552 (ad. L. *germanus,* said to be of Celtic origin).

GERMAN, GERMANE. M.E. (O.F. *germain,* ad. L. *germanus.* 'genuine, real')

adj. 1. closely akin. 'Own' (brother or sister). *obs.* exc. in BROTHER-, SISTER-GERMAN.
2. 'First' or 'own' (cousin). *obs.* exc. in COUSIN-GERMAN. M.E.
3. 'Closely related'; 'akin'—1657.
4. 'Closely connected'; 'relevant'—1602.

The phrase would be Germane to the matter: if we could carry Cannon by our sides. (*Hamlet* v.ii.165.)

Oxford English Dictionary

Contents

CONTENTS

Acknowledgements

I would like to thank the following for permission to quote extracts from their publications: Barrie and Jenkins Ltd for Michael Balfour, *The Kaiser and his Times* (Cresset Press); Oxford University Press for David Edwards, *Leaders of the Church of England*; Evans Brothers Ltd for Roger Fulford, *Dearest Mama* and *Your Dear Letter*; Weidenfeld and Nicolson Ltd for John Gross, *The Rise and Fall of the Man of Letters*; Yale University Press for C. F. Harrold, *Carlyle and German Thought*; Hamish Hamilton Ltd for J. Christopher Herold, *Mistress to an Age*; Macmillan and Co. for J. M. Keynes, *Economic Consequences of the Peace* and for Roy Harrod, *Life of J. M. Keynes*; Laurence Pollinger Ltd and the Estate of the late Mrs Freda Lawrence for D. H. Lawrence *A Propos of Lady Chatterley's Lover*; Max Niemeyer Verlag for Walter F. Schirmer, *Deutsche Einflusse auf die englische Literatur im Neunzehnten Jahrhundert*; Chatto and Windus Ltd for Basil Willey, *Nineteenth Century Studies* and *Samuel Taylor Coleridge*; Hector Bolitho for his book *Albert the Good*.

I would also like to thank, formally, the Institute of Contemporary History and Wiener Library and, personally, its director, Professor Walter Laqueur, for the assistance and encouragement I have been so generously given. Lastly, I would like to thank all those, English, American and German, who have helped with suggestions and advice, not least my wife who has borne the heat and burden of the day during the long gestation of this book.

Introduction

Politicians 'declare an interest' when they speak of matters in which they have a personal stake. Should less be required of historians and writers? Let me say, then, that this book is written with an eye as much to a personal as to a public concern: the concern of an individual Anglo-Saxon, and of Anglo-Saxons in general, with the matter of Germany. Why, the reader may ask, this overwhelming concern with Germany, and not, for example, with the United States, the Soviet Union, or the Third World? Certainly, it may be that it is what will happen in these countries—and let us add Japan and China for good measure—that will affect our national and personal destinies during the rest of this century. That an older generation of historians should have been preoccupied with German history and politics—from G. P. Gooch and Sir Lewis Namier to the generation that came to maturity between the wars: A. J. P. Taylor, Hugh Trevor-Roper, Alan Bullock, Veronica Wedgwood, Elizabeth Wiskemann, Gerald Reitlinger, Geoffrey Barraclough, John Wheeler-Bennett, and others no less distinguished—requires little explanation. Their childhood memories were of the Hun and of Flanders' Fields; their formative years saw the transition from the 'good' Germany of Weimar to the 'bad' Germany of Hugenberg, von Papen, and Adolf Hitler. Never has a generation of Anglo-Saxon historians, writers, and journalists been so absorbed, so obsessed with a single concern: but then never was the pull of the *zeitgeist* so importunate.

It is indeed a rich, many-talented galaxy. And we of a younger, post-war generation need to remember that such views of Germany as we hold will derive in large measure from the work of that generation. (We need to remember also, with due humility, that we are unlikely to witness such a constellation again.) But to return to my question: why Germany? Then, in the time of Auden's 'dark, dishonest decade', the question would have answered itself. But now, as I write these introductory words, the question may seem less urgent, even superfluous. It is more than a hundred years since the Princes of the Reich hailed Wilhelm I German Kaiser in the Hall of Mirrors at Versailles. The Reich had at last been united, *kleindeutsch* indeed, but an undoubted Great Power on the European scene. *Herrlichen Zeiten geht Ihr entgegen!* the second Wilhelm was to cry, in the vainglory of Germany's quickly growing strength, a generation later. 'Glorious times lie ahead of you!' Sad words these must have sounded to the generation of Langemarck, Verdun, Versailles, and the Inflation; still more so to the cowed and starving survivors of 1945. Yet, over a quarter of a century later, all may seem tranquil enough. The ruins have been tidied away; the shining new skyscrapers arisen in their place. Neo-Nazism is moribund as a political force—or so it would seem—and a new, less turbulent generation of students appears to have arrived in Germany's once famous universities. *Der König hat eine Bataille verloren—Ruhe ist die erste Bürgerpflicht:* thus were the inhabitants of Berlin admonished after the catastrophe of Jena. Has history repeated itself: 'The King has lost a battle —calm is the first duty of the Burgher'? Ah for that Germany of wine and song, of *Dichter und Denker*, of *Ruhe* and *Gemütlichkeit*! That is the Germany Anglo-Saxons used to love, the Germany of Albert and Victoria and our own great-grandparents. Is it still there? Is it—was it ever—the 'real' Germany? Can we say that past Bonn today—to give a twist to his *Lorelei* the impish Heine would surely have pardoned—*ruhig fliesst der Rhein*?

As I write, I have before me a cutting from an opinion poll which has been busy asking the good burghers of Britain what they think of their continental neighbours. The results are both depressing and instructive: indeed, they constitute perhaps in themselves a justification for attempting a book such as this. If the polls are right, to the average Briton in the seventies Wogs still begin at Calais; and the British people are still overwhelmingly the favourite of the British people (29 per cent). But there are Wogs and Wogs: the Dutch rate well as 'honest, friendly, clean, reliable, and not too interested in sex' (25 per cent). The French and the Italians rate much lower (20 per cent and 16 per cent), as is only right since the British people consider them 'dishonest, dirty, and too interested in sex'. A predictable result, if ever there was one: would the question have evoked a very different response in 1918, in 1871, in 1848, at Trafalgar or Minden, at Oudenarde or Crécy? Yet, ironically, there is something reassuring about such consistency, such perseverance in distaste. For the response is at least *consistent*. We *love* the French for their virtues and certain of their vices: but we do not, and never have, pretended to *like* them. Still, at least we know where we stand with one another (after all, they hold much the same view of us). Who, then, comes lowest on the popularity chart? Need one ask? Of course, the Germans—with 13 per cent—are England's least favourite people on the Continent. 'The traditional view of the Germans,' declares the commentator, 'still remains, with many people thinking them violent, lacking in tolerance, and unfriendly.' (Whether this *is* the 'traditional' English view of the Germans it is the task of this book to discover.) And, the commentator continues, 'surprisingly, the age-group which finds the Germans least friendly is the *18–24 year olds* . . .' (my italics).

One need not be sceptical about opinion polls to guess that this does indeed reflect the view of the man in the street over a quarter of a century after the second German defeat. (Incidentally, I would hazard that the French and Italians would rate a good deal higher among the intelligentsia, whereas the Dutch would rate lower; and the Germans, I fear, would rate a good deal lower still among the intelligentsia—particularly the left-wing intelligentsia—than among the population as a whole.) The only area where the Germans appear to score is that they are held to be 'hard-working'—something which the British people seem to see as a virtue in foreigners, though not overly so in themselves. Yet, are the Germans not, like the popular Dutch, also 'honest, clean and reliable'? On further questioning, I think many of the respondents would have agreed that the Germans are, at least, 'honest' and 'clean'—though not perhaps 'reliable'. But what is striking, surely, is that a generation born *since* the collapse of Nazism—and which indeed can hardly have become aware of Germany and the Germans at all until after Adenauer's departure from office in 1963—should

3

rate the Germans as distinctly 'unfriendly' (not at all how the Germans see themselves, or how our great-grandfathers saw them: that eternal figure of caricature in German newspapers, *der Deutsche Michel*, may be seen as comic; but no German would see him as *unfreundlich*).

No doubt too much should not be made of these results. But on two points they reflect, I believe, an attitude which—whether justified or not—is deeply ingrained in the Anglo-Saxon mind. It is a mistake to suppose that the Anglo-Saxon view of the Germans is going to change—in a favourable direction—by virtue of the healing processes of time: the response of the youngest generation shows that. Equally, it is clear that the 'unpopularity' of the Germans not only runs much deeper, *but is of a different nature*, from the distaste shown for the Latins. That this has often been so is easy to demonstrate historically, as this book will show. Yet what is at the bottom of it? To anticipate the main argument of this study, I shall suggest that the answer is to be found in the one word: 'unpredictability'. Your Frenchman and your Dutchman you may rate as you will; but both are assumed to be *predictable* in their general behaviour, whereas Germans are not—*les incertitudes allemandes*. (Again, this is not how the Germans see themselves: *Deutsche Treue*, 'German loyalty', even if in part an invention of the Romantics, is widely believed in today, and few things disturb the Germans more than to have this imputed attribute put in doubt. But then too few Germans appreciate that the motto of the S.S.—*Mein Ehre heisst Treue*, 'My Honour is my Loyalty'—has given the word a dubious ring in foreign ears.) And in personal relations 'friendliness', after all, rests precisely on a premiss of loyalty and predictability. On both the personal and the political plane, then, the curse the Germans bear is not that they are lazy, or dirty, or dishonest, or too interested in sex or, like *der Deutsche Michel*, at times clumsy and tactless, or boastful and brutal. They bear, in foreign eyes, the more ambiguous curse of unpredictability.

In saying this I have, I think, in effect answered the query: 'Why Germany?' The condition of Belgium, too, might be described as 'unpredictable' in the seventies; so might that of

Italy. Yet, somehow, it is not the same thing. Belgian unpre-dictability can be borne; a federal, Flemish-Walloon state would not spell disaster for Europe. Italy is in the throes of an industrial-social revolution which will strain her social fabric for a generation. But the spectacle of a Communist President receiving the blessing of the Vicar of Christ has ceased to be either comic or catastrophic in its implications. Italy survived Mussolini—and he held power twice as long as Adolf Hitler—remarkably unscathed. It will know how to survive those sheep in sheep's clothing, the Italian Communists, with no less poise and resilience. But Germany? Poise and resilience are not words often associated with her stance in the world. There may be *ruhe* in Bonn at present: but is there a single one of Germany's neighbours who, deep down, is confident that this mood will last?

I am not speaking here of the monstrous brutalities the past generation has witnessed. Those horrors, and the savage retribution that was taken for them, are scarcely likely to be forgotten or forgiven by the year 2000. If Adolf Hitler is remembered a thousand years from now—as he boasted that he and his Reich would be—it will be for these things; and Germans will have to learn to live with this greatest trauma of European history since the coming of the Goths and Vandals. Personally, I do not see that we need fear any recrudescence of Nazism in this generation or the next. But it does not follow that Germany has overcome her instability, her *incertitudes alle-mandes*. She is the most powerful industrial country in Europe—second only in power to the Soviet Union—the second most populous, and the most strategically situated. She is divided and, in military terms, impotent, without nuclear weapons of her own and to all intents and purposes—shades of von Tirpitz!—a landlocked country. Many will applaud this state of affairs: we have Germany where we want her, and long may she remain there, lest she do damage to herself and her neighbours!

But it is only logical that those who take this line should be the first to admit that Germany has her own interests and ambitions, that she is not—in Bismarck's phrase—*saturiert*, not a 'satisfied' country. Those with a strong sense of their own national self-respect—Gaullists, shall we say—ought to be the first to admit that others too have a right to national self-respect. That, of course, was an argument much employed by the pre-war appeasers in Britain and elsewhere. But it is not the less cogent for that. What was wrong with 'appeasement' was bad timing; it remains true that successful appeasement is the essence of diplomacy and high politics. If West Germany is now relatively stable, it is because of the skilful 'appeasement' practised by Truman and Marshall, Bevin and Schuman, and by that more fortunate reincarnation of Gustav Stresemann, Konrad Adenauer. Keynes, one feels, would have approved. His 'Economic Consequences of the Peace', he might perhaps have felt, had not been written in vain.

I have pointed out that the generation of historians, writers, and journalists born between 1890 and 1920 produced the most exhaustive and brilliant examination of German history and politics that has ever been attempted in this country. This book will be taken by some to be 'revisionist' in tone, to represent a different approach—and thus an implicit reproach—to the work of that generation. The reader must decide that for himself. But I think that would be to overdramatise the situation. Born later than most of them—in 1932, so that my earliest memories are of sirens and gasmasks—I would reject few of their assumptions. Yet this book will make one assumption which it strikes me—and may strike others younger than myself still more forcibly—is lacking in many even of the best books produced by the generation of our seniors. This assumption is that, no matter how disastrous the course it ran, it was as natural and inevitable that the Germans should develop a national consciousness (though not Nazism!) as it was that the peoples of Spain, France, and England should have done so; or, for that matter, the peoples of Algeria, Indonesia or Vietnam. Essentially, this is no more than a difference of emphasis, and one dictated by the passage of time. The body of writing I have referred to was written under the shadow of the British

dead of the Kaiser's war and the storm-clouds of its still
terrible sequel (much of it, of course, was only to con
maturity in the post-1945 years). It would be arrogant,
wholly unjustified, to claim that a subsequent generation is
to see more clearly; if we see further at all, it is because we s
on the shoulders of giants.

But too great a preoccupation with Germany can give ri
believe, to a view almost as single-mindedly pan-Germa
much of the Nazis' own propaganda. Luther—Frederi
Bismarck—Hitler: who insisted the more vehemently on
grim historical succession—Vansittart and Taylor, or Goel
and Himmler? An impudent query? Perhaps. But if the p
is harshly made, it is made with a purpose. To see Ger
history in wholly German terms is surely to stray dangero
close to the *Weltanschauung* of those one desires to comba
does not excuse Germany and the Germans if one insists
anti-semitism is found elsewhere, that Fascist and Commu
totalitarianism existed in half a dozen European coun
before Hitler came to power, or to point out that the excesse
nationalism in the Third World since 1945 make it difficult
non-European peoples to argue that this disease is a uniqu
European, or a uniquely German, phenomenon.

No, the Germans stand condemned for what Hitler did,
no German historian or writer of any standing has come
ward since 1945—how different from the years after 1918
who seriously denies the thesis his British contemporaries p
claim: namely, that German nationalism took on a peculia
twisted and self-destructive character in the course of
historical development. But they, too, write under a shado
they too are at times as pan-German in their anti-nationali
as were the Nazis in their crazed, hysterical *Teutschtümelei*. Th
Englishmen and others did not find German patriotism as su
repulsive (though Goethe did) until after 1871—in some ca
until 1914—is something I shall hope to illustrate in this stud
Yet, from the 1890s until the 1950s it is hard to see how a
decent Englishman could have seen German nationalism oth
than as a dangerous and malignant phenomenon. Still, witho

putting any undue faith in the *ruhe* of Bonn politics under Adenauer or Brandt or their successors, I believe it is impossible to deny to the Germans that right to patriotism we do not hesitate to claim for ourselves. This too is a political premiss: that we shall be safer with a healthily patriotic Germany than with a Germany that is forever swinging between the extremes of nationalist arrogance and anti-nationalist self-abasement. It is this premiss that I confess I miss in much of the work of the generation of which I have spoken.

That is why I have decided to begin my investigation with the first intimations of the existence of 'German Romance', as they appeared at the latter end of the 18th century to Coleridge and Wordsworth, Walter Scott, Byron, Shelley, and Carlyle. While there is relatively little question in this early period of 'influence' —an unfruitful variety of literary paper-chasing—there is something for our purposes more germane. Before 1800, it would be broadly true to say that the English had no definite concept of 'the Germans'. If they knew about Germans at all, it was as Prussians or Hanoverians, Rhinelanders or Tyrolese, Hessian or Württemberg mercenaries in His Majesty's service. Even of this Germany they had little real knowledge, as a perusal of Boswell and other contemporary diarists reveals. For Boswell, in 1764, visiting Germany on the very brink of her Golden Age, there was much sport to be had of a kind dear to his heart. He could—if he had heard of him—have met the great Lessing; in fact, he was most anxious to meet the legendary Frederick, but received the customary cool rebuff. For a Dr Johnson he had to scurry south-westward into Switzerland to force his acquaintanceship upon a reluctant Rousseau and a still more reluctant Voltaire.

Until about 1800, then, the English were largely unaware that the Germans had a *Kultur* at all: indeed the Germans were mostly unaware of it themselves. Viennese music, of course, was to be heard in the grander London drawing-rooms; and Handel was of course a national hero. But none of this was seen as belonging to a specifically German *Kultur*. It was only with Coleridge and his followers, and somewhat later with the

great figures of Carlyle, of Thomas and Matthew Arnold, of
G. H. Lewes and George Eliot, that *Deutsche Kultur* can be said
to have come into its own. Thackeray might laugh at it; and
even Coleridge was not above poking fun at inebriated German
Professors. But Germany had arrived. By 1827, according to the
O.E.D., the German student term of contempt, *philister*, had
entered the English language as 'philistine'—a usage that was
to be employed with devastating effect by the younger Arnold
in 'Culture and Anarchy'. From now on, then, it makes sense
to speak of 'influence'. The influence of Coleridge and Carlyle is
easily discernible in eminent Victorians of the stamp of
Frederick Denison Maurice, John Ruskin and, later, William
Morris and Walter Pater (and from Morris, incidentally, there
is a feed-back to the Vienna *Sezession* and Walter Gropius'
Bauhaus). Looking back across the abyss of hatred and contempt
of the past century—it was in early 1871 that Queen Victoria
wrote to her daughter, Crown Princess Victoria of Prussia,
that whereas the British people were formerly 'very German',
now they were 'very French'—we can distinguish an earlier
period when Germany was seen in a more tolerant light. Too
rosy a light, perhaps? Maybe. But as a challenge to so much
that has been said and written since perhaps a useful corrective.

The 19th-century Englishman's favourite German was Goethe,
and it is clear that Goethe was admired not only as his countrymen's greatest *Dichter*, but also as the embodiment of his
countrymen's virtues. Here, once again, there is a certain
discrepancy between the Anglo-Saxon and the German view.
Whereas the Anglo-Saxon valuation of Goethe has stood to this
day (so that for most laymen, and many professionals, Goethe *is*
German literature, rather as Shakespeare to most Germans *is*
English literature), to the Germans themselves there has always
been something disturbing, *unheimlich*, about the Master.
Schiller, who has never really entered the English canon, was
always the preferred *Charakter*: upright, high-minded, intro-
verted, chaste, intellectual, idealistic. Goethe, by contrast, was
unashamedly snobbish, promiscuous, extrovert, cynical, pagan
—in short, a permanent but unavoidable embarrassment to

9

that archetypal figure of German society, the German school-master. But if the English tended to admire a Goethe of their own creation, and largely ignored Schiller, there were a great many German writers of the Golden Age—roughly 1750 to 1850—who remained unknown to the eminent Victorians, and indeed still remain to be discovered today. Walter Scott translated Bürger's *Leonore*; Kotzebue—of all playwrights!—was a huge, though brief success on the London stage; and Schubert, Schumann and Hugo Wolf and other *Lieder*-composers put much of the best of the lyric poetry of the epoch to music. Heine, too, was well known; but for his early 'romantic' poems like the *Lorelei*, not for the witty perceptiveness of his prose-writings or for the greater, later poetry he was to write on his Parisian death-bed (*Aus der Matratzengruft*).

How much does this matter? I should say—at least in the context of this study—that it matters a good deal. True, the Germans also neglected many of those we now see as major figures of the period: Hölderlin, Heinrich von Kleist, Georg Büchner. The upshot was to give an image of the Golden Age that was too saccharine, too sentimental, too *gemütlich*. As Anglo-Saxons we can hardly be blamed for failing to see what most Germans failed to see, or perhaps did not wish to see. Still, deception or self-deception, the saccharine image of Germany accepted abroad throughout most of the 19th century made the reaction that has followed in our own century the more bitter. Of course, it is not possible to read the literature of the Golden Age today—not to speak of Schopenhauer, Wagner or Nietzsche—without seeing in it the seeds of much that was to come. This is not literary Vansittartism-with-hindsight: it is the only perspective open to us. But it belongs to our story because that story is so often one of misunderstanding and mis-interpretation, rather than of wilful ignorance or malign distortion.

A study such as this cannot but be selective. There are very many excellent historical studies in English dealing with the past century and a half—literature, alas, is less well served—and for the period 1900–45 it is a case of *embarras de richesse*. We know perhaps more about this second Thirty Years' War of

European history than we do about any comparable period. And there will be more to come, as the archives are quarried and yet more detail brought to light. I shall not attempt to retell that tale in this study. The reader will be better served in this case, I believe, by a more oblique approach, deliberately blending the political with the literary and biographical.

What more illustrative of the 'personal' difficulties between Germans and Anglo-Saxons (again so often based on misunderstanding) than the tragic contrast, spread over three generations, between 'Albert the Good'—so typical a product of liberal 'Young Germany' in the 1830s—his grandson, the mock-Prussian Kaiser, whom Northcliffe's jackals urged the Allies to hang during the Coupon Election of 1918, and the well-and-truly anglicised John Bull figure of Royal Teddy, his admired and envied uncle? Queen Victoria's affection for 'our dear little Germany' is well known. But one can trace the souring of that family affection in the letters of her daughter, Vicky, Crown Princess of Prussia and Consort to the ill-fated, excellent Frederick who—many have thought—might have steered Germany on to a different course from that pursued by his lamentable son, of whom Bismarck said unkindly that he 'combined all the vices of his ancestors with none of their virtues'. In studying the relations between those three generations we run the whole gamut of the souring of Anglo-German relations between mid-Victorian times and the disagreeable postures of the Age of Imperialism.

For my final section, I have chosen a symbolic central figure who may appear at first sight (having little personal interest in Germany, despite his famous and sympathetic sketch of Dr Melchior) to fit awkwardly into this scheme. Yet not only will the figure of John Maynard Keynes—or so I believe—loom larger to those who grow up in the last third of this century than almost any other intellectual-political figure of the first half of the century, the very fact that for Keynes and the Bloomsbury circle (except Forster*) German *Kultur* was not

* E. M. Forster was for a time tutor in the household of Countess von Arnim, the ironic author of 'Elizabeth and her German Garden'.

merely neglected, but likely to appear actively abhorrent, has an unspoken significance. Nietzsche had prophesied of Bismarck's Reich after 1871: *die Macht verdummt*, 'power stupefies' (a neat variation on Acton's 'power corrupts'). *Deutsche Kultur* faded rapidly in the period between the rise of the second Reich (though less so in music than in literature) and the revival of the early years of this century: Rilke, Hofmannsthal, the Mann brothers, the Secessionists, the Expressionists, the *Bauhaus*. But by the turn of the century, when Keynes and Strachey and Leonard Woolf were undergraduates at Cambridge, the world had lost interest in what might be coming out of Germany. For Bloomsbury it was French culture and the newly-discovered glories of Russian literature, music, and ballet that mattered. And Keynes, we know, fully shared their tastes.

Yet the book of Keynes that will surely come to seem most *politically* significant—'The Economic Consequences of the Peace'—is quite unsentimentally, yet centrally concerned with Germany: its message is 'without Germany, no Europe; without Europe, no Civilisation'. And we know that it was with the preservation of European Civilisation, as Clive Bell and his Bloomsbury friends saw it, that he was chiefly concerned, not only in that epoch-making pamphlet, but in all his work up to the final period when he assisted in Washington at the birth of the World Bank and the International Monetary Fund. As he wrote of pre-1914 Cambridge in retrospect:

> We repudiated all versions of the doctrine of original sin, of there being insane and irrational springs of wickedness in most men. We were not aware that Civilisation is a thin and precarious crust, erected by the will and personality of a very few, and only maintained by rules and conventions skilfully put across and guilefully preserved.

Keynes died, too early, in 1946. But if we agree that Civilisation is 'only maintained by rules and conventions', who can deny that he was indeed a 'guileful' and 'skilful' preserver of it? Can we doubt, for instance, that the Marshall Plan must be counted among his numerous intellectual brain-children, or that the policies pursued by the Allies after 1945 did *not*—in great part, surely, thanks to his warning ghost?—repeat the follies of 1919, and did indeed maintain Civilisation at what seemed to many the beginning of a new Dark Age?

'Without Germany, no Europe; without Europe, no Civilisation': that could be the motto of this book too. A century ago no one would have doubted the truth of this axiom. There are many today who doubt it all too readily. A younger generation might be inclined to question, not only whether a nation that could throw up an Adolf Hitler, but also whether a Europe which colonised and exploited three-quarters of mankind, has much right to claim to represent 'Civilisation'. Let me then declare my colours, since they too form a premiss of this study. I would claim to be 'a good European'—a European chauvinist, if you will—both in the sense of Nietzsche's *guter Europäer* and in that political sense which is implicit in Keynes' pamphlet, and has become explicit since the war in the preaching and practice of Jean Monnet and his collaborators. That there is something Faustian, not about *Deutsche Kultur* alone, but also about the whole story of European civilisation from the time of Nietzsche's beloved pre-Socratics to the tumults of our own day is not to be denied. Europe has destroyed much that was valuable in the cultures of other continents—do we need to think further than Cortez and Clive?—and in the first half of this century came close to destroying what is most valuable in its own. It has indeed been a century ripe for prophets of *Kulturpessimismus* of the stripe of Oswald Spengler and Arnold Toynbee.

Yet, over a quarter of a century after the holocaust, Europe has risen from her ashes economically stronger, and as inventive and as creative as ever. Whether or not she achieves political unity—and I am among those who look forward to that day—she is collectively stronger and more populous than either of her protector-rivals, the United States and the Soviet Union. And—stranger still—the repudiation of European values that apparently underlay the decolonisation of the Third World over the past two decades has been accompanied by a more rapid adaptation to European values on their part than at any earlier period. De-colonisation has not, after all, meant de-Europeanisation—not even in China or the Arab world—but, on the contrary, has aroused a ferocious desire to emulate a civilisation that is condemned alike, in their official ideology, by Communists and Nationalists. It is for this reason that the new-found *Kulturpessimismus* of the 'New Left' seems to me profoundly mistaken. The New Left claims to speak for the oppressed and silent millions of the Third World. But the facts, surely, speak louder: they give the lie to this new *Kulturpessimismus*. Imitation is said to be the sincerest form of flattery.

Yet clearly there can be no European civilisation without a sound political foundation, without a return to that *Staatensystem* which Ranke praised, and which Bismarck inherited and sought to maintain in the face of the potential Frankenstein he had himself created. That *Staatensystem* need not be idealised: all too frequently it broke down and brought destruction and misery to Europe—though never, since the Thirty Years' War, on the scale of the European civil wars of this century. But it offered a working arrangement, one which allowed steady progress in the arts and sciences and, if it did not bring in the millennium, took what the past had to offer it, intermittently with wisdom and occasionally with genius. Nation could speak unto nation; but nations were not required to love other nations as themselves. The business of civilisation was maintained only with 'skill' and with 'guile'; but it was maintained.

So it will be, I believe, in the Europe of the last third of the 20th century. Whether or not Europe achieves her unity, she must achieve harmony, and develop immunity to those twin cancers, which grew out of her own body politic over half a century ago, Fascism and totalitarian Communism. Great Britain and the two leading states of the old Reich—Prussia and Austria—belonged to Ranke's *Staatensystem*. But whereas Englishmen knew much of the character of the Dutch, the French, the Italians, the Spanish, the Portuguese, the character of the Germans remained largely hidden—hidden hardly less, as I say, from the Germans themselves—until the German Renaissance of the late 18th century and the political emergence of Bismarck's Reich a century later. I shall try in this book to examine the emergence of that character through English eyes, and to examine what lessons there may be for the future in this strange, ambivalent tale of mutual misunderstanding. The Germans are not required to love us; nor we to love them. But we are required to understand, if we are to survive; to fulfil Forster's categorical imperative—another suitable motto for this book—that he made the motto of his own very English, yet obliquely Anglo-German investigation, 'Howards End', with its Margaret-*Gretchen*, its Helen-*Helena*, and its ironically portrayed English Faust, Henry-*Heinrich*: 'Only connect . . .'

SECTION I

The Discoverers

CHAPTER ONE

In the Beginning: 1750-1815

Beginnings are arbitrary; and the date I have chosen—*c.* 1750 —as much so as any other. It is not quite true that the Germans and their *Kultur* were unknown to the English before that date, but it is as true as to make no difference. Individual Germans were known to individual Britons—Martin Luther, for example, or his disciple Martin Bucer, who came over at Henry VIII's invitation and assisted Cranmer with the Book of Common Prayer. And there were many Grand Tourists, like Sir Henry Wootton in the early 17th century, who found much to interest them in the Germany of the time. But these were individuals; and they were rare birds. Later, the German influx was to increase. Many Hanoverians had left their country in the wake of their Elector George, on his elevation to the Crown of Great Britain. (A Pomeranian, a certain Karl Friedrich Necker, whose descendant, Madame de Staël, we shall meet later, was endowed by Parliament with two hundred pounds per annum to set up an English school in Geneva.) But there is no question that educated Germans knew more of England and her ways at that period than vice-versa. As the 'German Renaissance' progressed it was to English masters that the Germans turned, to Milton and Richardson, Sterne and Young and, above all, to Shakespeare. Voltaire and Rousseau and the Encyclopedists were, of course, well known and highly influential in 18th-century Germany. There was no greater disciple of the En-lightenment in Europe than Immanuel Kant; no more famous zealots of Rousseau than Herder and the Goethe of *Werther*. But it was the introduction of English literature, fostered by Klopstock and Wieland, Lessing and Goethe, that broke the stranglehold (for so it came to be seen) of French classicism on the infant struggling to be born. It was English literature that stood godfather to the German literary revival.

Yet it was largely a one-way traffic. Not until the end of the period of 'Discovery' do we begin to see—in the age of Coleridge and Carlyle—something of a reverse traffic. Not until Victoria's reign, then, at a point when the Renaissance in literature, historiography, music, and philosophy in Germany was effectively over, do we find German *Kultur* firmly established on English soil: the property, for the first time in our mutual history, of the well-educated Englishman—and, still more, of the Scot. One observation we may risk even at this stage, for it is a recurring factor: the evolution of German intellectual life— *Deutscher Geist*—was seriously out of phase with English appreciation of it, with the result that the picture remained always a little cloudy, and at times very seriously distorted. There is no shirking, here, the vexing problem of translation. The 18th-century English gentleman was able (theoretically) to read his Homer, his Virgil, his Voltaire in the original: but few could speak or read German. All, therefore, depended upon the quantity and quality of translation. And it can be said without fear of contradiction that the chief difference between the first phase—1750–1815—and the period that followed the publication of Madame de Staël's *De l'Allemagne* (1813) is that the quality of translation in the early period varied from poor to catastrophic, whereas, with the advent of Carlyle and others, there was a marked improvement. Victoria could depend on most of her educated subjects knowing a good deal (though not necessarily the best) of German literature in reasonable translation; George III could not.

It was not, then, that the books were wholly unavailable; but rather that the selection was unfortunate, and even where happy, all might be spoiled by the quality of the translation. To the vagaries of English taste in the matter of selection we shall return: they shed much light on what the English wanted to know, as well as on the varying tastes of the publishers and translators involved. At the risk of boring the reader, here is a list of what was actually translated in the thirty years after 1750:

| 1752 | Gellert: | 'Swedish Countess' |
| 1757 | Rabener: | 'Satirical Letters' |

1761	Gessner:	'Death of Abel'
1762		'Select Poems from Mr Gessner's Pastorals'
		'Rural Poems from Mr Gessner's Pastorals'
1763	Gessner:	'Death of Abel' (a new translation)
	Klopstock:	'Messiah'
	Klopstock:	'Death of Adam'
1764	Gessner:	'Death of Abel' (a new translation)
	Schönaich:	'Arminius'
	Wieland:	'Trial of Abraham'
1766	Möser:	'Harlequin' or 'A Defense of the Grotesque'
1767	Bodmer:	'Noah'
1771	Klopstock:	'Messiah' (a new translation)
	Wieland:	'Dialogue of Diogenes of Sinope'
	Zimmermann:	'Essay on National Pride'
1772	Haller:	'Usong'
1773	Lessing:	'Fables'
	Wieland:	'Reason Triumphant Over Fancy'
	Wieland:	'Agathon'
1775	Wieland:	'Two Dialogues'
1776	Gessner:	'New Idylls'
	Gellert:	'Swedish Countess'
	Gellert:	'Swedish Countess' (a new translation)
	Sophie de la Roche:	'Lady Sophie Sternheim'
	Sophie de la Roche:	'Lady Sophie Sternheim' (a new translation)
1779	Goethe:	'Werther' (from the French)

With Goethe's *Werther* we reach, of course, the first landmark likely to be familiar to the layman, and it is noteworthy that it appeared in England in Goethe's thirtieth year. It comes, therefore, as something of a shock to discover that of the major works produced by Goethe up to his fifty-first year (1800) only the following had appeared in English translation:

1786: 'Werther and Charlotte' (a new translation)

1789: 'Werther' (a new translation)
1793: 'Iphigenia' (by William Taylor)
1798: 'Clavigo and Stella'
1799: 'Goetz' (by Walter Scott)
'Goetz' (by Rose Lawrence)
'Letters of Werther' (a new translation)

The pattern is plain: *Werther* remained the reading public's favourite, and it would hear of nothing else. It was translated afresh, twice in 1801, and again in 1802 and 1807. Eight *Werthers*! And the industry was evidently still busy putting them out at a time when Goethe had long since moved into his 'classical' phase, and was wishing that he had never put pen to paper—though Napoleon might have the book lying beside his camp-bed—only to be known to all Europe solely as 'The author of *Werther*.'

The balance was corrected in part by the appearance of 'Hermann and Dorothea', that delightful epic in praise of the peasant, pastoral virtues, in 1801, and again in 1805. But 'Hermann and Dorothea' was neither well received nor well understood. *The British Critic*, as was its custom, attacked Goethe as 'a supporter of revolutionary principles', and 'an enemy of all social order' (the exact opposite of Goethe's intention, who had written *Hermann und Dorothea* in 1797 largely out of disgust at the excesses of the French revolution). *The Monthly*'s judgment must seem to us still more peculiar, since if *Hermann und Dorothea* has a fault—to English ears—it is that it is perhaps somewhat too placid and low-keyed:

This performance is purely and characteristically German, and cannot possibly be admired by those who have not a true German taste . . . It deserves however to be commemorated as a very remarkable instance of perverted taste both in nations and in individuals since the poem is much read in Germany (1802).

But how much that is precious of those fifty years of Goethe's life never came to light! There was, certainly, Shelley's partial rendering of *Faust* in 1815; and the translation of *Iphigenia* (a 'classical' work) by William Taylor of Norwich, the most indefatigable propagandist of German literature before Carlyle, must be reckoned a very reasonable translation. On the other hand, we have little idea how far it was noticed by the intelligentsia or the reading public; it was certainly not performed. Still, on the principle that publishers do not publish what they do not think will sell (and vice-versa), it seems likely that the very early Goethe *did* sell—*Werther* and *Goetz*—and that interest in Goethe never got much beyond this juvenile phase (as he would have seen it by 1800) until the post-1815 period. This was the Goethe the public wanted; and this was the Goethe that it got.

That this is so is supported by the spate of Schiller translations, starting in 1792 with 'The Robbers' (the *Sturm und Drang* play *par excellence*), followed by two further 'Robbers' in 1799, and another in 1801. True, Coleridge had tried his hand at 'Wallenstein' in 1800; and 'Cabal and Love' and 'Don Carlos' had appeared in 1795, and *Maria Stuart* in 1801 (none of these, it appears, was performed on the London stage). Most of the translations were very poor. But at least it could be said that some of his major works, including his historical studies 'A History of the Thirty Years' War' (1799), and 'The Rise and Progress of the Belgian Republic' (1807: for 'Belgian' read 'Dutch') were obtainable in English, unlike the majority of Goethe's works. Nevertheless, there is good reason to suppose that Schiller continued to be seen as another *Sturm und Drang* writer throughout the period and not, as he came to be seen in Germany, as a 'classical' writer in the Weimar mould.

As the *Edinburgh Review* was to put it in 1816, on the eve of a more fruitful period:

The astonishing rapidity of the development of German literature has been the principal cause both of its imperfections and of the enthusiasms of its warmer admirers. About five and twenty or thirty years ago, all we knew about Germany was that it was a vast tract of country, overrun with Hussars and Classical Editors; and that if you went there, you would see a great tun at Heidelbergh; and be regaled with excellent old hock and Westphalian hams; the taste for which good things was so predominant as to preclude the slightest approach to any poetical grace or enthusiasm. At that time, we had never seen a German name affixed to any other species of writing than a Treaty, by which some Serene Highness or other had sold us so many head of soldiers for American consumption, at a fair and reasonable market price; or to a formidable apparatus of critical annotation, teeming with word-catching or billingsgate in Greek or Latin.

As can be seen, when the English first began to taste German *Geist*, the public went for figures who would now be considered very minor (though one should remember that in Germany the real impact of Lessing, Klopstock, and Goethe did not come until the sixties and seventies). But it does appear that *two distinct sorts* of German writing appealed to the English: works of religious piety, and the gentle, pastoral work of the pre-*Sturm und Drang* writers—or their opposite, the violent, often incoherent emotionalism of the *Sturm und Drang*, and later, of the Romantics. One is almost tempted to see in this division of taste the origins of that familiar dichotomy between the 'good' and the 'bad' Germany which was to become so popular a hundred and fifty years later. This division would certainly not provide an accurate guide to the real course of development of the German Renaissance, which was a rather more complex affair. But it does suggest an embryonic English reaction to things German which was to have important effects in years to come.

There was, then, an ambiguity in the English response. Why, for instance, did the English take to Wieland, an author much read in his time in Germany, but now strictly relegated to the teaching syllabus?

That Wieland was in so many ways not a typical German was probably one of the chief reasons for his popularity in England. He imitated English writers, especially Sterne, and was also much influenced by contemporary French philosophy. He soon became popular in France and this also facilitated his introduction to English readers. The ease and lightness of his style obviated the prejudice against the heaviness and dullness of German works (V. Stockley 'German Literature in England 1750–1830', Routledge 1929).

What of a fine if—compared to Lessing—minor writer of the period: what *did* the English see in Gellert? Miss Stockley (to whom I am much indebted for this and other information) comments on a review in *The British Critic* (1805):

> Typical of the first period is a review of Gellert's 'Moral Lessons'. Gellert is compared to Cowper, and Mrs. Douglas congratulated for bringing to public notice 'the life and writings of so truly amiable and Christian an author'—but warns readers not to expect anything very original, new or profound in Gellert's lessons.

The Annual Review was less inclined to be charitable: in the English view even piety can be overdone, and preachifying is still less favoured:

> They will find, however, purity and tenderness of sentiment and chaste and elevated piety. It was wise to select the devotional writings of Gellert, for provided books abound with pious aspirations and conscientious apprehensions, the religious public care little how feeble the eloquence or how trivial the truisms.

Here, then, we begin to see something of the nature of the English ambivalence. We have seen that Klopstock—fine poet though he is, not quite the 'German Milton' he was proclaimed at this period—was one of the earliest and most translated of poets (he appears to have been often confused with his much inferior contemporary Gessner, whose 'Death of Abel' was sometimes attributed to him). What was the appeal of Klopstock to the English? The phrase 'the German Milton' was certainly an invitation. But there was more to it than that. In a curious pamphlet, published in 1776, 'Thoughts Upon Some Late Poems, particularly the Death of Abel and the Messiah', we find the (presumably clerical?) writer recommending these two books to young ladies as the 'best reading after the Bible and the Book of Common Prayer', indeed as an almost infallible means of Salvation:

> Whoever is acquainted with these pieces early in life and acquaints herself with them thoroughly, and reads them over at least once a year; and is never tired of them, but still resumes them, and still reads them again, till she is perfect mistress of each of these pieces, and has a full comprehension of them so that she can readily call to mind, or lead into discourse any material circumstance in them—such a young person will be timely instructed in true piety and virtue; will scarce ever be at a loss for any point of conduct, great or small; will have a competent store of real knowledge; and will find herself gradually enabled to write and to discourse, to live and die as a Christian.

It is an interesting sidelight on the period that the author takes both pieces to be really English originals, though given to two German masters with hard names:

> It is probable that the names are only mentioned as a trial of the taste of the times, and for a stroke of raillery on that nation which was never eminent for epic poetry.

Whereas *The Critical* (1776) remarks sourly that it is surely but a

> puff to recommend the heavy dung-carts of German poetry which are daily perfuming the Metropolis.

Once again, it must be said that the translation was miserable; but the comment certainly suggests that public interest in German writings was increasing. Again, it goes to show that the Germans were a people credited with both a strong national morality, and with a degree of immoral outspokenness, or even blasphemy, which horrified (or perhaps titillated) those who were to flock to the plays of Kotzebue and Iffland in the nineties. We should also remember that these were the years when, in the 'Messiah' and so many other works, Germany gave Britain her greatest composer, a composer very much in the Miltonic tradition, identifying his adopted country with the Chosen People. (It was also in these years that John Wesley underwent conversion on a voyage to America at the hands of some German Moravian brethren; and he and his brother Charles were already busy translating some of the most famous Lutheran hymns, now seldom thought of as German, into English.) For many, Germany must have seemed the fount of true Protestantism and Piety. As to the translation of Klopstock's 'Messiah', it was indeed excruciatingly bad, as this rendering of its opening couplet makes clear:

Sing, unsterbliche Seele, der sündigen Menschen Erlösung
Die der Messias auf Erden in Seiner Menschheit vollendet

is rendered by the translator as

Inspired by thyne immortality, rise, O my soul, and sing the honours of thy Great Redeemer: honours obtained in hard adversity's rough school—obtained by suffering for the sins of others himself sinless.

These lines were not calculated to encourage the English reader to proceed, however great the degree of his piety. Not surprisingly, when Coleridge and Wordsworth on their visit to Germany in 1798 went to visit the old man near Hamburg, Klopstock

spoke with great indignation of the English prose translation of his 'Messiah'. All the translations have been bad, very bad —but the English was *no* translation—there were pages and pages not in the original and half the original was not to be found in the translation. Wordsworth told him that I intended to translate a few of his Odes as specimens of German lyrics— he then said to me in English, 'I wish you would render into English some select passages of the "Messiah" and *revenge* me of your countrymen'. It was the liveliest thing he produced in the whole conversation. (Coleridge, 'Letters'.)

Already, at this date, we seem to find a fatal compound of ignorance and ambivalence bedevilling Anglo-German relations. German piety might be ridiculed at one moment; German 'immorality' the next. Even *Werther* was a doubtful case. Was this a 'suitable book to put into the hands of a young person': might not Werther's suicidal escape from his troubles set off an imitative wave? (This charge was actually made.) The famous concluding line, *Kein Geistlicher begleitete ihn* ('No Pastor accompanied him on his way'): was not that near-atheistical? Even *Hermann und Dorothea*, surely the most moral and least impious of Goethe's works, might be regarded with suspicion. Yet it is possible to detect another strain. The 'sentimental and moral' tale 'from the German' had certainly won an English audience, though probably not a very numerous one. Few of these works are of literary merit, and most are forgotten today in their country of origin.

But there was a market, and it was an appreciative one, which allowed a view of the Germans—in itself perhaps a little sentimental, and frequently to be echoed in the following century—that was favourable in the extreme. An early example of such a 'German Tale' is *Henrietta von Gerstenfelt*, 'A German Story' (1789). And from a remark in the *Critical* we see why publishers and authors found it expedient from time to time to attach the label 'A German Tale' to certain works. The most famous example is perhaps 'Monk' Lewis's 'The Bravo', which the *Critical* hailed as a 'Germanico-terrifico-Romance' (it appears that a large part of 'The Bravo', which was to enjoy a great success on the London stage, was in reality Lewis's own work). Of this latter-day Ossian, who had written 'Tales of Wonder' in 1801—some from Scott, some borrowed freely from all possible sources—a contemporary wag wrote:

> The Monk has published 'Tales of Wonder';
> The public calls them 'Tales of Plunder'.

Nevertheless the *Critical* had commented on Lewis's earlier effort:

> Is it in consequence of our common ancestry that we feel a congenial warmth for everything of German origin? Or do we approve of their writings because of the strong sound good sense which is observed on every page?

That this argument from 'our common ancestry' had an appeal can be seen in the reaction to Scott's 'Goetz' (Goethe's *Goetz von*

Berlichingen mit der eisernen Hand, 1773). Even though, as usual, the translation may be faulted, the general feeling of the play comes through well enough in Scott's translation, so that it is not surprising that the *Critical* can write (1799):

> The author has not only imitated Shakespeare's irregularity and medley of character, but also shows the same distinguishing and powerful genius. No Englishman capable of understanding dramatic excellence can peruse it without delight.

The key, then, to the first period of enthusiasm for the 'New German Drama' is evident enough. The English were hearing Shakespeare played back to them, as it were, through the medium of another language. And bearing in mind the melodramatic style in which Shakespeare was performed in England in that period, it is not surprising that there should have grown up a sudden, if short-lived, passion for the 'Germanico-terrific', stimulated by ballads such as Bürger's *Leonore* (no less than six translations, one by Walter Scott himself), and plays such as Schiller's 'Robbers' (said to have been commended by Pitt), as well as Goethe's *Werther* and *Goetz*. It was also, of course, the age of the Gothic Novel, which undoubtedly received impetus from the writers of the German *Sturm und Drang*, an impetus which lasted until Mary Shelley's 'Frankenstein' well into the 19th century. What was unfortunate for the future appreciation of the German Renaissance was that the playwright who took London by storm in the 1790s should have been a man whose works were really a parody of the worst tendencies of the period: Kotzebue.

The culprit, it appears, was no less a man than the eminent Sheridan. Sheridan adapted an English translation of Kotzebue's *Menschenhass und Reue* ('Hatred and Remorse') in the early nineties. The play was an immediate success, and soon outdid even Shakespeare's plays in popularity. Covent Garden produced in the same season 'Lover's Vows', which enjoyed forty-two performances and, in the following year, no less than four of Kotzebue's comedies. (Jane Austen was evidently parodying 'Lover's Vows' as 'Lovers' Vows' in 'Mansfield Park', much as she had parodied 'The Mysteries of Udolpho' in 'Northanger Abbey'.) The extraordinary success of Sheridan's 'Pizarro' (1799), adapted from a translation by Geisweiler into French of Kotzebue's *Die Spanier in Peru*, is also recorded. It went through as many as twenty editions in one year, and drew crowded houses for no less than sixty-seven nights at Drury Lane. (There was a presentation as far off as Athlone in Ireland in 1837 in which the play was praised as 'Shakespeare's celebrated play of Pizarro'!) It was much the same with the novels. 'The Constant Lover', or 'William and Jeanette' (1799), was enthusiastically reviewed in the *Critical*:

> Such are the talents of this wonderful author that we can scarcely wish him to correct more lest he should write less.

But the frenzy of this reaction to the English version of the *Sturm und Drang* was not to last. It found a formidable enemy in Canning's *Anti-Jacobin*. Indeed, Herford comments in his 'Age of Wordsworth' that the *Anti-Jacobin* parody 'The Rovers', in 1798, killed German drama in England for many years. It certainly appears to have pre-empted a stage performance, much to his chagrin, for Walter Scott's beloved *Goetz*. And soon the tide of critical comment was to set firmly against what a few years earlier had been so indiscriminately praised. By 1806 the *Critical*, reviewing Kotzebue's 'Travels in Italy', is already referring to 'the pompous trifles of this strutting sentimentalist'. It would appear, then, that the attempted transplant of the new German literature withered at the first sign of Anglo-Saxon ridicule. No doubt it was all most unfair. But we must remember that Goethe and Schiller would not have disagreed. They themselves delightedly parodied what the *Anti-Jacobin* had in mind to parody. Another Conservative periodical, *The Meteor*, also published a skit on 'The Robbers', advertised as:

> 'The Benevolent Cut-Throat', trans. from an original German drama written by the celebrated Klotzboggenhagen, by Fabius Pictor.

In the *Gentleman's Magazine* there occurs an 'Ode on the Prevalence of German Drama' (1800):

Say from what cause proceeds the modern rage
Of German dramas on the English stage?
Must British tears for ever cease to flow
Save through the fount which streams from German woe?
And laughter lose its empire o'er the pit
Except when forced from heavy German wit?

And the writer goes on to ask how Sheridan can 'banish Avon's Bard for Kotzebue'. Even as late as 1811 a burlesque on German drama was given at the Haymarket with great success. Its title runs: 'The Quadrupeds of Quedlinburgh or The Rovers of Weimar. Tragico-comico-anglo-germanico-hippo-ono-Romance.'

Clearly, the first attempt to introduce the new German literature to the English had floundered in ridicule. Whether a better understanding of the German Renaissance, or better translations, would have helped to remedy the situation, it is difficult to decide. Certainly, there was a political misunderstanding, in that the anti-revolutionary English took the new literature to be of a revolutionary nature (which it had possessed, perhaps, twenty years earlier). It is evident with the benefit of hindsight that the reverse was the truth. Goethe and Schiller had become resolute anti-revolutionaries; and the generation we call the Romantics, emerging around 1800, was if anything still further to the Right. (Indeed, historians of Nazism have not found it difficult to discover embryonic traces of it in the work of Kleist, Novalis, the Schlegels, and other writers of the anti-revolutionary, patriotic Romantic Age that came to dominate Germany's literature and philosophy after the turn of the century.) It is relevant that after 1815, during the second 'period' of discovery, the Germans were seen by the English as natural Allies and the French as potential political enemies; this factor must in part account for the readier understanding of German philosophy and literature characteristic of the later period. It is therefore of some interest to hear the views of a contemporary Englishman, who was then living in Weimar, had known Goethe, Wieland, Schiller and others, and was also an intimate friend of the group around

Coleridge and Wordsworth, Lamb, Leigh Hunt, and De Quincey. In the *Monthly Register* in 1801, Henry Crabb Robinson gave his opinion freely:

> I have for the present but one observation; you know nothing of German literature. Kotzebue's and Iffland's plays are not German literature. Though popular German works, they are not considered classical here.

Of this first period, then, the most one can say is that it had stimulated the English appetite, that it had produced some good translations in William Taylor's version of Lessing's 'Nathan the Wise' and Goethe's 'Iphigenia', Richardson's translation of Lessing's 'Fables', Scott's 'Goetz', and Coleridge's 'Wallenstein'. But one would have to add that these attracted little attention among literary men, were never performed, and that nothing of what was truly original in the philosophy of the period—Kant, Fichte, Schleiermacher or Schelling—achieved translation into English (except, at second remove, through the work of Coleridge). Perhaps it is unfair to conclude that the first voyage of exploration implanted little more in the English mind than that there might be something more to Germany besides beer, brass-bands, and plump, blond maidens. But let the last word on the period rest with a German traveller, Herr C. A. G. Goede (1802):

> It is a fact indeed that Kotzebue's plays having been well received, herds of wretched translators introduced a heap of ridiculous German novels to the attention of the public. A few good works followed; but they were so dreadfully mutilated that the rage died away. . . . Many English consider German literature immoral and dangerous. But they have formed this hasty opinion on some trifling German novels which too easily find their way from circulating libraries to the toilet of beauty . . . Pitt's admiration of 'The Robbers' gave it celebrity, but *Werther* is the only work really popular. . . . The English are thus strangely perplexed in forming an adequate conception of Germany.

CHAPTER TWO

Kultur-Walküre

The Karl Friedrich Necker whom we have already met as a
protégé of the King-Elector, George I, was to leave behind a
remarkable progeny. The man whose forefathers had lived for
generations as Lutheran pastors on the meagre soil of Prussian
Pomerania was to find fortune in Geneva; elected Professor—
and thus admitted to the closed circle of 'Burghers of Geneva'—
he was soon to be writing his name Charles Frédéric Necker.
Of his two sons, both became millionaires; and one the effective
ruler of France in the twilight years preceding the revolution.
Indeed, Necker is often apostrophised as the man who might
have 'saved France from revolution'—which, had Genevese
virtue alone sufficed, he might just possibly have done. This is
not the place to dispute the subject: it is enough to say that
there is powerful evidence to show that his financial talents were
not matched by equal talents in the political sphere. Why
should so many Frenchmen have seen in this taciturn, high-
minded, severe Genevese the possible saviour of France?
Un-French? Certainly, to our received notions of what a
Frenchman should be. But this is to forget that in the declining
years of the 18th century the French—and especially the Third
Estate—looked back on the frivolities of the Age of Watteau
and Fragonard, to Clive Bell so seductive, with something
approaching contempt. Henceforth, France should emulate the
stern virtues of the Republic of Rome—or of Geneva. In this
new scheme of things there was a place for a Jacques Necker.

Whatever his virtues and faults, Jacques Necker remains an
historical figure of the first importance. But his personality and
impact on events, though not irrelevant, are essentially
tangential to our story, which is that of his adored and adoring
daughter Germaine Necker, better known as Madame de
Staël. From all that we know about her—and we perhaps

33

know more than is good for us or for her—one fact stands out: Germaine was politically and intellectually her father's daughter. Yet, despite their common interests, it is evident that emotionally she was in many ways quite as much her mother's daughter (though she came early to hate her mother). She was, unlike her dour father, a highly strung, at times hysterical, personality. Nor was her morality exactly Genevese. The most charitable thing to be said about her deportment in sexual matters is that she did not see these matters—though they took so large a place in her life—as pertinent to that social, financial, and political morality of which the great Necker was both propagandist and examplar. There are at least two facets to the many-sided phenomenon of Madame de Staël—almost certainly the most remarkable woman of her time—which we shall not pursue in this brief study: the intricate story of her love affairs, and the no less intricate story of her dabblings in high politics. (The curious reader may be referred to Mr Christopher Herold's superb 'Mistress to an Age' for a study in depth of these matters.) Not that we can eschew politics altogether, since it is not possible to distinguish her political intriguing, at times, from her utterances on literary matters. It is the Madame de Staël of *De l'Allemagne* who concerns us; and it is arguable that in writing this book she pulled off the most remarkable coup of her stormy career.

Madame de Staël's trip to Germany in 1803 was largely a matter of accident—the accident that, after years of political intrigue in her salon (not all of it unsuccessful: she saw to it that her lover Talleyrand was made Foreign Minister), she had at last met her match in Napoleon Bonaparte. Father-adoring as she was, not surprisingly she had a unique insight into men— particularly into the workings of men's minds—and a unique gift of compelling them to do her bidding. The list of her lovers would fill an impressive album; and she was continually writing, and still more talking, of Love: the very embodiment of that 'enthusiasm' (a key word in her vocabulary) which she saw as the chief end of human existence. That she was promiscuous on an heroic scale has never been denied. But though she could be quick to drop a lover, if better game were in sight, she was always kind and appeared strangely indifferent, even unfeminine, in her reactions when a lover chose to drop *her*. And drop her in the end they mostly did—from sheer exhaustion. For she selected as her lovers mostly men as effeminate in character as she was, in essence, masculine. Many of her lovers were no less intelligent than she—Benjamin Constant, say, or Monsieur de Talleyrand—but it is plain that she was far too demanding a character emotionally for any lasting relationship. A further consequence of this psychological make-up was that she had no luck with more masculine men, who too often found her lacking in feminine charm and, for all her intelligence, a slightly ridiculous figure. The three men of whom this is most obviously true were Napoleon, Goethe, and Byron. Thus, exasperated at her endless intrigues, Napoleon forbade her to live in France. She had a choice of exile open to her: England, Switzerland, and Germany. She chose Germany.

What did she know of Germany? Almost nothing: but that, to a woman of her temperament, was probably the strongest motive for setting out on a new voyage of discovery. Though her grandfather had been a Pomeranian, she had no German: she was a thoroughbred Genevese. (A thoroughbred Genevese, one might add, who regarded herself, when it suited her, as a Frenchwoman, who never ceased to regard the Parisian salon as the cradle of civilisation.) She came, therefore, to Germany with very little real knowledge, and with a good many preconceptions. These are worth recording, since they tend to be smoothed over in *De l'Allemagne* for the sake of the argument; and indeed she changed her opinions as her course progressed. What she thought about Germany and the Germans in earlier years is evident from the following utterance (she had been invited to meet the illustrious Wieland in 1796 in neighbouring Zürich):

> To go to Zürich to see a German author, no matter how famous he may be, that's something I shan't be guilty of. I believe I already know as well as any German what the Germans are up to, and even what they'll be up to fifty years from now . . .

On her arrival in Frankfurt, she expressed her distaste for

the country she was setting out to discover in no uncertain terms to her current companion Villers, a French émigré who had become enthusiastic about the new German philosophy:

> Shall I give you my impressions, like a real Frenchwoman, of a country I have spent only a couple of days in, and don't yet know? I've already listened to someone torturing a piano in the smoky public room of an inn, with woollen clothes put out to dry on the oven. That's the way everything seems to me: a concert in a smoke-filled room, all the poetical feeling you could ask for, but none of the outward graces.

She wrote, with haughty indignation (and, it must be admitted, some insight), that the introspective Germans

> lock away their thoughts and feelings, like objects never to be used, not even on Sundays. . . . All they do is eat, and all they ever talk about is food. Except for the educated minority, the Germans, if judged by French taste and sensibility, barely belong to the human race.

Villers patiently attempted to initiate Germaine into the world of her new-found enthusiasms:

> Only since Voltaire's time has justice been done in France to the admirable literature of the English. All that is needed now is for a genius to be inspired by the profound originality of certain German writers, and then the French will understand that the Germans have not only revealed the profoundest thoughts, but have also expressed the emotions with a new energy . . .

Did Villers hope that Germaine might be that genius? Her initial reaction hardly suggested it. She was willing to accept his assertion that 'the intellect of Mankind' was temporarily residing in Germany, but she did not know what to make of Villers' assertion that

> The Germans are fundamentally kind, benevolent and hospitable; unlike the Parisians . . . they have not refined the arts of enjoyment . . . but they are natural, they are calm, and they are good.

36

This, which one might call the 'Hermann-and-Dorothea' view of Germany—that 'good' Germany we shall meet from time to time—is likely to have puzzled Germaine. But, the German expedition once *en marche*, it had to be followed through.

Frankfurt had been dreary in the extreme (a view some of us would hold to today). Rich bankers—Germaine's own class of people, after all—did not care to discuss Kant over dinner, and showed a philistinism and a materialism that Germaine must have found disillusioning. But the forward journey—through Hesse and the hills of Thuringia to Weimar—began to work on Germaine's sensibility. She saw German *Gemütlichkeit* for the first time; and became, almost, *gemütlich* about it herself. Here is Mr Christopher Herold's account:

> The journey to Weimar took them across the pine-clad, snow-covered mountains of Thuringia through tiny medieval towns, through Eisenach, Luther's birthplace, where they watched the young men singing Christmas carols under the frosted yellow-glowing windows, their black cloaks sharply outlined against the snowy, deserted street. This was a quite different Germany from philistine Frankfurt. Germaine was strangely moved by the indefinable poetic atmosphere, 'that interior life, that poetry of the soul, which characterises the German people.' At least, that is how she recalled it in her book on Germany, where all is transmuted. Almost all Germans were musical, Germaine asserted. 'At times, entering a smoke-blackened dwelling, I found not only the housewife, but also her husband improvising on the spinet, just as Italians improvise poetry.'

The news that the famous author of *Delphine* was on her way to Weimar gave rise to varying degrees of apprehension. Goethe's mother had been visited by her in Frankfurt, and that sprightly old lady had written to her son, 'What on earth does she want with me? I'm not an Encyclopedia!' On November 30th, 1803, Schiller had likewise written to Goethe:

> Madame de Staël is already in Frankfurt, and we may expect her here at any moment. If only she understands German, I am confident that we can get the better of her;

but if we have to listen to our creed being recited in French, and with typical French glibness, I fear it may be too much for us.

It is some evidence of the shrewdness of Schiller—so often presented as a creature of pure spirit, a German Shelley, soaring in the empyrean—that he should have foreseen that it might very well be rather a case of Madame de Staël expounding *their* philosophy to *them* (and in French!) than of the eminent exponents of the new German *Geist* expounding *their* philosophy to *her*. Goethe, no less apprehensive, replied to his friend's warning:

> I've been thinking things over, for I don't want to be upset; and I have decided I should remain here. In this unpleasant time of year, I've just enough physical strength to survive.

That Goethe had some reason to be apprehensive can be judged from a scribbled note to Villers of Germaine's first encounter with him. She had expected him to resemble Werther; but Goethe was now a man of fifty-four:

> Goethe is not Werther. He is getting fat—in parentheses, that's one of the German vices—and he isn't much to look at.

There were other German vices, too, she noted—though the following remark is typical also of her ambivalence towards France:

> A Frenchman always has something to say, even when he has no ideas at all; while a German always has more ideas in his head than he knows how to express.

We can see how this comment cuts both ways. But, as she wrote to her father at Coppet, the real trouble was that all these new ideas—by which she came to be fascinated—had no real relation to their common passion, politics:

> Goethe and Schiller have their heads stuffed with the craziest metaphysics that you can imagine, as they live all by themselves and are much admired, they go on thinking their own thoughts and are taken terribly seriously. . . . The

great minds of Germany will indulge in the most violent arguments concerning the world of ideas, and won't allow anyone to interfere with their speculations. But as far as the real world goes, they are only too eager to submit to authority.

A curious three-cornered correspondence ensued. Schiller wrote soothingly to Goethe:

> She is all of one piece and there isn't a single false note or pathological trait in her nature . . . As far as philosophy is concerned, particularly in the nobler sense of the word, we will never understand each other, no matter how long the conversation lasts. But her instincts are better than her metaphysics, and her intellect, which is first-rate, is capable of rising to certain heights. She wants to explain everything. . . . She can't conceive of any dark or intangible forces and what she can't light up with her torch might just as well not exist.

But then, brandishing the torch of Reason, had she not already snubbed the youthful Henry Crabb Robinson, then resident in Weimar (and who had been giving her German lessons), when he had remarked, 'Madame, you have not understood Goethe, and you will never understand him,' with the remark, 'Monsieur, I understand everything that deserves to be understood, and what I do not understand is nothing.' Was she an arrogant woman, and perhaps a bit of a fraud into the bargain? She was certainly the first: but Schiller's judgment stands: 'She is all of one piece and there isn't a single false note in her nature.' She was, in fact, remarkably good-natured; and not at all, as might appear, malicious in character. But she was a stubborn child of the Enlightenment, of her father and of his *philosophe* friends who had crowded Madame Necker's salon before 1789. Her egocentric, yet essentially generous nature comes out, indeed, in what she has to say about Schiller:

> I warmly defended the superiority of the French drama over that of all other nations. . . . In the beginning I used French weapons to defeat him; I was amusing, and I was vivacious. But very shortly I made out from what Schiller was saying that he had a good many ideas even if he didn't know the French

for them. . . . I found he was so modest about his own success, and so compelling when he was defending what he believed to be the truth, that I could not help admiring the man.

Her claim, on arriving in Weimar, was that 'Intellect Personified' was converging on that delightful town to welcome her. But, as Mr Christopher Herold notes, this was not strictly true:

Intellect had either taken to its heels or gone to ground. Goethe, on a thin pretext, had left for Jena. Schiller, who had barely one more year to live, was terrified at the prospect of having to interrupt the writing of 'William Tell'. . . . And it was only on the Duke's command that he undertook it. He wore full court-dress, and Madame de Staël mistook him for a General. Herder was on his deathbed when Germaine arrived, and Goethe somewhat callously expressed his envy of such an easy escape.

What seems to have shocked Goethe and Schiller was Germaine's lack of inhibition in discussing, not so much the most private matters in public, as the most public matters in private. Such things were not for the chatter of the boudoir or the drawing-room: indeed, one might almost say that Germaine was too earnest for the Germans. Germaine, they were aware, was essentially a journalist on the prowl: they knew they were going to be written up. Germaine's first meetings with Goethe did not go off well. He had been summoned back by the Duke from his hide-out in Jena, and after the third meeting

He let it be known that he had a cold and could see nobody. Germaine, though she had planned to go to Berlin early in January decided to outlast his cold. . . . Relations were resumed only three weeks later, and from then until the end of Germaine's stay they improved steadily.

Goethe, like Byron later, decided that he would play the game his own way: he would tease her. A contemporary witness depicts the scene:

At one time Madame de Staël would make a pronouncement

40

on Art, and Goethe would be paralysed with shock: then
Goethe would make a cutting remark on false sentimentality and the confounded moralising intent that soiled the
purity of Art, and Madame de Staël would shake with
indignation at such heresy. Attraction and repulsion alter-
nated between them, and thus the conversational minuet
continued along endless diverging lines until it ended with
two deep bows.

And it was Goethe who, much later, most charitably and justly
summed up Germaine's contribution to the *zeitgeist*:

> Whatever one may think of the events I have been describing,
> we must realise that she was a woman of tremendous
> influence. She drove a breach in the Chinese Wall of pre-
> judice that separated us from France, so that we grew to be
> appreciated, not only across the Rhine, but even across the
> English Channel. I think that we should look upon all the
> inconveniences we were put to as a blessing, even if the
> conflict of national characteristics did not seem beneficial at
> the time.

Goethe was right, even though his friend Schiller, at the time,
took a distinctly less sympathetic view: in Mr Herold's words

> Schiller, who had been wondering if Benjamin and Germaine
> would know when to leave, was pleasantly surprised on
> March 1st, 1804, to hear that Constant was setting out for
> Switzerland, and she for Berlin. 'I feel', Schiller wrote to
> Goethe, 'as though I were recovering from a severe illness.'

Berlin, after Weimar, was bound to be a disappointment.
She had got on best, in Weimar, with the septuagenarian
Wieland—the same she had refused to meet in 1796—who was
very much a man after her own taste: that is, a man of the
18th-century Enlightenment. The Peace of Amiens was still
more than a scrap of paper: but Berlin was (as we now see it)
a city *entre deux guerres*. She was quick to complain:

> The two classes of society—the Scholars and the Courtiers—
> are completely divorced from each other. . . . As a result the

Scholars do not cultivate conversation, and mundane society is absolutely incapable of thought.

But, as it happened, the moment she had chosen to descend on Berlin was not well chosen. Novalis was already dead; Tieck was away; Brentano, Arnim, E. T. A. Hoffmann had not yet arrived; Heinrich von Kleist was there, but unknown; Schelling was teaching at Würzburg, Schleiermacher at Halle, Hegel at Jena. 'Intellectual Berlin', then, was less able to be put on parade in authoritarian Prussia than in the sleepy, pacific Duchy of Weimar. Yet Berlin was, with 'Romantic Heidelberg', the epicentre of the 'Romantic Movement' that had sprung up, not at all to Goethe's delight, in the five years preceding. (To avoid confusion, since the English and the German words do not quite correspond, it is preferable to use the German term *Die Romantik* for these writers, rather than the vaguer, Anglo-Saxon term 'The Romantics'.) She did, however, meet the very *spirituelle* Rahel Levin, one of the great hostesses of *Die Romantik*, was much impressed with her, and assumed as ever that the sympathy was reciprocated. Alas, after their first meeting, Rahel was constrained to remark, 'Poor woman, she has seen nothing, heard nothing, understood nothing.' That this was not mere feminine malice is suggested, I think, by the blunt comment of Crabb Robinson a few weeks before that 'she would never understand Goethe'. But we must remember that years of coaching by the arch-Romantic August Wilhelm Schlegel lay ahead of her, before *De l'Allemagne* was ready for the press.

Still, Germaine had already decided that a book could be made out of Germany; and that she was destined to write that book. Germaine was a woman who appears to have been born without many of those inhibitions that are the lot of the rest of us. Thus, when she met the philosopher Fichte in Berlin (whose 'Discourses to the German Nation' were to provide an intellectual foundation for German Nationalism), she behaved as a true *Walküre*. She asked the Professor, in her most winning way, to explain to her his doctrine of the 'Absolute Ego' (*Das Ich-Ich*), which she declared she only imperfectly understood, 'as briefly as possible, in a quarter of an hour, for instance'. Fichte gulped, spoke briefly of his doctrine, only to be interrupted by Germaine:

Oh, that will do, Monsieur Fischt. . . . I understand you completely. Your system may be illustrated admirably by one of the tales of Baron Münchhausen.

While Fichte looked vaguely amazed and the company embarrassed, Germaine explained how Baron Münchhausen, having come upon a large river, managed to cross it by firmly taking hold of his left sleeve with his right hand and swinging himself to the other shore.

This, if I understand you correctly, Monsieur Fischt, is exactly what you have done with your '*Ich*'?

Hair-raising though this may sound as a conversational gambit, she did contrive to make the same impression in Berlin as she had in Paris and Weimar, and was later to make in Rome and London: you might say what you liked about her, but Germaine was a phenomenon. She was not to be resisted. And Berlin, far from being the end of her journey of exploration, was to prove its beginning. For it was there that she met the ineffable August Wilhelm Schlegel, scion of an eminent literary family, and with his brother in the very vanguard of *Die Romantik*. He was a vast repository of information about the latest permutations of the German *Geist*—and, indeed, about everything else. She offered Schlegel a position at Coppet, nominally as tutor to her three children. It appears that August Wilhelm had fallen a little in love with Germaine—though probably not Germaine with him. But the man was now indispensable. He was more than a trifle hesitant. True, the Neckers had money; but would it not demean him in the eyes of the world to take up a position at Coppet as a mere resident tutor? Then, out of the blue, came the news that Necker was gravely ill, and had asked for her immediate return to Coppet. 'He is dead!' cried Germaine. She drove quickly home, had her trunks packed, and sent off a note to the undecided Schlegel: she would call for him at 9 a.m. the following morning. When she called, prompt at 9 a.m., Schlegel was ready: henceforth, his life was determined: he was but one among the many treasures that the indefatigable *Kultur-Walküre* had added to her collection. 'You were unhappy', he wrote to her later, 'and everything was decided in an instant.'

The next few years were spent, of necessity, at her father's house at Coppet. Her father was indeed dead upon her arrival; and there were the estates and M. Necker's huge fortune to be managed and, after all, Napoleon had banned her from Paris. Dauntless, she decided that if she could not meet the world in Paris, the world should come to meet her at Coppet. Soon, the house was full of English Grand Tourists, French refugees, German intellectuals, and that small central core of her court, composed of Constant, Schlegel and Sismondi (it was, one cannot help thinking, the Napoleonic equivalent of Lady Ottoline Morell's—and Keynes' and Strachey's—Garsington a century later). From our point of view, Schlegel is of course the key figure, since, while he did his best to tutor the children, his most important function was to feed Germaine with information about the latest movements of the German *Geist*. This has led some writers to assert that *De l'Allemagne* is really Schlegel's book, and not Germaine's. But this is to underrate Germaine: whatever her critics may have condemned in it, *De l'Allemagne* is most certainly her book. It was of course written with a political purpose in mind: she would be the Tacitus of Napoleonic France. By exalting the culture of England and Germany she would implicitly attack the nationalist spirit that had grown up in France, the 'Chinese Wall' of French chauvinism. She intended in her book to annoy Napoleon. She did not fail.

When *De l'Allemagne* was finally completed in 1810, she still hoped—perhaps naïvely—to have the book published in France. But she cannot have been altogether surprised when, on September 25th, the police seized every copy that had been run off the presses, and also the plates. On the 27th, the Prefect of Loire et Cher, M. de Corbigny, who had often enjoyed Germaine's hospitality, appeared. His orders were to confiscate every last sheet of proof and scrap of manuscript. It was also his duty to inform her that she must leave France immediately. But he was too late. Proof and manuscript had already been handed to

young Albert de Staël, who scrambled over the garden wall
with the treasure. He handed it in turn to August Wilhelm
Schlegel, who was to race to Vienna and confide it to the safe
keeping of his brother Friedrich. (This was the Schlegel—in
fact, the more original thinker of the two—of whom Constant
noted, Garsington-style, that he seemed to prefer living in
countries where there was no freedom of the press, and that the
true reason was that this meant his own works would not then
be open to criticism.) The truth is, of course, that whereas in
her young girlhood before the Revolution the French had been
responsive, even eager to learn from other nations, the Revolution had aroused a nationalism which persuaded the French of
what they had never really doubted—that it was they who
should be not merely the physical, but the spiritual masters of
Europe. The vendetta between the Corsican and the Genevese
(neither strictly French) was therefore not a purely personal
one—though a personal vendetta existed too. At first, she had
tried to woo Napoleon. As early as 1797 she had entered upon a
one-sided correspondence with the General, whom she recognised to be the Coming Man. According to Napoleon, Germaine
had compared him to both 'Scipio and Tancred, uniting the
simple virtues of the former with the brilliant deeds of the
latter'. 'This woman is mad,' the hero is said to have commented, 'I have no desire to answer such letters.'

Later, at a ball in Paris, observing her well-developed bust,
he asked whether (as a good disciple of her fellow Genevese, Jean-Jacques Rousseau) 'she was not in the habit
of breast-feeding her babies?' In a further attempt at the conquest of the First Consul, she asked to be admitted to his residence
in the Rue Chanteraine. The butler explained that the Citizen-
General was taking his bath. 'No matter,' cried Germaine,
'genius has no sex!' Napoleon was not amused. Now, having at
last got the woman out of Paris, he was confronted with a
challenge from the flank. On September 20th, 1810, having
leafed through the proofs of *De l'Allemagne*, he wrote to his
newly appointed police chief, Savary:

Has she really the right to call herself a baroness? . . .
Suppress the passage about the Duke of Brunswick and three-

fourths of the passages where she makes so much of England. That unfortunate infatuation of hers has already done us harm enough.

There followed the seizure of the plates and, on October 11th, a deliberately insulting—but surely most revealing—note from the Duc de Rovigo:

> Your latest work is not French. . . . I have the impression that the climate of this country does not suit you—and you must know that we have no idea of modelling our civilisation on that of the nations you admire.

In 1812, Napoleon gave orders that she was not to travel more than two leagues from Coppet; and Schlegel was ordered out of Switzerland. Apparently, his crime was to have compared, in his Vienna 'Lectures on Art and Literature', Racine's *Phèdre* unfavourably with that of Euripides.

Madame de Staël decided she must escape from the tyrant's clutches. She made her way through Austria and Moravia into Poland—then, in 1812, within the sphere of Napoleonic power —and thence into Russia (where she was compelled to make a lengthy detour to avoid the Napoleonic invasion) and from St Petersburg to Stockholm. In Sweden she was known at Court, since the husband to whom she had been briefly and unsatisfactorily married, M. de Staël, had been Swedish Ambassador to France. A new plan now hatched in her fertile brain. Bernadotte, formerly one of Napoleon's Marshals, was now King of Sweden and about to change horses, with a little encouragement from the British Exchequer, by joining the anti-Napoleonic Coalition. Bernadotte was to be her man; *he* should rule France according to English constitutionalism and Genevese probity! Bernadotte duly landed at Stralsund and played an important part in shattering Napoleon's armies at last in the three-day Battle of Leipzig. But otherwise he was to prove a sad disappointment. He was no great politician, and evidently had no ambition to be what Germaine wanted: her very own, puppet-King of a new France. He did not even go to Paris, but turned back for Sweden once the Allies had crossed the Rhine. Germaine proceeded to London, leaving behind her the newly uniformed and patriotically zealous August Wilhelm to win military glory in the service of Bernadotte.

In London, Germaine enjoyed a triumphal reception. The Prince Regent, the Queen, the Duchess of York, the Duke of Gloucester received her almost as visiting Royalty. To meet a Cabinet Minister, it was said, one had to go to Madame de Staël's rooms in Hanover Square. At Lord Lansdowne's, men and women climbed on tables and chairs to see her. After all, she was the only continental power to have resisted Napoleon as steadfastly as England. She signed a contract with John Murray, who bought her manuscript of *De l'Allemagne* for fifteen hundred guineas (so that *De l'Allemagne* in fact made its first appearance in England). Its publication in October, 1813 made her the literary, as well as the social and political lioness of the season; it sold out in three days. The reviewers were less enthusiastic than the general public. The *Edinburgh Review* remarked:

> A scoffer might with some truth tell us that German philosophy is founded in a repugnance to every system which has experience for its basis, or happiness for its end.

But the reviewer in the *Critical* for January, 1814, reveals the general ignorance of German literature—especially of the richness of German lyric poetry—when he comments severely:

> It is, however, in her delineation of the intellectual character of the Germans that her sketches are the most faulty. She says that it is imagination more than intellect that characterises the German. . . . We are convinced that they who are conversant with the writings of the German literati, will allow that they are marked by profundity of intellect, and that it is the absence of imagination which renders them so unpalatable to a foreign taste. . . . Were the Germans to give greater scope to the imagination, and emancipate themselves from the cumbersome trammels of metaphysics, their literature would rise in the estimation of Europe, and would recover from that degradation under which it at present labours in England.

47

Germaine would not have been Germaine if she had not still feuded from time to time. Her most intimate acquaintance appears to have been Sir James Mackintosh, whom Constant had known in his University days at Edinburgh and who, having served in India, was now a Member of Parliament. But the great attraction of London—and like her father Germaine had always been a passionate anglophile—was the 'noise'. She was a restless, hyper-active creature, and had once remarked to her husband revealingly, 'What I love about noise is that it camouflages life.' Noises, however, might be of several kinds: there were kind and unkind noises, everything from rant and the sighs of rapture to delicious gossip and the sound of verbal gunfire. Thus she clashed with Godwin, who had defended Cromwell against her. 'It is curious to see,' she remarked acutely after he had made his departure, 'how naturally these Jacobins become the advocates of tyrants.' Yet, bafflingly, it seemed that what Englishmen resented most in her was her admiration for England. Henry Crabb Robinson, whom she had known from Weimar days, called her 'a bigoted admirer of our government, which she considers to be perfect'. More fruitful was her encounter with Wilberforce whom she assured of her support in the struggle for the abolition of the slave-trade. Like many before him, Wilberforce was profoundly impressed with her conversational prowess. 'The whole scene was intoxicating, even to me. The fever arising from it has not yet gone.'

Germaine, we know, could be exceedingly formidable. But she had her failures. Napoleon had cold-shouldered her; Goethe had made gentle sport with her; Byron she had yet to confront. When it came to it, Byron was as ready to chaff her as Goethe had been. 'Poor De Staël,' Byron wrote to Lady Blessington,

she came down upon me like an avalanche, whenever I told her any of my amiable truths, sweeping everything before her with that eloquence that always overwhelmed, but never convinced. . . . Madame de Staël was certainly the cleverest, though not the most agreeable woman I have ever known. . . .

48

There is an obscurity that leaves the impression that she does not perfectly understand what she endeavours to render intelligible to others. She *thinks* like a man, but alas! she *feels* like a woman!

At Coppet he had teased her almost beyond endurance. He declared that her two—largely autobiographical—novels, *Delphine* and *Corinne*, were

> Very dangerous productions to be put into the hands of young women. . . . The virtuous characters in the latter novel were dull, commonplace and tedious, and what was this but a most insidious blow aimed at virtue, and calculated to throw it into the shade? She was so excited and impatient to attempt a refutation that it was only by my volubility that I could keep her silent. She interrupted me every moment by gesticulating, exclaiming, '*Quelle idée!*' '*Mon Dieu!*' '*Ecoutez donc!*' '*Vous m'impatientez!*' . . . I was ready to laugh outright at the idea that I, who at that period was considered the most *mauvais sujet* of the day, should give Madame de Staël a lecture on morals, and I knew that this added to her rage.

It was devilish of Byron, to be sure; but had she not asked for it and, in the end, paid for it? 'The fire', Mr Herold remarks, 'was nearly burnt out.' The face she showed to the world might look haggard and tired; but from her lips and eyes the fireworks blazed forth as always. She appeared in the eyes of London Society as the familiar Germaine. Byron was to write in 1821 (after her death four years before) that though he had come to esteem her qualities, she did not know the meaning of the word tact:

> She interrupted Whitbread; she declaimed to Lord Liverpool; she misunderstood Sheridan's jokes for assent; she harangued, she lectured, she preached English politics to the first of our English Whig politicians the day after her arrival in England; and . . . preached politics no less to our Tory politicians the day after. The Sovereign himself, if I'm not in error, was not exempt from this flow of eloquence.

Yet Byron admitted her good nature; and indeed did not

quarrel with her political views. Her political outlook was, in a sense, very English—as her father's had been. She was a born moderate, a liberal Whig. She had supported the Girondins against the Jacobins before the September massacres; and the *Directoire* against the Jacobins because they would preserve the fruits of the Revolution, while bringing order to the country. She was usually right, and always courageous, in her judgment. But she lacked, as her father had done, the power to implement herself, or to find others to implement, what she saw to be necessary. In this she was, it is not unfair to say, the spiritual mother of many other 19th-century Liberal revolutionaries.

To present *De l'Allemagne* as a book composed simply to spite a political regime would, of course, be quite wrong. She came in for a good deal of criticism; and a good deal of it was deserved. As Mr Herold remarks:

> She was convinced until death that Ossian was the father of English literature, that the Irish were Germans and that Spinoza was an Italian. . . . Her German critics gently took her to task for her superficial scholarship, though conceding that for being French and a woman she was uncommonly profound and serious.

As Schiller had told Goethe, she had almost no ear for poetry; and none at all for music. She thought Mozart's *Requiem*, 'not sufficiently solemn for the occasion'; decided that Haydn was too intellectual for his own good; and contrived to overlook Beethoven entirely. And she wrote in *De l'Allemagne*,

> There are few remarkable buildings in Germany. For the most part all one sees in northern countries are Gothic monuments.

So much for Cologne, Naumburg and the glories of Rococo *Vierzehnheiligen*! Again, in philosophical matters, Byron was not alone in gaining the impression that Germaine had not always seized the core of the matter she was expounding. Yet, for all its imperfections, *De l'Allemagne* marks a watershed in the history of European thought. For it was quite true that the emergence of new modes of thought had made Germany temporarily the Abode of Intellect, as well as a Temple of the Muses. And she was fortunate in her timing in that the end of the Revolutionary era opened up the channels of communication in Europe again shortly after her book appeared. No one should suppose that because the book would not stand up to criticism today that *De l'Allemagne* is not a serious book. It has a coherent intellectual framework, not one invented for the occasion, but very much that which Germaine had elaborated almost twenty years before in her 'Literature considered in its Relationship to Social Institutions'. When Goethe teased her with his assumed *l'art pour l'art* view, her indignation was genuine enough. For Germaine believed that all art ought to be *engagé*, to use the modern term; and she was not alone in rejecting Goethe's deliberate immoralism in such matters (Schiller, after all, would have been quite closely in agreement with her). Knowing that she held such views, it was a wicked shot—but on target—for Byron to declare that *Delphine* and *Corinne* were not fit books 'to put into the hands of young women'. For both heroines are modelled on herself; and there can be little doubt that she saw herself as having inherited the mantle that Necker and the great Jean-Jacques Rousseau—and let us throw John Calvin into the bargain—had once proudly worn.

It is too often assumed that because Madame de Staël introduced the German Romantics to Western Europe, she was herself a Romantic. The impression is heightened, of course, by the 'romantic' life she chose to lead: forever on the move, intriguing in love, in politics, and in literature. But examining her life more closely, one sees that at bottom she remained a moderate, a child of that Enlightenment which she had seen displayed before her in the flesh, sitting as a small girl at her mother's side at Necker's famous Friday *salons*. A Rousseauvian and a Rationalist: is that not a contradiction in terms? The trouble is that most of us have a picture of Rousseau that is little more than a caricature. Let me quote Mr Herold once again:

Germaine's cult of sensibility, of the passions, and of enthusiasm, did not conflict in the least with the commonplaces of the Enlightenment. To ascribe this cult to the exclusive influence of Rousseau is a persistent error. It was Locke, not Rousseau, who first vindicated the just demands of the passions. It was Shaftesbury who argued, before Rousseau, that man had a natural sense of right and wrong and an innate sympathy for his fellows; who extolled the benevolent passions; and who wrote a 'Letter concerning Enthusiasm' that anticipated everything Madame de Staël said on the subject. It was Diderot, Shaftesbury's translator and commentator, who pleaded even more eloquently than Rousseau the case for the natural passions of man—and Diderot was one of the familiars of Madame Necker's drawing-room.

Thus, far from being the man who pleaded for a divorce of heart from intellect, Rousseau was in truth the only *philosophe* to argue for a reconciliation of the passions and the intellect. Seen in this light, far from being intellectually inconsistent, Germaine was in the direct line of descent from the *philosophes* of the 18th century.

The basic concept underlying *De l'Allemagne* runs something like this. There are two opposing attitudes to life among the peoples of Europe: on the one side, clarity, sunlight, a happy, colourful, sensuous imagination—the Southern, pagan, classical, Mediterranean world; on the other side, there is the misty, melancholy, sensitive, Christian, Northern world. The complete Rousseauvian man would need to be a synthesis of both. Stated thus, the proposition may sound a trifle simplistic; and it is clearly not difficult to fault this opposition of qualities (is the North *really* more 'Christian'? Is the South *never* melancholy, ever happy and sunlit?). But it was always easy to make Germaine appear slightly ridiculous: indeed this was how she appeared to most of her contemporaries, in London and in Weimar as much as in Paris. Yet such an evaluation would be mistaken. There was always method in her madness, in philosophy as in life:

To understand Germaine's flirtation with the Romantics, one must read 'On the Influence of Enthusiasm' which concludes the book. What the Germans possessed and the French had lost was the faculty of Enthusiasm. By Enthusiasm, she understood the vivifying force of generous emotions—never fanaticism. The incredible creativeness of Germany in the age of Goethe would have been impossible without Enthusiasm—as would have been its noblest synthesis: Schiller's 'Ode to Joy' in Beethoven's Ninth Symphony. It was here that the humane ideals of the Enlightenment, faith in the future, and romantic Enthusiasm found their unique expression—and this was the romanticism that Germaine, despite her deafness to poetry and music, understood and defended. (Herold.)

It is clear, then, that Germaine was not the woman to have her book ghosted for her by an August Wilhelm Schlegel, useful as she found him as a source of information. As regards *Die Romantik*, it is clear that she could go only so far with it and no further. In Mr Herold's words:

She championed Romanticism because it fitted into the theory she had formulated. . . . She remained distrustful of German metaphysics, hesitatingly toyed with mysticism, only to discard it in the end, recoiled from the glorification of Catholicism, and looked to the Middle Ages as an inspiration rather than a model. In no respect is the cleavage between Germaine and the arch-Romantics so striking as in their attitudes towards Medieval Catholicism. She believed in indefinite progress: they believed in a return to the past. Her Romanticism was never reactionary.

The truth is, *De l'Allemagne* is one of those epoch-making books that owe their impact more to the larger-than-life personality in whose shadow they stand, than to high merit as literature. That much of *De l'Allemagne* is confused has long been granted. That much of it is thinly veiled propaganda against Napoleon, and against French smugness and insularity in general, is also true. Her indifference to music was unfortunate, to say the least, at a period when the musical genius of the German people had come to fruition. And the same is true,

of course, of her deafness to the charms of lyric poetry—
arguably the field of literature in which Germany has most to
offer. But Germaine, one needs to remember, was essentially an
autodidact, for all the somewhat un-Rousseauvian intellectual
hoops her blue-stocking mother (who nearly married Gibbon)
had put her through as a child. She was also, as Byron recognised, even if Napoleon did not, first and foremost a *woman*: she
worked by instinct and intuition rather than by ratiocination.
This was both a strength and a weakness. Schiller was right
when he predicted to Goethe, 'She will never understand our
philosophy.' She never did. But her intuition told her that
something was stirring in the Germany of the age of Goethe,
Schiller, and *Die Romantik*, and that many ideas hatched in
smoky German studies or beery *Burschenschaften* would profoundly influence the thinking of 19th-century Europe. Here, we
can see now, her intuition did not fail her. She would have had
no sympathy with the ideas of a Karl Marx; but his ideas came
from the same environment, and are discussed from China to
Peru. When she died in 1817, she had arguably done more to
form the intellectual ideas of the rising generation than any
other European writer, French, German, or English. She once
asked Talleyrand whether Napoleon was intelligent, or whether
he did not think her the more intelligent. He is said to have
replied, 'I cannot say, *Madame*. But I think that you are the
braver.' He was a great diplomat.

54

CHAPTER THREE

De l'Allemagne and After

Writing to Goethe in 1829, his eightieth year, Crabb Robinson summed up the position—perhaps a little unfairly—as he saw it then, almost thirty years after his own discovery of Germany:

> The slow progress your works have until lately been making among my countrymen has been a source of unavailing regret. Taylor's 'Iphigenia in Tauris', as it was the first, so it remains the best version of any of your longer poems. Recently a man called Des Voeux, and Carlyle, have brought other of your greater works before our public—and with love and zeal and industry combined. I trust they will yet succeed in redeeming *our* literature rather than your name from the disgrace of such publications as Holcroft's 'Hermann and Dorothea', Lord Leveson-Gower's 'Faustus' and a catchpenny book from the French, ludicrous in every page, not excepting the title—'The Life of Goethe'.

Carlyle had himself already been in correspondence with Goethe, and Crabb Robinson was not able, or was perhaps unwilling, to see that with the arrival of Carlyle on the scene a new age had dawned. For, with the exception of Coleridge, Carlyle was the first man of letters of the first rank in Britain not only to acquire a profound knowledge of the language, but to appreciate the true importance of the German Renaissance which, by 1829, stood out in high relief and could at last be seen as a whole. There are still a number of omissions— notably Hölderlin and Kleist—but the whole tone in which German literature is spoken of has undergone a change. Carlyle himself attributes the change to the publication of Madame de Staël's *De l'Allemagne*:

> The work indeed, with all its vagueness and shortcomings,

must be regarded as the precursor, if not the parent, of whatever acquaintance of German literature exists among us.

And the tone of the Introduction to his anthology 'German Romance' (1827) suggests how firmly Carlyle considered German literature to have taken root by this time:

. . . The dead wall which divides us from this as from all other provinces of German literature, I must not dream that I have anywhere overturned: at the most, I may have perforated it with a few loopholes, of narrow aperture truly, and scanty range; for which, however, a studious eye may perhaps discern some limited, but, as I hope, genuine and distinctive features of the singular country, which, on the other side, has long flourished in such abundant variety of intellectual scenery and product, and been unknown to us though at our very hands. For this wall, what is the worst property in such a wall, is to most of us an invisible one; and our eye rests contentedly on Vacancy, or distorted *Fatamorganas*, where a great and true-minded people have been living and labouring, in the light of Science and Art, for many ages.

'German Romance', a collection of *Novellen*, was published in 1827—which may be taken as the high-water-mark of our second period—and it is said that Carlyle postponed publication of the work by a year, since no less than six anthologies of German Tales had been offered to the public the previous year (three 'Fairy Tales', or *Märchen*, were published in 1827 by Albert Ludwig Grimm—no relation of the famous Brothers Grimm, whose *Märchen* had already appeared between 1823 and 1826, with illustrations by Cruikshank). What had once been a trickle—if one excepts the rage for Kotzebue—the efforts of Madame de Staël and others had transformed into a flood. One sign that a new age had dawned was the enormous improvement in the quality of translation (a point that Crabb Robinson should have recognised). Another sign was that Enthusiasm, which Carlyle certainly possessed in large measure, did not preclude a more critical approach. Carlyle seems to have been one of the first, for example, to point out that the strength of German literature lay in *lyric* poetry—the most inaccessible field, alas, for the foreign reader:

> The strength of German literature does not lie in novel-writing; few of its greatest minds have put forth their full power in this department; many of them, of course, have not attempted it at all. . . . Klopstock, Herder, Lessing, in the eighteenth century, wrote no novels; the same might almost be said of Schiller, for his fragment of the 'Ghost-Seer' and his Magazine-Story of the 'Criminal from loss of Honour', youthful attempts, and both, I believe, already in English, scarcely form an exception.

Carlyle, in the same preface, makes the important point that we should no more expect German novels or other writings to resemble our own, than we should expect it of those of the French or Italians:

> On the general merits and characteristics of these works, it is for the reader and not me to pass judgment. One thing it will behove him not to lose sight of: they are German Novelists, not English ones; and their Germanhood I have all along regarded as a quality, not as a fault. To expect, therefore, that the style of them shall accord in all points with our English taste, were to expect that it should be a false and hollow style. Every nation has its own form of character and life: and the mind which gathers no nourishment from the everyday circumstances of its existence, will in general be but scantily nourished.

As for the supposed difficulties of learning the language, they are

> little more than a bugbear. They can only be compared to those of Greek by persons claiming praise or pudding for having mastered them. To judge from the signs of the times, this general diffusion of German among us seems a consummation not far distant. As an individual, I cannot but

anticipate from it, some little evil and much good; and look forward with pleasure to the time when a people who have listened with the most friendly placidity to criticisms* of the slenderest nature from us, may be more fitly judged of; and thirty millions of men, speaking in the same old Saxon tongue, and thinking in the same old Saxon spirit as ourselves, may be admitted to the rights of brotherhood which they have long deserved, and which it is we chiefly that suffer by witholding.

Not for the first time—or the last—we meet with the argument that as 'Saxons' the English have, or ought to have, some special affinity with the Germans. Madame de Staël herself thought that this was the reason for the greater interest in things German she detected among the English than among her own people. What truth, if any, is there in assertions of this kind? The question does not admit, certainly, of a simple yea-nay response. That the languages have a common root is no convincing argument, since they have developed in different directions, and the huge infusion of Latinisms, from the Norman Conquest to the Humanists of the English Renaissance, has given English a variety of inflexion and choice of wording that does not exist in German or French (indeed, the vocabulary available to the English writer is about double that available to the French or German writer). To most Englishmen learning the language for the first time, the difficulties of German, *pace* Carlyle, do indeed appear a bugbear. But this is very largely attributable to the fact, not that German has more genders and cases (so have French, Latin, and Greek), but to the fact that we are conditioned to so many items in the French vocabulary, because they are identical with our own, or easily to be guessed at from such scraps of Latin or Greek as we may have acquired at school. Thus, in chemistry, *Wasserstoff* and *Sauerstoff* seem perversely difficult. Yet for the German child who knows that 'Water-stuff' means hydrogen, and 'Sour-stuff' means oxygen, they are the easiest thing in the world. (Ask an English child studying chemistry what the

* Carlyle's reference to 'criticisms' is possibly a reference to Père Bouhours' satirical inquiry, *Si les Allemands peuvent avoir l'esprit?*

root meanings of hydrogen and oxygen are, and you will get a poor response.) The fact that Shakespeare, in the famous Schlegel-Tieck translation (on which August Wilhelm was working at Coppet), sounds better in German than he is inclined to in French, may point to some deeper affinity between the two languages. Yet that the affinity between the two languages is the outward sign of an inner affinity of *Geist* must seem a questionable proposition.

The truth is—and here I speak from personal experience —that German is decidedly more difficult to translate into English than are the Latin languages. The root of the difficulty lies in the rigid and over-formalised sentence structure, with its many-comma'd clauses, each with its verb situated firmly at the end. It could be argued that this rigidity reflects a certain aspect of the German character: certainly, the way German children write is very different from the way they speak—it is almost a different language. Certainly, too, the syntactical structure of English is infinitely more flexible: there are far fewer rules, and it matters less if you break them. But it makes for many headaches and much head-shaking when the translator goes to work. A few writers—Kafka, for example—read surprisingly well in English, and not only because Edwin and Willa Muir were his translators. Rather, writers like Kafka use German in a way that is assimilable into English; if Kafka is obscure, it is not because of his use of language. But despite Ralph Manheim's brilliant translations of Günter Grass or Michael Hamburger's of Hölderlin and other German poets, it would be true to say that we still lack translations of Goethe, say, or of the majority of German literature which are of the first rank. And this, of course, is most clearly and most sadly true of the richest vein of all: German lyric poetry. To speak from the experience of this translator, then, I would say that there is little plausibility in the contention that there is any mystical affinity between the two Saxon tongues. But this is not to play down the fact that many of the first discoverers of intellectual Germany *thought* that there was some such affinity; and that this idea may have played a larger part in making the English more susceptible to the tag 'Made in Germany' than would otherwise have been the case.

It is certainly of sociological significance that the cause of German literature, while it flourished in London, should have received so strong an impetus from certain provincial centres. These were, in order of importance: Edinburgh, Norwich, Bristol, and Liverpool. The role of the Scots in the work of discovery hardly requires emphasis: from Macpherson, of 'Ossian' fame, to Sir James Mackintosh, the friend and adviser of Madame de Staël; from Walter Scott to his son-in-law Lockhart; from the publishers and editors Murray and Constable to the great Scottish Reviews; and later from De Quincey, who had lived in Edinburgh, to Gillies and Carlyle. Not surprisingly the Germans have always felt an affinity with the serious-minded, well-educated, puritanical, philosophical Scots; and over this whole period the regard appears to have been returned.

Norwich is an interesting, and perhaps a more surprising case. But Norwich, like Edinburgh, enjoyed a considerable intellectual and artistic revival around the turn of the century with Amelia Opie, William Taylor, George Borrow, Cotman, and John Taylor's remarkable daughter, Sarah (the two Taylor families are unrelated), who carried on the work of enlightenment into the 1840s. William Taylor we have met, and probably no man did more to promote understanding between the two cultures before Carlyle. It was he who had advised the youthful Henry Crabb Robinson to go to Germany in 1800, he who had first translated a 'classical' play of Goethe (*Iphigenia*), and he who taught German to Sarah Austin, George Borrow and many others. Bristol was at the same period a lively place—a great port like Liverpool—and Southey, Wordsworth, and Coleridge had repaired there. Their friend and Maecenas, Joseph Cottle, lived there; and in Thomas Lovell Beddoes, the son of Dr Beddoes, and author of 'Death's Jest-Book', Bristol produced a remarkable writer who was certainly influenced by German models, and was to spend much of his life in Germany—a loss to England, since this most Germanised of writers of the period exerted very little influence in his native land. The Liverpool circle, if less rich in distinguished names, was productive in the field of translation: Felicia Hemans, Anne Swanwick, and Thomas Roscoe—who was in turn a friend of Sarah Austin's cousin, Edgar Taylor of Norwich.

The provincial emphasis is interesting because it corresponds closely to the social pattern in Germany itself. There were, despite the undisputed dominance of Weimar, at least a dozen centres where important work was being done in these years: Jena, Heidelberg, Tübingen, Göttingen, Frankfurt, Berlin, Königsberg, Dresden. The sociological point is that not only was the new German literature very much a product of the rising German middle class—and largely of the *Protestant* middle class—but it evidently appealed in Britain to much the same class which at that time was active and creative in its ancient and strongly Protestant strongholds, and had not yet been submerged by the Industrial Revolution or been absorbed into the Great Wen of London. (A point of no small interest is that in this story Oxford and Cambridge are conspicuous by their absence.) A great debt, then, is owed to these early groups who laboured to bring the new literature and philosophy to England, unsupported by any official institution (their German contemporaries were, after all, often salaried lecturers at universities).

Indeed, it was this realisation of the stagnation of intellectual life at English (again, less so at Scottish) universities and schools that helped to set in motion the project of a 'University of London', which would be open to all classes, demand no religious 'tests', and encourage free research. It was not until the seventies that the Reform battle was finally won at Oxford and Cambridge, and dons and undergraduates were released from the necessity to swear on matriculation to the Thirty-Nine Articles of the Church of England. The prime movers in the London enterprise were Henry Crabb Robinson and Thomas Campbell, another product of the Edinburgh circle. Campbell knew the German system at first hand from his experiences at Bonn University, founded in 1818 and soon to be Prince Albert's Alma Mater. Under the patronage of Henry Brougham they determined to set up a University of the same kind in England.

More exactly, what they set out to do was to realise the ideals of Schleiermacher and Wilhelm von Humboldt as expressed in the newly-founded University of Berlin in 1810 (Schleiermacher is usually regarded as the father of modern 'liberal' Protestant theology). According to Schleiermacher's precepts, 'particular areas were not to be studied in isolation, but in association with related subjects, with the aim of achieving a more universal view'. The various sciences were to be studied and understood as forming an 'organic unity'. His second demand was that there should be complete freedom of teaching and research, i.e. no interference from Church or State. Again, both teacher and taught were to be allowed complete freedom in the selection of fields of study. Great emphasis was to be placed on the university as a place of creative activity and research; while the ultimate aim, to be constantly kept in view, was the formation of a balanced, harmonious personality. When one considers the condition of Oxford and Cambridge at this time, the attraction of these new ideas to progressive-minded men in England is evident (still more so in America, which was quick to learn from the new model). The moment of conception of the new university can be traced to a letter in *The Times*, February 9th, 1825, 'A Proposal of a Metropolitan University in a letter to Henry Brougham Esq.' The authorship is Campbell's—or Campbell's in association with Crabb Robinson—and the source of the ideas it contains is evident enough. There shall be 'no religious controversy, no political and party and national spirit . . .

It is a vestige of barbarism in our language that learning only means in its common acception knowledge of the dead languages and mathematics. . . . The knowledge of foreign languages, domestic and foreign statistics and of political economy ought to enter fully into the education of a British merchant of superior grade.'

This doffing of the cap to the traditional ruling classes of

English society is significant. The thought is un-Humboldtian, certainly, but the motive is obvious: where was the money to come from? The emphasis is placed deliberately—doubtless with an eye to the English in general and the commercial classes in particular—on the practical, rather than on the ideal aspects of education:

> The plan which I suggest is a great London University effectively and multifariously teaching, examining, exercising and rewarding with honours in the liberal arts and sciences the youth of our middling rich people.

Later, as the project got under way, Campbell was called to the Rectorship of Glasgow (where he played a similar role), and Lord Brougham became the moving spirit behind the enterprise. Campbell's place, essentially advisory, was taken over by Crabb Robinson, who had given his views on the differences, back in pre-Humboldtian days, between the English and German university in a letter to his brother (1801):

> The German university is not at all like the English, a Seat of Discipline, a sort of School for grown Gentlemen. They are mere places of assembly where Professors are nominated to give lectures on all the Sciences and branches of Learning. They have no prayers, no Costume, no obligation to attend lectures, no Tests, few Examinations and then only when Degrees are conferred and they deserve the name of University much better than the English Colleges as all the practical Sciences are introduced. . . . They are cheap, hence there are very many poor students.

Crabb Robinson was one of those fortunate mortals who, in the course of a very long life, was able to observe a number of his youthful ideals come to fruition. 'University College'— as it became after the foundation of the rival, Anglican King's College in 1831—was the first English university to set up a Faculty of Science, and the first to introduce English as a regular subject. 'Tests' were abolished, evening classes set up for those gainfully employed during the day, and (perhaps less fortunate) the old Oxbridge tutorial system was done away with. The 'God-less University', as the pious called it, or the 'German University', as those who saw it as an undesirable foreign intrusion knew it, flourished despite all criticism (and criticism there was: Dr Pusey, of the Oxford Movement, was later to declare that in his opinion 'all the troubles of the Church since the Reformation can be ascribed to German Professors'). Later, the emphasis shifted from research back to the old examination system, and Crabb Robinson duly protested. But he remained active in the service of the University until his death in 1857, and regarded it always as 'the main business of my life'.

Here, then, we have an excellent example of how powerful 'the new German ideas' could be when introduced into an English context—and, equally, evidence both of the *middle-class* ambience in which these ideas could flourish best, and of the way in which the more 'idealist' German ideas could be gently transformed by the more pragmatic spirit of the English. The twenties can be described as altogether the most fruitful period of intellectual interchange between England and Germany: this was the period when Goethe, in his final period, returned to the enthusiasms of his youth and found in Byron a new hero, with whom he corresponded, and whom he was to apotheosise as 'Euphorion', the child of Helen and Faustus, in *Faust II*. In truth, Madame de Staël had opened the floodgates to a vast increase in the demand for general knowledge about Germany, and she was indirectly the Fairy Godmother of that typical Victorian phenomenon, the Handbook. A random sample from the time of publication of *De l'Allemagne* in 1813 to the accession of Queen Victoria reveals the extent and variety of the new infatuation:

1816	F. Hare Naylor	'The Civil and Military History of Germany'
1820	R. Hodgkin	'Travels in the North of Germany'
	C. E. Dodd	'An Autumn near the Rhine'
	W. Jacob	'A view of the Agriculture, Manufactures, Statistics and State of Society in Germany'

1822	G. Donne	'Letters from Mecklenburg and Holstein'
1827	M. Sherer	'Notes and Reflexions during a Ramble in Germany'
1828	J. Russell	'A Tour in Germany in 1820, 1821 and 1822'
1831	W. Beattie	'Journal of a Residence in Germany in 1822, 1825 and 1826'
1834	Anne Jameson	'Visits and Sketches at Home and Abroad'
1836	John Strang	'Germany in 1831'

Nor did the flood cease at Victoria's accession—Mary Shelley's 'Rambles in Germany and Italy in 1840, 1842, and 1843' was still to come. Nevertheless, the interest in Germany which had thriven so luxuriantly from 1813 into the 1830s began to slacken off (through no fault of his) at about the time 'Albert the Good' married Victoria in 1840. Fortunately we possess John Murray III's account of how the famous Handbooks came to be written. A handbook by a Mrs Starke had been published in the twenties, the accuracy of which Murray was able to test for himself on a trip to Germany in 1831:

The errors in the German part of it are innumerable, and I have taken great pains, ever since I went abroad to collect information, to improve it . . .

Much later in life (*Murray's Magazine*, 1889) John Murray III wrote of the origins of these exemplary, indeed essential, Handbooks:

Having from my early youth been possessed of an ardent desire to travel, my very indulgent father acceded to my request, on condition that I should prepare myself by mastering the language of the country I was to travel in. Accordingly, in 1829, having brushed up my German, I first set foot on the continent at Rotterdam, and my 'Handbook for Holland' gives the results of my personal observations and private studies of that wonderful country. . . . At that time such a thing as a Guidebook for Germany,

65

France or Spain did not exist. Mrs. Starke's work is of real utility because, amidst a singular medley of classical lore, borrowed from Lemprière's Dictionary . . . She has an elaborate theory on the origins of *Devonshire cream*, in which she proves that it was brought by Phoenician colonists from Asia Minor into the West of England . . .

Decidedly, Mrs Starke would not do. But Murray was not to be daunted:

Sorry I was when, on landing at Hamburg, I found myself destitute of such friendly aid. It was this that impressed on my mind the value of practical information gathered on the spot. I set to work to collect for myself all the facts . . . which an English tourist would be likely to require. These notebooks (of which I possess many dozens) were emptied out on my return home, and arranged in Routes. Finally, I submitted the project to my father . . . He had known nothing of my scheme, but thought my work worth publishing, and gave it the name 'Handbook', a title applied by him for the first time to an English book.

These routes were worked out with the utmost thoroughness and ingenuity, and friends were asked to take them with them to test their reliability. Murray's travels took him to parts of Europe at that time scarcely penetrated by the English traveller: from Budapest and Belgrade to the gorge of the Danube at the Iron Gates; from the Turkish frontier in Wallachia across Hungary to Carinthia, Carniola, and the Tyrol. In July, 1830, he is writing home from Bordeaux; on August 7th from Venice; on August 20th from Salzburg; on August 31st from Munich. John Murray III could be said, with some accuracy, to have been the Grand Tourist to end Grand Tourism—for with such expert guidance all the world could, and did, take up Grand Tourism, not least the 'middling rich people'. Yet his thoroughness and integrity are admirable throughout, and soon no English tourist could fail to be recognised on the continent as such by the tell-tale little red volume open in his hands. The first Handbook, comprising

Holland, Belgium, and North Germany, was published in 1836, and followed at short intervals by South Germany, Switzerland, and France—all written by Murray himself and illustrated by his friend William Brockedon. For later volumes outside help was called in: Scandinavia in 1839; the 'Handbook to the East' in 1840; and in 1842 Sir Francis Palgrave contributed his 'Guide to Northern Italy'. Later in the forties— perhaps most distinguished of the whole brood from a literary point of view—came Richard Ford's 'Spain'. By the fifties— to paraphase Madame de Staël—one could say that what the possessor of a little red guide did not know was not worth knowing.

There can be no doubt that this physical opening up of Central Europe—soon to be expedited by the coming of the railway—was the 'rambler's' counterpart to the great flood of translations that was let loose by Murray the elder's publication of *De l'Allemagne* in 1813. Let us tabulate further progress of German *Geist* in England from that time:

1815	Goethe	Faust (extracts, by Shelley)
	A. W. Schlegel	Lectures on Dramatic Art
1817	Gessner	Selected Tales and Idylls
1818	Fouqué	Undine (by Soane)
	Kotzebue	Patriot Father
	F. Schlegel	Lectures on the History of Literature (by Lockhart)
1819	Müllner	Guilt (by Gillies)
	Müllner	Guilt (by W. E. Frye)
1820	Fouqué	Sintram (by J. C. Hare)
	Goethe	Faust (extracts, by Soane)
	Görres	Germany and the Revolution (by J. Black)
	Grillparzer	Sappho (by Bramsen)
1821	Fouqué	Minstrel Love (by Soane)
	Goethe	Faust (Part I, Anon)
	Klopstock	Messiah (by Egestorff)
	Schiller	Don Carlos (Anon)

		Specimens of German Lyric Poetry (by Beresford and Mellish)
1823	Goethe	Memoirs (from the French)
	Goethe	Faust (extracts by Lord Leveson-Gower)
	Schiller	Song of the Bell, etc. (by Lord Leveson-Gower)
	Schiller	Ravenna, or Italian Love
	Wieland	Graces (by Sarah Austin)
	Wieland	Crates and Hipparchia (by C. R. Coke)
1824	von Chamisso	Peter Schlemihl (wrongly attributed to Fouqué)
	Brothers Grimm	Popular Stories (by E. Taylor)
	Fouqué	Outcasts (by Soane)
	Goethe	Wilhelm Meister's Apprenticeship (by Carlyle)
	E. T. A. Hoffmann	Devil's Elixir
	Kotzebue	The Poachers
	Schiller	Fiesco (by Dr. Reinbeck)
	Schiller	Maria Stuart (by H. Salvin)
	Schiller	Maid of Orleans (by H. Salvin)
	Schiller	Friedolin (by J. P. Collyer)
1825	Fouqué	Magic Ring (by Soane)
	Klinger	Faust (by George Borrow)
	Lessing	Fables and Epigrams
	Tieck	Pictures (by C. Thirlwall)
	Tieck	Betrothing (by C. Thirlwall)
	Schiller	Wilhelm Tell (by S. Robinson)
	Carlyle	Life of Schiller
1826	Engel	Lorenz Stark (by I. Gans)
	Klopstock	Messiah (by Miss Head)
	Kotzebue	Graf Benjowski

Tales from the German (by R. Holcroft)
Specimens of German Romance (by Soane)
German Novelists (by T. Roscoe)
German Stories (by Gillies)

With Carlyle's 'Life of Schiller' we come to the first serious
attempt to assimilate, rather than merely observe or register,
the onrush of German *Geist*. The correctness of Carlyle's view
of Schiller and Goethe is a matter we shall have to go into
later in more detail. But it is clear that, by 1825, Carlyle was
able to assume a reasonably wide knowledge of Schiller
among the reading public (though not on the stage, from
which German plays had almost disappeared in this second
period). True, many of Schiller's philosophical writings,
particularly his essay on 'The Aesthetic Education of Man',
had not been translated; though this does not prove that they
were unknown to, say, Coleridge or Carlyle or others with a
knowledge of the language. The picture of Lessing was still
very incomplete—though De Quincey's (partial) translation
of the *Laocoön* was to appear in the *Edinburgh Review* in 1827.
Some of the old favourites from the earlier period are still to
be found: Gessner, Kotzebue, Wieland. But they have to a
great extent been replaced by new favourites from the era of
Die Romantik: Fouqué, E. T. A. Hoffmann, Tieck, Chamisso,
and the Schlegels. Knowledge of Goethe is still very patchy;
the translations are still—except for Shelley and Carlyle—not
good, and it cannot be said that by Goethe's death in 1832,
Goethe had been adequately served by the efforts of his
translators.

Still, in general, the quality of translation shows a certain
improvement from the earlier period, with Shelley, Soane,
Gillies, Borrow, De Quincey, Hare, and Carlyle himself. Gaps
certainly existed: Novalis, Lichtenberg, Hölderlin, and Kleist,
and the great historians (Niebuhr, Ranke) and philosophers
of the time (Kant, Fichte, Schelling, Hegel). No doubt some
of those were read in the original by those sufficiently interested.
We know, for example, that Coleridge read Kant, that Carlyle
read Fichte, that Dr Arnold read Niebuhr. But without
adequate translations from the new German philosophy, it
was hard to appreciate just how far the 'German Renaissance'
was bound up with a new approach to philosophy; and in fact
it was not until the sixties and seventies that 'German Idealism'
came into fashion at the senior British universities. Neverthe-

less, it can be said that by Goethe's death in 1832, though German plays might no longer be the rage in the London theatre, a general knowledge of the language was growing. The German governess was not yet a power in the land. But in the Brontë sisters' library at Haworth there are to be found German books both in translation and in the original—indicating that German literature was certainly by this time to be found 'in the hands of young ladies'.

One could sum up this second phase, then, by pointing simply to the names of Scott, Shelley, Coleridge, Borrow, De Quincey, and Carlyle. German literature, though not the other German arts (with the exception of music), had found a serious audience at last among the intelligentsia—something that was entirely lacking before 1800. This was bound to lead to a quite new phase, a period of digestion and consolidation, and perhaps ultimately of synthesis, in which one can begin to speak with confidence of German 'influence' on English literature and philosophy—this is the phenomenon we shall be looking at in the next two sections, and I will not anticipate. More material, at this point, is the evidence that at some time during the thirties the general public's interest in German literature began to wane, and by mid-century it was (except for the discovery of Heine in 1835, who was to remain very popular among the Victorians) to German science, historiography, and theology that attention was directed. In itself, this change is natural enough, since between the death of Heine in 1855 and the rebirth of German lyric poetry in the late nineties (Hofmannsthal, Rilke, Stefan George), German literature went through a somewhat depressing period. The one towering literary figure Germany produced during this period—Nietzsche—had vastly greater influence in France than in England (though there is evidence of influence on Walter Pater, on Shaw—the 'Superman'—and on Orage and his circle at the *New Age*).

Such, briefly, was the course taken by German *Geist* in England during the rest of the century. Something had been absorbed, chiefly Goethe (or Coleridge's and Carlyle's interpretation of him). But it is open to question how far the

German Renaissance had been correctly assessed—how far, for example, the deeply reactionary outcome of German Romanticism had been appreciated. Was German influence 'progressive'? Madame de Staël clearly thought so; so did Dr Pusey, who had studied in Germany, though for him this was reason to combat it. These are questions we shall have to investigate. But at least up to 1871, and to some degree right up to 1914, knowledge of German was spreading and Germany was 'on the map' in a way that it had never been before 1800. By the end of the century, for example, it is probable that the educated Englishman knew as much German as he knew French—though that is not, perhaps, to say very much. (Still, if I may intrude a personal note, I know that my grandfather went to Germany in the 1870s to study Chemistry and romantically met his bride, a Canadian 'doing Europe', on a voyage down the Rhine. And my father was still able to recite from memory the German poems he had learnt as a child in the nineties seventy years later. Since there were no special ties, familial or otherwise, with Germany, it may well be that this was a common pattern. It was only after 1914 that the teaching of German declined, and the linguistic link was broken.)

But there were other reasons why enthusiasm for things German began to decline among the British public after the great activity of the period between Waterloo and the accession of Queen Victoria. That there were still enthusiasts, who preserved the memory of the new planet that had swum into their ken earlier in the century, is suggested by a figure like De Quincey, who had first studied German in (not *at*!) Oxford in 1805. A few years later he was to write

> German literature is at this time beyond all question, for science and philosophy properly so-called, the wealthiest in the world. It is a mine the riches of which are scarcely known by rumour in this country.

De Quincey first read Herder, Kant, Jean Paul, and later Lessing and Goethe. He translated Kant's 'Essay on National Character', and did a partial translation, as we have seen, of

Lessing's *Laocoön*. In 1827 appeared his 'Last Days of Kant'. His interest never ceased; and we hear of him at seventy climbing a hill 'like a squirrel', discoursing the while of German literature.

But one, at least, of the later-comers—Sarah Austin, one of William Taylor's disciples—began to move away from her youthful germanophilia in later life. She had done much to carry on the Taylorian tradition. In 1831, after being introduced to her, Carlyle described her as 'a true Germanised screamikin'. In 1833, she published her 'Characteristics of Goethe', in memory of the dead poet, and had fallen fully under the Carlylean spell. In 1841, she brought out her 'Fragments from German Prose Writers'. Meanwhile she had turned to the translation of German historiographical works. In 1840 her translation of Ranke's 'History of the Popes' appeared; and in 1845 his 'History of the Reformation'. Macaulay reviewed the former for the *Edinburgh Review*, praising the translation, and apostrophising Sarah Austin as 'an interpreter between the mind of Germany and the mind of Britain'. In 1842 Murray tried to persuade her to write an updated version of Madame de Staël's *De l'Allemagne*, but she felt bound to excuse herself. She had travelled much with her barrister husband, John Austin, in Germany in previous years. Why, then, had her enthusiasm waned?

A hint may be gleaned from an unfavourable notice by John Austin of List's 'National System of Political Economy' in the *Edinburgh Review* (1843):

> Dr. List labours to diffuse a spirit of exclusive and barbarous nationality in the country of Leibnitz, Kant and Lessing.

Sarah Austin made much the same criticism of the Prussian historian Droysen's account of the 'Wars of Liberation': though these men would have called themselves Liberals, the tone was clearly too nationalistic for the Austins' taste. The truth is, the idyllic picture of Germany as the *Land der Dichter und Denker* which Germaine and Carlyle had so assiduously propagated was from this time on to be greeted with growing scepticism. Certainly, Bismarck was not yet on the scene, the

1848 meeting at the *Paulskirche* in Frankfurt had not yet collapsed in ignominy, and German nationalism still had a strong Liberal tinge. But Germany *was* changing, and it was acute of the Austins to spot this transition from the Age of *Geist* to the Age of Blood and Iron so early, for the legend lingered on until the time of Matthew Arnold and beyond, only finally to be shattered by the tragic years leading up to the catastrophe of 1914.

SECTION II

The Road From Ecclefechan

CHAPTER ONE

The Young Carlyle

It is said that each generation rejects its predecessor. Does each century do something of the same kind? Certainly, the men of the Enlightenment recoiled from the religious atrocities and doctrinal disputations of the 17th century. The French Encyclopedists were quite convinced (a view which Newton himself would have repudiated) that Newton had taken the Universe to pieces and demonstrated how it might be put together again, without assistance from Above. A First Cause might be postulated; but, once correctly wound up, the watch would run on with no need of a Watchmaker, keep good time, measurable, and rationally comprehensible to the student of Nature. We are so accustomed to dating the 'clash' between Science and Religion to Lyell's Geology, and Darwin's Evolution, that we forget that this was a drama that had its roots deep in the 17th and the 18th century, with Bacon, Hobbes, Locke, and Hume as its progenitors in England, and Voltaire and Diderot in France.

Where, in all this, did Germany stand? During most of the 18th century her philosophers, like her writers and architects, had been only too ready to subordinate themselves to foreign, and especially to French influence. There is no more touching monument to the spirit of the *Aufklärung* than Lessing's 'Nathan the Wise'. Goethe and Schiller, after they had emerged from the anti-rationalistic turmoil of the *Sturm und Drang*, fell back—or advanced, as you will—towards the 'classical' spirit of the *Aufklärung*. Yet Lessing was also the man who liberated the German theatre from the tyranny of France, by appealing to the example of English Shakespeare. The role of this rediscovery of Shakespeare, to the point where Germans were inclined to think that the countrymen of Shakespeare did not deserve him, and that he was secretly one of themselves, has often been told, and as often derided. Goethe's 'Goetz with the Iron Fist' and Schiller's 'Robbers' are among the first fruits of this rediscovery, as are so many of the works of the lesser *Stürmer und Dränger*, of the unfortunate Kotzebue and, towards the turn of the century, of *Die Romantik*. With Tieck's and August Wilhelm Schlegel's famous translation Shakespeare had indeed become almost German property. This was fundamentally the doing of Lessing and Goethe; and it represented an attempt to break the bonds of what Germans increasingly felt to be a constricting subordination to the norms of French culture.

But the revolt, as it gathered pace towards the latter half of the 18th century, was not wholly, or even primarily, aesthetic. It was a revolt of the national Spirit, of the national *Geist*. There is no reason to suppose that there was at first any general feeling of hostility towards France before the Revolution broke out. France had fought Frederick's Prussia in the Seven Years' War; but Austria had been France's ally. If anything, there was a tacit understanding that France was the natural protector of Protestant Germany against the power of the Habsburgs. But the moment at which Germany fully entered the modern world—the age of Kant and Lessing, Mozart and Beethoven, Herder and Goethe, Schiller and Niebuhr—is surely of the utmost significance. It was the moment when the Enlightenment must either fail, and become the property of scattered, and perhaps persecuted scholars and students—not unlike, say, the Humanists of the age of Erasmus —or when it would take hold of the mind of the rising middle classes, and lead to dire political consequences for Church and State. That had happened in England; and the French *philosophes* were the pupils of the English. Might not the same thing happen in France? Might not another King's head fall under the axe? And, if so, what would be the reaction of the Germans, their Kings and Princes, Emperors and Grand Dukes, and of her newly-awakened middle classes?

The question, of course, is more easily stated than answered. Some philosophers and writers were at first enthusiasts for the Revolution. There is the tale of Hegel, Hölderlin and their friends, dancing round a maypole as young students at

Tübingen. They were, after all, the contemporaries of Wordsworth and Coleridge, and felt themselves also to be living at a time when

> Joy was it in that dawn to be alive,
> But to be young was very heaven.

Goethe was *interested* (he had witnessed the battle of Valmy in the Duke's army) but, as ever, detached and uncommitted. Schiller was at first an enthusiast, but by the time the *Légion d'honneur* had found its way to him in 1796, he too had become a resolute opponent of the Revolution. The Romantics, of a younger generation, reacted much more strongly. Berlin had been the capital of the German *Aufklärung*. Now Tieck and Wackenroder, Novalis and the brothers Schlegel were passionate against the whole 'shallow philosophy' of that movement. Not surprisingly, then, Germany soon became—with Pitt's Britain—the upholder of Legitimate Sovereignty. And, in the main, her young intellectuals agreed. The Revolution was not the dawn of a new day for humanity; it was rather a fulfilment of the Apocalypse. The infidel spirit of the 18th century had become flesh in the persons of Robespierre, Danton, and Napoleon. Inevitably, then, the German patriotic reaction, when it came, would have a strongly reactionary tinge in politics and religion. Goethe (and later Heine) might stand apart. But the German Renaissance had been diverted on to a path that was to lead to a right-wing nationalism, in many ways unlike the new nationalisms of Italy and Poland and the smaller nations that Napoleon had helped to throw off an alien yoke. Not wholly incorrectly did the Nazis (and their forerunners) see themselves as men whose mission it was to reverse the consequences of the French Revolution.

The two men I intend to consider in the following chapters differed much from one another; and it may seem, at first glance, arbitrary to link their names. Yet Carlyle and Coleridge had at least one property in common: they were, to the English middle classes of the Victorian age, if not to us, Prophets and Sages. And they were regarded—rightly or wrongly—as prophets in a quite special sense: they were, or seemed to be, lights in the darkness of religious doubt. It would, of course, be possible to treat Coleridge and Carlyle as Men of Letters, as critics of literature who happened also to be critics of life—and this is indeed standard procedure in our English faculties. But what if the thesis is reversed? What, in other words, if theology is taken to be the fundamental object of their preoccupations, and not merely the setting up of new aesthetic categories? After all, Coleridge wrote as much, if not more, on matters of religion—though these books are little read today—than on literary matters. The same may be said of Matthew Arnold; and neither would have seen a dichotomy here, but rather a rational and necessary continuation of their attempt to examine and exhibit the Good Life. And the same is true of Carlyle, in his successive preoccupations with German literature and philosophy, and later with history and social criticism. What I am asserting, then, is that these men—and one could reasonably add the names of Blake, Wordsworth, F. D. Maurice, and Newman—are the English equivalents of those German scholars and writers who represent essentially the reaction of the 19th century to the 'godlessness' and immorality and materialism of the 18th century.

I shall treat first of Carlyle, not the earliest in time, but in the Victorian era perhaps the more powerful influence. Certainly, there is an initial difficulty. Whereas Coleridge (and Matthew Arnold) have risen in intellectual estimation during the last fifty years, so that they are now possibly more highly regarded than they were in their own time, Carlyle's reputation has never really recovered from the slump that had set in even during his lifetime. The reason usually given for this is his ostensibly too intimate relations with the *Kultur* of the national enemy. It is on this that his stylistic extravagances are blamed, as well as his thought (or lack of it). As early as 1933 the late Professor Sir Herbert Grierson published a book with the title 'Carlyle and Hitler'. The book is based on his Adamson Lecture at the University of Manchester, given in December, 1930, and originally entitled 'Carlyle and the Hero'. Whether Professor Grierson had the future Führer in mind when he delivered it, I am not certain. (The elections of September, 1930, were the first great Nazi victory on their road to power.) But he certainly had in mind the kind of social and historical conditions which existed in Germany at the time, and which are likely (according to Carlyle) to be favourable to the emergence of a 'Hero'; and by 1933 he must have seen his prophecy come painfully true. But the reader should not be misled by the choice (or change) of title: Professor Grierson's book is essentially an apologia for Carlyle, a demonstration that his writings and prophesyings have a relevance for today which should not be overlooked.

What, then, of Carlyle's Germanism? We shall see that it has not only been greatly exaggerated and badly misunderstood, but that it almost certainly played a much less important part in his 'conversion', and in the general development of his views, than is commonly assumed. Professor Harrold, in his excellent study, 'Carlyle and German Thought' (1927), remarks that:

> It is undoubtedly true that a great many of the books which Carlyle mentions he knew only by name . . . His knowledge of the German nation as a whole was never very rich; he was nearly sixty years old when he first visited Germany in 1852—twenty years after he had given up periodical writing on German themes.

Since it is not my intention to burden the reader with a biographical résumé of what is perhaps already too widely known (the noisome cocks next door at Number 6, Cheyne Row; the 'silent room'; the endless quarrels with Jane; the better-avoided impotence controversy) I shall give only a brief account of Carlyle's perambulations. But one or two facts in his life story are certainly vital to the understanding of the development of his mind. As is well known, the 'Ecclefechan peasant' had enjoyed—if that is the word—a Calvinist upbringing as strict as any to be had in Scotland. If Edinburgh disappointed him (he shone—oddly, perhaps, in view of his later revulsion from abstract, systematic philosophy—chiefly in the field of logic and mathematics), this account by Leslie

Stephen of his first sight of the Great Wen describes the young Calvinist's early view of life:

> Carlyle received strong impressions from his first view of London society. He judged it much as Knox judged the court of Mary, or Saint John the Baptist the court of Herod. He is typified by Teufelsdröckh: 'A wild seer, shaggy, unkempt, like a Baptist living on locusts and wild honey.'

And if the reader has any doubts about the power Calvinism held, and never ceased to hold, over Carlyle, his mind will be set at rest by this further biographical fragment, from the same author, on the woman Carlyle was to marry:

> Jane Baillie Welsh was descended from two unrelated families both named Welsh. They had long been settled at the Manor House of Craigenputtock. Her father, John Welsh, descended through a long line of John Welsh's from John Welsh, a famous minister of Ayr, whose wife was the daughter of John Knox.

Carlyle, then, was as true a son of Geneva as the great Necker, or his famous daughter, whose *De l'Allemagne* was soon to open the path for him into 'German Idealism'. But now something happened—around 1818—that was to happen with increasing frequency to other men, greater or less, in the course of the 19th century: Carlyle found that he had lost his faith. Had he sinned grievously? It would seem that he had done no more than read Gibbon:

> I have studied the evidences of Christianity for several years with the greatest desire to be convinced, but in vain. I read Gibbon and then first clearly saw that Christianity was not true.

A Jesuit confessor would not have wasted too much time on this, surely venial, lapse. There were plenty of other arguments in the Catholic armoury and there would have been—what the Calvinist must abhor—Confession: even mortal sin is subject to divine grace in that sacrament, and who is to say that a man's momentary doubt constitutes even mortal sin?

But, of course, there is no such way out for the Calvinist. For loss of faith implies something infinitely more terrifying: that one is not of the Elect. This, surely, is why many of the 'honest doubters' later in the century—such as John Sterling or Leslie Stephen—could take their loss of faith so comparatively lightly. They could always comfort themselves with something resembling Pascal's wager: if there be a God, then good works will make up for loss of faith; if there be none, to have done one's portion in improving the world is not dishonourable, and is in effect self-justifying. It is only when we put ourselves back into the mind of a man, so recently and securely rooted in the iron soil of Calvinism, that we can truly understand the state into which the young Carlyle was now plunged.

One, among all too many, difficulties in studying Carlyle's work is that by mid-century he had become—and it surprised him, too, for he considered much of his work too obscure for the general market—a popular author and a Sage. As R. H. Hutton was to write:

For many years before his death Carlyle was to England what his great hero, Goethe, long was to Germany—the aged seer whose personal judgments on men and things were eagerly sought after and eagerly chronicled and retailed. To those who were young in the thirties and forties, to those especially who were adrift in the cross-currents of Newmanism and Benthamism, and had lost their sense of direction, Carlyle's early prophesyings (notably 'Sartor' and 'Heroes') came with the force of a revelation, and 'Carlyle is my religion' was heard as often as 'Credo in Newmanum'.

The puzzle to us must be how Carlyle achieved this position. Yet the fact that he did so is part of the history of the mind of England and America in the 19th century; and it requires explanation and careful examination. Reviewing 'The French Revolution' in the *London and Westminster* in the year of Queen Victoria's accession—that is to say, very shortly after the appearance of the book—John Stuart Mill could enthuse:

This is not so much a history, as an epic poem; and notwithstanding, or even in consequence of this, the truest of histories. It is the history of the French Revolution, and the poetry of it, both in one: and on the whole no work of greater genius either historical or poetical has been produced in this country for many years.

Mill, as much a pupil of Carlyle's as any son of James Mill could hope to be, is here perhaps giving 'The French Revolution' something of a puff. But the cult grew. So sharp a critic as George Eliot could write of Carlyle twenty years later in an unsigned piece for *The Leader* (October, 1855):

It is an idle question to ask whether his books will be read a century hence: if they were all burnt as the grandest suttees on his funeral pyre, it would only be like cutting down an oak after its acorns have sewn a forest. For there is hardly a superior or active mind of this generation that has not been modified by Carlyle's writings; there has hardly been an English book written for the last ten or twelve years that would not have been different if Carlyle had not lived. The character of his influence is best seen in the fact that many of the men who have the least agreement with his opinions are those to whom the reading of 'Sartor Resartus' was an epoch in the history of their minds.

The historian J. A. Froude—Carlyle's biographer, admittedly —was to reminisce later in the century in the same vein:

Amidst the controversies, the arguments, the crowding uncertainties of forty years ago, Carlyle's voice was to the younger generation of Englishmen like the sound of 'ten thousand trumpets' in their ears, as the Knight of Orange said of John Knox. . . . I, for one, was saved by Carlyle's writings from Positivism or Romanism, or Atheism or any other of the creeds or no creeds which in those years were whirling about us in Oxford like leaves in an Autumn storm.

We are dealing here with three intellectuals of great significance, each in his or her field, during the reign of Queen

Victoria. They can fairly be considered typical of the thinking England of that age. They also have in common a personal history typical of the age: all—even Mill, as any reader of the 'Autobiography' knows—had passed through an acute religious crisis of some kind. They arrived at different destinations: Mill was shaken, but not toppled in his Atheism. J. A. Froude —the younger brother of Newman's intimate, Hurrell Froude— was almost persuaded to say *Credo in Newmanum*, but lapsed finally into agnosticism as did, coming from the opposite, Evangelical direction, George Eliot. They also have in common that at a crucial period of their lives they were tempted to say 'Carlyle is my religion'.

CHAPTER TWO

The Style and the Man

There can be no doubt, then, about the extent of Carlyle's
influence; and he was, we should remember, almost as much
an author for the people as Dickens or Samuel Smiles. His
appeal lay, very obviously, in the 'religion' he could offer his
disciples, and they were legion. But it would be misleading to
suggest that he lacked contemporary critics, and critics of no
mean standing. What is likely to strike the modern reader is
that the criticisms of his contemporaries are in many ways
precisely those we would be inclined to make. To simplify
matters, I shall deal with the various areas of criticism, not in
strict chronological order, but under certain heads which
seem to me logically connected: style; Carlyle's 'conversion';
the nature of the 'German' influence on him; and, finally, the
closely interrelated question of his approach to History and
his doctrine of the Hero.

To take, first, the famous controversy about Carlyle's style.
In his day, some were prepared to admire him precisely
because of this. Thus Emerson, in an unsigned review for *The
Dial*:

> One more word respecting this remarkable style. We have
> in literature few specimens of magnificence. Plato is the
> purple ancient and Bacon and Milton the moderns of the
> richest strain. Burke sometimes reaches that exuberant
> fullness, though deficient in depth. Carlyle in his strange
> half-mad way, has entered the Field-of-the-Cloth-of-Gold
> . . . the indubitable champion of England. Carlyle is the
> first domestication of the modern system with its infinities
> of details into style. We have been civilising very fast,
> building London and Paris, and now planting New England
> and India, New Holland and Oregon. . . . Carlyle's style

is the first emergence of all this wealth and labour, with which the world has gone with child so long.

'Obscure'? 'Teutonic'? Thoreau, at any rate, was ready to absolve him from such a charge:

> Not one obscure line, or half line, did he ever write. His meaning lies plain as the daylight. . . . He utters substantial English thoughts in plainest English dialects . . . all the shires of England, and all the shires of Europe are laid under contribution to his genius. . . . And yet, no writer is more thoroughly Saxon. . . . And if you would know where many of those obnoxious Carlyleisms and Germanisms came from read the best of Milton's prose, read those speeches of Cromwell which he has brought to light, or go and listen once more to your mother's tongue. So much for his German extraction (1847).

A contemporary critic, Mr John Gross, is also ready to offer an apology for Carlyle's style ('The Rise and Fall of the Man of Letters', 1969).

> No English prose of this period apart from Dickens' has more body—or, on occasion, greater delicacy. Legend suggests otherwise: what has come to be the stock notion of Carlylese takes far too little account of all the really subtle quicksilver effects at his command, to say nothing of his genius for serio-comic caricature . . . He has been made to pay altogether too heavy a price for his verbal excesses. Strip away the rant and what remains is a daring chiaroscuro prose, flecked with satire, opening up vistas that still have the power to startle.

But detractors started up, and have on the whole carried the day, as soon as 'Sartor Resartus' was published (the early 'Life of Schiller', most of the early essays, and the felicitous 'Life of Sterling' are commonly, and rightly, excused). Some were as rude as Mill, Froude and George Eliot were polite.

An early example—again American—is Edgar Allan Poe's outburst:

> I have not the slightest faith in Carlyle. In ten years—possibly in five—he will be remembered only as a butt for sarcasm. His linguistic Euphuisms might very well have been taken as *prima facie* evidence of his philosophic ones; they were the froth which indicated, first, the shallowness, and secondly, the confusion of the waters (1846).

But there were those prepared to struggle through the verbal jungle of 'Sartor Resartus' and 'The French Revolution', and come up with treasure of a kind. Thus, Thackeray, in an unsigned review for *The Times* (August 3rd, 1837):

> But never did a book sin so grievously from outward appearance, or a man's style so mar his subject and dim his genius. It is stiff, short and rugged, it abounds with Germanisms and Latinisms, strange epithets and choking doublewords, astonishing to the admirers of simple Addisonian English. . . . A man, at the first onset, must take breath at the end of a sentence, or, worse still, go to sleep in the midst of it. But these hardships become lighter as the traveller grows accustomed to the road and he speedily learns to admire and sympathise; just as he would admire a Gothic cathedral in spite of the quaint carvings and hideous images on the door and buttress.

Thackeray has his fun at the expense of the Germans in the Pumpernickel-Weimar episode in 'Vanity Fair'. But it is easier for us perhaps than for Thackeray to see why Carlyle became —in Meredith's words—'A heaver and not a shaper'. Just as Carlyle himself was a self-made man (and most of his Heroes are cast in the same mould) so must his style be self-made, self-created. Some of his contemporaries also saw the matter in this light: for Emerson this was a new style forged for a new age. But Carlyle could hardly have accepted Emerson's interpretation in its entirety; for the 'civilising' process of which Emerson speaks is precisely what Carlyle is against.

The real reason for Carlyle's elaboration of this style—and

we cannot have Carlyle without his style—is surely to be found elsewhere; I mean, in his new-found 'religion'. The 'Addisonian Style' is the very epitome of what he disliked in the 18th century; it is the style of Materialism, Rationalism, and Godlessness. In intention, Carlyle is attempting to do for prose what a previous generation had done for poetry. He aspires to be the prose-Wordsworth of the new age, not its Addison. And here we approach the heart of the matter. The old coinage must go, be melted down, and re-minted into new images, symbols and forms. But whereas Wordsworth and Coleridge had tried—or claimed that they had tried—to mint a new language for poetry by going back to the plain language of simple men, to the unworked ores of Cumberland and Westmorland, Carlyle went about it a different way. If ever there was a concocted language, it was that of Thomas Carlyle. Annandale lies forty miles or so from the Lake District; and the dialect spoken on both sides of the border cannot have been so very different. Thus critics who pointed to (and, in his time, laughed at) his Lowland inflexions, are almost certainly right in finding many a Scotticism in his prose. But this will not quite do; for the Lowlander, when sober, is very sober indeed— indeed likely to strike the Sassenach as dour. He was, and is, a man of plain speech and few words: not qualities we associate with Carlyle (there is Lord Morley's famous quip that 'it had taken Carlyle twenty-four volumes into which to compress his doctrine of Silence'). We are reduced, then, to the two other obvious sources, the Bible and 'Germanism', and it would be safe to say that a great deal of both must have gone into the making of the pudding, with rather more of the Bible, I would say, and rather less of the German than has been generally assumed. Nevertheless, when allowance is made for these and other borrowings, it remains true that in Carlyle *le style c'est l'homme*. His disciple Froude remarked that 'he had no *invention*. He had a powerful imagination. It is possible to have both, of course; but the distinction is important.' That is the point: Carlyle needed his new style to convey the particular message he felt—especially after his 'conversion'—that he was elected to convey; but the words and the art were lacking.

Interestingly, it is from one of those who most loved Carlyle and found his affection returned, John Sterling, that we get the most frank and—to our ears—most acute and devastating contemporary criticism. On 'Sartor Resartus' he speaks out plainly:

> The language is often positively barbarous. 'Environment', 'Vestural', 'Stertorous', 'Visualised', 'Complected' . . . are words, so far as I know, without any authority; some of them contrary to analogy; and none repaying by their value the disadvantage of novelty . ..

Ironic that two of these neologisms should now be standard English! But Sterling is no less severe—and he had a gentle temperament, as different from Carlyle's as it is possible to imagine—on the syntactical curios which, he sees, are both so dear to Carlyle, and yet so damaging to his philosophy:

> The incessant use of odd superfluous qualification of assertions; which seems to give the character of deliberateness and caution to the style, but in time sounds like a mere trick or involuntary habit. . . . Something similar may be remarked of the use of the double negative by way of affirmation, or of the composition of words, such as 'snow-and-rosebloom-maiden': an attractive damsel doubtless in Germany, but, with all her charms, somewhat uncouth here.

One is never entirely clear about Sterling's own standpoint on matters of religion: he was never quite sure about it himself. But his general views would most likely have resembled those of his great fellow-Coleridgean, Frederick Denison Maurice, co-founder of the Apostles in their Cambridge days (we shall hear more of the Apostles later, and rather different things, when they formed the core of the original Bloomsbury group). As it was, Sterling died young, and we cannot know whether he would have lost his faith entirely, like Leslie Stephen, or whether the combined influences of Coleridge and Carlyle and Maurice might have drawn him back into the fold. But that he saw to the heart of the matter, in the case of Carlyle, there can be no doubt. Carlyle had indeed something to say; but he was not going about saying it in the most effective way:

> A style may be fatiguing and faulty precisely by being too emphatic, forcible and pointed; and so straining the attention to find its meaning, or the admiration to appreciate its beauty. . . . In short there is not a sufficient basis of the common to justify the amount of peculiarity in the work.

Sterling sums up; and stresses, once again, the link between the style and the underlying *Weltanschauung*:

> The sum of all I have been writing . . . may of course be quite erroneous: but granting its truth, it would supply the one principle which I have been seeking for, to explain the peculiarities of style in your account of Teufelsdröckh and his writings. . . . The life and works of Luther are the best comment I know of on this doctrine of mine.

Luther as an antidote to Carlyle and his Teufelsdröckh? At first glance, this may appear bizarre, a case of coals to Newcastle: would not the cure have proved worse than the disease? Yet, of course, the suggestion is uncannily right. For Luther is all that Carlyle is striving to be and, as Sterling realises, fails to be. Luther, by any standard, must be accounted one of the great prophets in the history of Christendom, indeed in the whole history of religion. He is a great preacher; that is, he has a powerful conviction of faith, and he has the gift of tongues. It is a truism that Luther's translation of the Bible is as great a work of literary art as the Authorised Version, and that it had a still profounder influence on the shaping of the German mind than the King James Bible on the Anglo-Saxon. Indeed, it can be said to have created modern German, as Goethe and Schiller knew it, and we know it today: Luther's precision, lucidity, and sheer poetic power have never been denied. Yet, although the German Renaissance lay two and a half centuries in the future, Luther's prose and verse—his great hymns—did not have the crushing effect that Shakespeare, for example, may be said to have had on the development of dramatic poetry in English. What Coleridge unkindly said of Schiller's blank verse—'it moves like a fly in a glue-bottle'—is all too close to the truth. But Schiller's prose writings, like those of Goethe or Lessing, are models of clarity and lucidity and—except where they sound too 'metaphysical' to the Anglo-Saxon ear—do not in the least resemble the Carlyle whom Sterling, quietly but firmly, felt bound to chastise (probably the chief culprit, though he was scarcely known in England at the time, who accounts for the more outrageous 'Teutonisms' in Carlyle was Jean-Paul Richter). But what Sterling does not spell out is nevertheless implicit in the remark he tosses off about Luther. In Luther the style elevates the man and message; in Carlyle the style diminishes both.

CHAPTER THREE

'Conversion'

We are thus confronted with the problem of Carlyle's 'religion' —the basis, I have suggested, of his enormous impact on Victorian England. Sterling makes a remark about 'Sartor Resartus' which is intended, I think, as praise:

> The style . . . coheres with, and springs from, the whole turn and tendency of thought.

But if what Sterling has been saying about style is true—and I fear its truth is undeniable—does not this comment imply an extremely negative verdict upon the nature of Teufelsdröckh's (or Carlyle's) 'religion'? This is the point we have now to examine. Carlyle's own account of his 'conversion' is familiar: we have no doubt that when Teufelsdröckh speaks we are also listening to the voice of Carlyle:

> Thus had the Everlasting No (*das ewige Nein*) pealed authoratively through all the recesses of my being, of my Me: and then it was that my whole Me stood up in native God-created majesty and with emphasis recorded its Protest . . . The Everlasting No had said: 'Behold, thou art fatherless, outcast and the universe is mine (the Devil's)': to which my whole Me now made answer: 'I am not thine, but Free and forever hate thee!'

Happiness, the great criterion of Bentham and the Utilitarians, is of course anathema to Carlyle. It is a kind of presumption— Calvinistically seen—on the part of Man:

> There is in man a Higher than love of Happiness; he can do without Happiness and instead thereof find Blessedness. . . . On the roaring billows of Time thou art not engulfed, but borne aloft into the azure of Eternity. Love not Pleasure,

93

Love God. This is the Everlasting Yea, wherein all contradictions are resolved: wherein who so walks and works it is
well with him.

'God' here, we notice, makes only a brief entrance from the
wings. It is the 'Everlasting Yea' and *das ewige Nein* that really
seem to matter. But then Carlyle dares a further step:

How thou fermentest and elaboratest, thy great fermenting
vat and laboratory of an Atmosphere, of a World, O Nature!
—Or what is Nature? Ha! Why do I not name thee God?
Art thou not the 'Living Garment of God'? O Heavens,
is it in very deed, He, then, that ever speaks through thee;
that lives and loves in thee, that lives and loves in me?

'Why do I not name thee God?' Why not, indeed? Perhaps
the strange confusion is indeed allowable, perhaps even
commanded from Above. Or perhaps it does not very much
matter what name we give to the Ultimate, the Infinite, the
All Highest? But there is also, as Carlyle must have known,
a Biblical command no less compelling: 'Thou shalt not take
My name in vain.' The question turns, then, on what kind of
God Carlyle believed in himself, and exhorted his followers
to believe in. We know that Carlyle considered himself to have
been raised up from the gloomy depths of death and damnation
by Goethe. There are two recognisable semi-quotations from
Faust in the passages quoted above: *der Gottheit lebendiges
Kleid* ('Living Garment of God') and Mephistopheles' *Ich bin
der Geist der stets verneint* ('I am the Spirit that denies'). But
Goethe never was, and never pretended to be, any kind of
Christian. He did not explicitly *deny* Christianity—though it
is said that he could not even bear the sight of a crucifix on
a wall—but rather tolerated it, in accomplished Olympian
style, as something that must have something good in it since
it had been going on for such a very long time. How, then,
was Carlyle 'saved' by Goethe from the threat of despair and
damnation? Carlyle wrote later:

I understood well what the Old Christian people meant by
their 'conversion', by God's infinite mercy. . . . I then felt,

and still feel, endlessly indebted to *Goethe* in the business; he, in his fashion, I perceived had travelled the steep rocky road before me—the first of the moderns.

The test, then, appears to be that a man should have gone through a 'crisis' in the course of his life. And there is no doubt that Carlyle saw in Goethe's progression from the 'despair' of *Werther* to the 'serenity' of the latter sections of *Wilhelm Meister* and *Faust* (we have to bear in mind that Carlyle— that hater of Dry-as-Dust scholarship—read very selectively) a progression which no man in this Vale of Tears can hope to escape—a progression from utter despair to the blessed certainty of Election. We see, further, that he judges people according to this criterion: his judgment on Coleridge in 'John Sterling' is indeed surprisingly harsh. Coleridge had

> skirted the deserts of infidelity . . . but had not had the courage, in defiance of pain and terror, to press resolutely across such deserts to the new firm lands of faith beyond.

Where had Coleridge gone wrong? According to Carlyle, he had

> lingered fatally round the starting point, and succeeded only in starting strange spectral Puseyisms, monstrous illusory hybrids and ecclesiastical chimeras which now roam the earth in a very lamentable manner.

By which, of course, he is implying that the Oxford Movement had its roots in Coleridge—a partial truth, certainly, but no more. But he is also implying something that the Tractarians in their day, and we in ours, can scarcely allow to pass: he is implying that Coleridge—unlike, presumably, Carlyle—while 'having skirted the deserts of infidelity . . . had not had the courage . . . to press resolutely across such deserts to the new firm lands of faith beyond'. This, and not mere spite, explains for example his outburst against the most famous literary Scotsman of his day, Sir Walter Scott. Leslie Stephen comments:

> He strives to do justice to the pride of all Scotsmen . . . but his real judgment is based upon the maxim that literature

must have higher aims 'than that of harmlessly amusing indolent, languid men'. Scott was not one who had gone through spiritual convulsions, who had 'dwelt and wrestled amid dark pains and throes', but on the whole a prosperous easy-going gentleman who found out the art of 'writing impromptu novels to buy farms with . . .'

But this kind of abuse is likely to be counterproductive in the long run—especially in that long run in which, as Keynes has it, 'we are all dead'. Nietzsche, whose name is so often coupled with Carlyle's, had nothing but scorn for Carlyle's prophetical pretensions: it is all English humbug; and it is *Carlyle* who has not had the courage to cast off his 'Hebrew Old-Clothes':

Carlyle stupefies himself by means of the fortissimo of his reverence for men of strong faith, and his rage over those who are less foolish; he is in sore need of noise . . . at bottom he is an English atheist who makes it a point of honour not to be so.

Nor was Sterling convinced. He admits that he has himself experienced something of the state of mind of poor Teufelsdröckh. But what he misses in Carlyle's doctrine is any kind of affirmation of a *personal* God, and any hope of redemption through Him. He craves for himself and for his fellow men

the clear, deep, habitual recognition of a one Living *Personal* God, essentially good, wise, true and holy, the Author of all that exists; and a reunion with whom is the only end of all rational beings. . . . What we find everywhere, with an abundant use of the name of God, is the conception of a formless Infinite whether in time or space; of a high inscrutable Necessity, which it is the chief wisdom and virtue to submit to. . . . And in this state of mind, as there is no true sympathy with others, just as little is there any true peace for ourselves. There is indeed possible the unsympathising factitious calm of Art, which we find in Goethe. But at what expense is it bought? Simply, by abandoning altogether the idea of duty, which is the great witness of our personality. And he attains his inhuman ghastly calmness by reducing the Universe to a heap of material for the idea of beauty to work on . . .

Carlyle would have had no quarrel with Sterling's rejection of aestheticism; no line leads from him to Matthew Arnold and Pater and Bloomsbury, as it does from the man he resembles in so many ways, Coleridge. Professor Harrold remarks:

> He had no taste for Goethe's and Schiller's philosophical dissertations, and indeed shyed away from their implicit aestheticism. Thus he altered Goethe's phrase from '*Im Ganzen, Guten, Schönen*' to 'The Whole, the Good, the *True*'— evidence of his readiness to find a moral emphasis in unlikely places.

Unlikely places! Yes, indeed. It so happens that we know Goethe's reaction; and who shall challenge the word of the Master? Goethe had remarked to Eckermann, after having had some correspondence with his new English admirer, that

> it is remarkable that when he is passing judgment on our German writers, it is always the moral and spiritual content that is uppermost in his mind (1827).

though he confessed that 'Carlyle is a moral power of considerable importance'. As ever, we return to Leslie Stephen— himself a de-convert from Christianity—as arbiter:

> The critics have had an eye for nothing but the harshness and gloom, and have read without a tear, without even a touch of sympathy, a confession more moving, more vividly reflecting the struggles and the anguish of a great man, than almost anything in our literature.

Leslie Stephen's judgment was not wrong, surely, in seeing that what was real in Carlyle was the suffering and the agony of soul—and adjectives such as 'dyspeptic' or, latterly, 'psycho-somatic' are not going to help. But what he also saw—and here I would not dissent—was that Carlyle's experience, whatever its nature, was not 'conversion' as the 'old Christian people' understood it:

Conversion . . . is a process which must be very exceptional with all men of real force of character. Carlyle, it is plain, was so far from undergoing such a process, that he retained much which would have been little in harmony with the teaching of his master. For, whilst everybody can see that Goethe had reached a region of philosophic serenity, we must take Carlyle's 'royal and supreme happiness' a little on trust.

'A little on trust'—already the Bloomsbury tone! Beneath the great shadow of Leslie Stephen there is a Lytton Strachey ready to pounce (although Strachey did not in fact include Carlyle among his 'Eminent Victorians'). But, even if we must take the famous 'conversion' in this way, we can accept that Goethe meant more to Carlyle than perhaps to any other English writer (including Coleridge). But it is likely that Stephen was right in doubting whether the Goethe Carlyle believed in was the real Goethe, or whether that Goethe had ever existed:

> The serenity of Goethe probably attracted him by the contrast to his own vehemence. Goethe . . . showed that the highest culture and most unreserved acceptance of the results of modern inquiry might be combined with a reverent and truly religious conception of the universe.

That Carlyle himself ever found serenity would certainly seem open to doubt. But it is equally open to doubt whether, if he did, his German studies had much to do with it. Professor Harrold makes the excellent point that

> It is probable that, in this first crisis of his life, the works of Schiller and Goethe played no part whatever. . . . Goethe was not for Carlyle a point of departure, but a *point d'arrivée*.

and he observes:

> That the Bible was the real basis for Carlyle's thought is revealed in the quotations from Ecclesiastes and the Fourth

Gospel in the last and climactic sentences of that chapter in 'Sartor Resartus': 'Whatsoever thy hand findeth to do, do it with all thy might'; 'work while it is called Today; for the Night cometh wherein no man can work'.

CHAPTER FOUR

Carlyle and Gurty

In Gissing's 'In the Year of Jubilee'—that is in 1887—there is a somewhat fatuous character, Samuel Barmby, who swears by 'Carlyle and Gurty', sources of all true knowledge and wisdom. He is, of course, ridiculed by Gissing. But it is implied that there are many like him. And that their names should be linked is natural enough: it was certainly Madame de Staël and Carlyle who effected the introduction of Goethe into England. Previously there had been other candidates for the post of German Laureate—Klopstock and Kotzebue, Lessing and Schiller. To have demonstrated in his 'Essays' (mostly written for the *Edinburgh Review*) that *Goethe* was the true and towering genius of the German Renaissance is to Carlyle's everlasting credit. We have seen, further, that Carlyle ascribed his 'conversion' to the good offices of the great German poet who had, he felt, doubted and suffered like himself, and yet triumphed over doubt and despair. It is, therefore, quite as much in the *man*, as in his works or 'philosophy', that Carlyle sought, and found, his salvation. But we have noted that this is not quite the end of the matter. For, as Sterling realised, Goethe's nature was essentially pagan; his religion, if he had any, amounted to a kind of Spinozistic pantheism, not unlike that of Wordsworth. Again, Carlyle's knowledge of German literature and philosophy was patchy. He was never the German 'expert' that his public took him for; but then, in his time, there were few to challenge him, since the public's knowledge of things German, as we have seen, was a great deal patchier. Yet, since Carlyle (with Madame de Staël) did so much to form the English idea of what Germany was all about, it is clearly important to know how well he himself understood those whom he declared to be his masters.

The three men besides Goethe whom he saw as his mentors were the philosophers Kant and Fichte, and the Romantic mystic Novalis. That there is a relation between Kant and Fichte is certainly true; though whether Carlyle understood its real nature seems improbable. There is also a relation between Fichte and Novalis, in that much of the substance of Fichte's thought finds aphoristic expression in the writings of perhaps the most original of the German Romantics. On the other hand, it is difficult to find much in common between the work of these three men and that of Goethe. Yet this is precisely what Carlyle is determined to do. He wishes to compound the thought of all four men—indeed of the whole German Renaissance—into a single unity, henceforth to be labelled 'German Idealism'. Professor Schirmer remarks in his invaluable study *Deutsche Einflüsse auf die Englische Literatur im Neunzehnten Jahrhundert* (Halle, 1947: the product, ironically, of a seminar conducted by him in the year of disgrace 1940, yet without a trace of Nazi influence, or, for that matter, of Communist, though Halle—Handel's birthplace—had by 1947 become part of the Soviet Zone):

> In his epoch-making essay for the *Edinburgh* in 1827, 'The State of German Literature', Carlyle puts together a largely fictitious, and certainly highly eclectic 'German Idealism', whose prophets are Goethe and Fichte. His discovery of Fichte's philosophy had led him towards the idea of the poet as Hero and Prophet; and as a result Goethe is apostrophised not only as a seer, but a spiritual leader and a moral teacher. In *Wilhelm Meister's Wanderjahre* Carlyle emphasises particularly the pedagogic element: Goethe speaks of suffering, and therefore we ought to follow this 'divine doctrine of suffering' and learn *Entsagen* ['renunciation'].

Clearly, much turns on what Goethe really meant by *Entsagen*, as well as on what Carlyle understood by it. It is well to bear two facts in mind: first, that Carlyle had a habit of seizing a phrase that took his fancy and placing rather more weight upon it, philosophically, than it was intended to bear.

It is also well to remember that Goethe and Carlyle had at least one thing in common: neither possessed a philosophical mind in the strict sense of the word. Both abhorred abstractions and system-building; and Goethe was certainly perturbed at the frantic system-building going on all about him—much of it, of course, at near-by Jena university. Schiller perceived this, and gave classical expression to it in his oddly named essay: *Über das Naive und das Sentimentalische in der Dichtung*. By naïve he did not, of course, mean simple-minded. Far from it, for he employed the concept to define the nature of the genius of his great friend over the hill, Goethe. He is implying that Goethe's genius, like Shakespeare's, possesses a certain immediacy, a certain naturalness, which is not present in the more cerebral, generalising (*sentimentalisch*) character of his own mind. He does not place the one above the other: he merely notes the distinction; and we can see that in English terms it corresponds roughly to the distinction between the nature of the genius of Shakespeare and Milton, and still more so to that between the mental processes of Wordsworth and Coleridge. Thus Professor Schirmer can write:

> Carlyle's chief debt was to German thought, either expressed in formal treatises like those of Kant and Fichte, or imaginatively stated in the poetry of Schiller and Goethe, or condensed in memorable phrasing in the *Fragmente* of Novalis or in the didactic passages of *Wilhelm Meister*.

Indeed, as Professor Harrold points out, this was the basis of the whole 'conversion' experience:

> The great influence which came to Carlyle through Goethe was primarily psychological: 'My greatly most delightful reading is where some Goethe musically teaches me.' What Goethe fundamentally taught him was faith in himself.

Yet, while this view seems to me correct, we are confronted with the paradox that, if Carlyle was not *sentimentalisch* in the Schillerian sense, he was certainly no aesthete either. Professor Harrold notes:

> He is much less interested in the artist and his art than in

the artist's philosophy and moral approach. . . . Thus we are not dealing with 'influence' in the old sense of the word, but rather with an attempted absorption of German philosophy in the course of which much of it has to be bent to suit Carlyle's argument. In fact one could say that he is only interested in other authors insofar as they lend support to the principles which he himself has extracted from Goethe.

According to Carlyle, his father had often expressed his distaste for the aesthetic in traditional Calvinist fashion:

Poetry, fiction in general he had universally regarded as not only idle, but false and criminal.

That this attitude was very much alive in his son is evident in the following passage:

It is expected in this Nineteenth Century that a man of culture shall understand and worship Art: among the windy gospels addressed to our poor Century there are few louder than this of Art.

One can hardly see Goethe—or Schiller, or Novalis—appreciating this blast of the Calvinist trumpet. The doctrine of the supremacy of Art may be said to have been held by practically all those writers and thinkers lumped together by Carlyle under the heading of 'German Idealism'. But what did Carlyle understand by 'German Idealism'? He had decided after reading Gibbon as a very young man that—in Nietzsche's phrase—'God is dead'. That is to say, the Calvinistic God of his childhood. Yet Carlyle needed a God. He needed Him to sustain his ethical teaching, and here he could derive some comfort from Kant, though Kant had used his 'categorical imperative' to sustain his argument for the existence of God, not the other way round. But Carlyle needed Him, too, not only as a transcendent Calvinistic Taskmaster, but to support that notion of God's immanence in the world which is no less fundamental to Calvinism, as it must be to any Incarnational Theology. Here he found himself rejecting Kant though, as

Professor Schirmer shows, this rejection was really based on a misunderstanding of Kant's teaching:

> Carlyle interprets Kant's epistemology as teaching that the material world is simply the symbol and veil behind which there exists an infinite and incomprehensible Spirit. That is, of course, an arbitrary interpretation of Kant: first, because Kant does not maintain that space and time are mere illusion; and secondly because Carlyle is interpreting his 'Infinite Spirit' as *essentia* in a theological sense, and not simply epistemologically as *Ding an sich*.

The truth is that whereas he found Goethe—in so far as he could bring himself to disagree with the Master—somewhat too 'materialistic' for his taste, he found this admittedly mis-interpreted Kant too little so. But he derived comfort from Fichte's concept of *Offenbarung* ('revelation'), in which he saw the doctrine of the Immanence of the Divine reasserted. In Professor Harrold's words:

> Carlyle took Fichte's concept of *Offenbarung* to be a step whereon he could pause in his reaffirmation of the deity; it helped him to recomprehend the doctrine of immanence. . . . Thus it released him from the tyranny of 'ancient matter'; it confirmed his belief in the God behind the vesture of the external.

The notion of *Offenbarung* was important to Carlyle, partly no doubt because he felt his own 'conversion' to have been a species of revelation, but also because of its bearing on Hero worship, and on the relationship of Hero worship to History (a matter to which we must soon turn). But he also considered himself indebted to Fichte for a quite different concept, which he was to make fundamental to his 'religion'. This was the concept of 'self-denial', fundamental, of course, to the religion of his childhood. Thus Fichte writes in his *Die Bestimmung des Menschen*:

> The faculty by which we lay hold on Eternal Life is to be attained only by actually renouncing the sensuous and its

objects, and sacrificing them to that law which takes cognisance of our will only, and not of our actions.

Or, again, in his *Anweisung zum Seligen Leben*, where Fichte declares that a man must

renounce himself as the true negation—and then he is wholly absorbed in God. . . . It is this self-renunciation, this love of God, that extirpates personal Self-Love.

Whether Carlyle actually read these passages is less important than their obvious general resemblance to the ideal of self-denial or renunciation he was searching for. Had not Carlyle—in the guise of Teufelsdröckh—experienced something of this sort as a necessary step in his own spiritual progress?

Here, then, as I lay in that centre of INDIFFERENCE; cast, doubtless by benignant upper influence, into a healing sleep, the heavy dreams rolled gradually away, and I awoke to a new Heaven and a new Earth. The first preliminary moral Act ANNIHILATION of SELF (*Selbsttödtung*) had been happily accomplished . . .

Now the deliberate use of the term *Selbsttödtung* is highly significant; for it is the term used by Novalis to express the doctrine of Fichte, though it acquires a more mystical meaning at Novalis' hands. (The term Fichte himself uses for 'renunciation' is *aufgeben*.) This may appear to be no more than a semantic point; and certainly the two words are interchangeable in normal speech, as 'self-denial' and 'renunciation' are in English. But what makes for real trouble is that Carlyle evidently equates both with *Entsagen*, the key word in Goethe's *Wilhelm Meister's Wanderjahre*. This word became a great favourite with Carlyle. But, alas, it is all too evident that he entirely misunderstood its Goethean significance, which Professor Harrold defines as follows:

In it there is no absolute denial of any part of ourselves or of life. The denial is wholly relative; all parts are permitted expression at the proper time. . . . We need only remember that Lothario, the ideal man, the embodiment of the principles of work and renunciation, had nothing of the Puritan in him. . . . The renunciation, therefore, of which Fichte and Carlyle write, was something almost wholly foreign to the ideal which Goethe desired. The idea of absolute denial of anything was repulsive to him.

Entsagen is most certainly central to Goethe's philosophy of life. For it is part and parcel of his concept of *Bildung*, of the formation of the individual mind and character. *Wilhelm Meister* is, of course, the '*Bildungsroman*' *par excellence;* and the essence of the philosophy expressed in it is that as a man grows up he must learn to discipline his wilder speculations, passions, and ambitions. He must become, to borrow a Jungian phrase, 'an integrated personality'. Goethe's is therefore a fundamentally optimistic philosophy; and is indeed at bottom a restatement of the classical ideal of the Golden Mean. It is quite certainly not compatible with the doctrines of Fichte and Novalis, which represent a mystical (if not necessarily Christian) point of view. But the Calvinist is bound to abhor mysticism, since the idea that a man can communicate directly with a Transcendent God is repugnant to his whole way of thinking. Here, indeed, is confusion confounded, as Professor Harrold drives home:

> This application of Goethe's word to Novalis's belief that life demands an acceptance of suffering is characteristic of Carlyle's treatment of doctrines and terminology. First he interprets Novalis's theory according to his ethical pre-occupations; then he identifies the doctrine, thus interpreted, with Goethe's *Entsagen;* finally he applies both terms, *Entsagen* and *Selbsttödtung*, to his own doctrine which is, strictly speaking, neither Novalis's nor Goethe's.

Of course, this does not necessarily mean that Carlyle's own doctrines were untrue; only that he misinterpreted the doctrines of his sources, and thus misled his readers seriously as to the nature of 'German Idealism'. The conclusion must be, in the same author's words:

> In Carlyle's dealings with Fichte and Goethe and Kant, Carlyle remains himself, a monist when he reflected, a

pluralist, even a Manichean when he acted and felt. Throughout all his study of Goethe and Fichte, he retained a sense of Puritan realities—of sin, punishment, humility before 'the great Taskmaster'.

CHAPTER FIVE

Heroes and History

What is the popular view of Carlyle today? It is, I suppose, that he was an Eminent Victorian, who wrote in a highly eccentric manner, and introduced notions of 'Hero-Worship' which have borne evil fruit in our time, though fortunately not in our own country. In other words, the charge against Carlyle is that he was a fascist before Fascism and, in particular, that he was some kind of forerunner of Nazism. Did not Hitler ask for the passage in 'Frederick the Great', in which the accession of the Empress Catherine saves Prussia from destruction in the Seven Years' War, to be read out to him in his last hours in the *Führerbunker*? The charge, then, laid against Carlyle is that laid against Nietzsche: that they bear a great burden of guilt for the use to which their ideas were put in the following century.

What truth is there in this? In neither case, I think, very much. Nietzsche, as is well known, was as much opposed to anti-semitism as he was to nationalism. However dubious his notion of the Superman, it is quite certain that he intended it in an existential, ontological sense—man overcoming himself, realising his full potentiality, somewhat after the fashion of Goethe in the *Wanderjahre*. We shall see in a moment that Carlyle's concept of the Hero has altogether different roots. Nevertheless, it is undeniable that Carlyle at his worst—in 'Past and Present', and some of his occasional writings—could show a callousness and harshness which may be Calvinist but are hardly Christian. He defended Governor Eyre in his brutal putting-down of the slave-revolt in Jamaica; and he detested 'philanthropy' because he saw it as a mere palliative, whereas the root of the trouble lay in the *laissez-faire* he so deeply hated.

Mr John Gross, in his 'Rise and Fall of the Man of Letters', while prepared to defend elements in Carlyle's style, is expressing both the popular and sophisticated view of Carlyle when he remarks:

> It would be a mistake to write him up as an isolated special case. On the contrary, he was very much a portent. He points forward, not indeed to fascism itself, since after all he never crossed over into the realm of active politics, but to the *trahison des clercs*, the long procession of artists and intellectuals whose hatred of the modern world has led them to flirt with brutally authoritarian regimes or to clutch at obscurantist dogma.

This strikes me as altogether too harsh. For it is possible to set against it passages which show how deep was Carlyle's sympathy, as a poor man's son, with the lot of the poor. Indeed, it is possible to argue that, through his influence on Ruskin, and Ruskin's on William Morris, he can also be seen as a forerunner of modern socialism. However, at the beginning of 1843 he had a literary break. He turned aside from the big historical work and wrote 'Past and Present' without difficulty in six weeks. He was appalled at the social misery of the age:

> . . . Eleven thousand souls in Paisley alone living on three ha'pence a day, and the governors of the land all busy shooting partridges and passing Corn-laws the while . . .

It was one of those powerful and passionate works which change public attitudes and promote progressive laws. Without such opinion-makers as 'Past and Present' and 'Unto this Last' harsh or absurd theories of Political Economy cannot be undermined nor Factory Acts introduced. He certainly did not number the Scottish Nobility, whom Sir Walter Scott had so profitably mythologised, among his Heroes:

> It is noteworthy that the nobles of this country have maintained a quite despicable behaviour from the time of Wallace downwards. A selfish, famishing, unprincipled set of hyenas, though toothless now, still mischievous and greedy beyond limit.

Nietzsche was fond of propagating the fiction that his family was of Polish aristocratic descent (the name itself points to a

Slav original). Not so Carlyle. Carlyle was far closer to Cobbett, to the populist tradition in England that flared up with the Luddites and the Chartists, than he would probably have cared to admit. His greatest Scottish hero, after John Knox, was after all his fellow-peasant, Robert Burns. His criticisms of *laissez-faire* have much in common with the thinking of Coleridge and Maurice and the Christian Socialists—though, again, he might not have admitted it. His denunciation of the 'cash-nexus' between man and man was, after all, only another way of pointing to the manner in which Capitalism was destroying the older bonds between man and man which personalities as different as Disraeli, Marx, Keble, and Kingsley would have seen as among the positive features of the Middle Ages, the age of Faith:

> All this dire misery . . . of our Chartism, Trades'-Strikes, Toryisms, Corn-laws and the general downbreak of laissez-faire . . . May we not regard it as a voice from the dumb bosom of Nature saying to us: 'Behold! Supply-and-Demand is *not* the one law of Nature; cash-payment is not the sole nexus of man with man—far from it!' Ah me, into what waste latitudes in this Time-voyage have we wandered. . . . The haggard despair of Cotton-factory, Coal-mine operatives . . . in these days is painful to behold; but not so painful, hideous to the inner-sense as that brutish, God-forgetting Profit-and-Loss philosophy and Life-theory which we hear ¹angled on all hands. . . . Laissez-faire on the part of the governing Classes, we repeat again and again, will with whatever difficulty have to cease; pacific mutual division of the spoil and a world well let alone will no longer suffice. A Do-nothing Guidance; and it is a Do-something World.

But this 'populism', pointing surely to Socialism of a kind, was not first aroused by the spectacle of Chartism; it was present in Teufelsdröckh's toast of ten years before:

> Lifting his large tumbler of Gug-guk, and for a moment lowering his tobacco-pipe, he stood up in full coffee house . . . and there with low soul-stirring tone and the look truly of an

angel, though whether of a white or of a black one might be dubious, proposed this toast: *Die Sache der Armen in Gottes und des Teufels Namen!*—'The cause of the poor in Heaven's name and the —'s!'

Not a sentiment one would have heard from Nietzsche's lips, certainly; and in Germany, in Carlyle's generation, perhaps only from those of Heine and Young Germany. But the sentiment was fundamental to Carlyle's outlook and, though he did not see the remedy in philanthropy, his espousal of 'the cause of the poor' was no doubt one more reason why he became a 'popular author', especially during the first half of Queen Victoria's reign. Here, for example, is his reaction to the Peterloo affair:

> Who shall compute the waste and loss, the obstruction of every sort, that was produced in the Manchester region by Peterloo alone! Some thirteen unarmed men and women cut down—the number of the slain and maimed was very countable: but the treasury of rage, burning hidden or visible in all hearts ever since, more or less perverting the effort and aim of all hearts ever since, is of unknown extent.

Mr Gross's comment on this restores, I think, the correct balance:

> There are some ugly moments in 'Past and Present' but on the whole the tone is humane; and if Carlyle had died at fifty, he would almost certainly be thought of today, with a few qualms and reservations, as having been on the side of the angels.

But we have not yet disposed of the matter of the Hero; and no idea of Carlyle's perhaps has caused his modern readers greater embarrassment. How do we reconcile his apparent approbation of Cromwell's or Frederick's cruelties with his espousal of 'the cause of the poor'? Professor Grierson comments in 'Carlyle and Hitler':

> What I wish to indicate is that Carlyle's cult of the Hero had its roots in both his religious and his social conclusions and convictions. Thus Jesus Christ is not God, in the sense in

which he had been taught to believe—but the divine spirit
was revealed in him and in other great men.

Now at first sight it might seem perverse, not to say blasphemous, for Carlyle to place Mahomet, Frederick the Great,
Cromwell, and Napoleon in such company. But seen in the
context of Carlyle's view of history, and of the true function of
historiography and biography, the offence appears less heinous.
For once correctly, Carlyle understood that it was of the
essence of the German Renaissance, and therefore of 'German
Idealism', to view the world *historically*. To be precise, there
were two different modes of apprehending history, which
arose in Germany at more or less the same time. There was the
introduction of 'source-criticism' (*Quellenforschung*) by pioneers
such as Niebuhr, and later Ranke. But this revolution in
historiography, while it influenced Dr Arnold (whose 'History
of Rome' was based to a large extent on Niebuhr's work on the
same subject), and ultimately the whole methodology of
European historiography in the 19th century, did not greatly
interest Carlyle. While he went to the sources—Cromwell's
speeches to Parliament or the journalists who reported the
French Revolution at first hand—he certainly did not practise
Niebuhrian source-criticism, which indeed would have appeared to him as the world of Professor Dry-as-Dust. Indeed,
as we shall see, when this new method was applied to *him*, by Professor Merivale and others, he comes off very much second best.
    It was rather the other tradition, that hinted at by Professor
Grierson, which appealed to Carlyle. He had been troubled by
the meaninglessness of men's lives, if God were dead, and the
world mere matter, destined to inevitable decay and destruction. But for his 'conversion' to be complete it was not only his
faith in himself, but also his faith in the reality and God-given
nature of the material world that had to be restored. But to
what end? Goethe had taught him 'musically' that man's task in
this world is work and self-development (it is remarkable how
Carlyle, while misunderstanding Goethe's doctrine of *Entsagen*,
nevertheless arrived at much the same ethical conclusions).
Goethe's doctrine had given back to Carlyle the faith of his

fathers that a man's actions in this world are meaningful, because performed beneath the never-sleeping eye of a stern Taskmaster. But a man's actions must, plainly, be directed to some end. Here he found help once again in the thinkers of the German Renaissance. Gibbon had seen no teleology in history, certainly none that Carlyle could accept and use as material for the 'religion' he was determined to fashion. Friedrich Schlegel harshly criticised, as Carlyle would have done, the British historians of the 18th century—Gibbon, Robertson, and Hume—not only for their irreligious interpretation of history, but for their neglect of the phenomenon of *development*. If the old Hebraic teleology was to be abandoned—and Carlyle was forever talking of casting off 'Hebrew Old-clothes'—there must be found another teleology for the historian to work with. We need not trace the course of this new doctrine in Germany in detail (and, once again, we can never be sure how much Carlyle really knew of it). But there is a clear line of development from Lessing's 'Education of the Human Race' (1780), through Herder's 'Thoughts concerning a Philosophy of the History of Mankind' (1784–91), Kant's 'Concept of a Universal History' (1784), to Schiller's Inaugural Lecture as Professor of History at Jena 'To what End do we study Universal History?' (1789) and his later (1795), 'Aesthetic Education of the Human Race'. Professor Harrold comments:

> Schiller offered several points which later appear in Carlyle's theory: that great blanks in history can never be filled; that history is at best only a collection of fragments; that only the infinite Spirit can survey it in its entirety; that teleology can alone make history intelligible; that only the philosophical historian and never the routine and uninspired fact-gatherer can hope to seize and recreate the past. . . . But it is not surprising that what contributed most substantially to Carlyle's philosophy of history was Schiller's practice in his 'Revolt of the Netherlands'.

That this tradition was carried forward, through Fichte and Schelling, to its culmination in Hegel—and through Hegel to Marx—points to the extreme tenacity of this search for a new

or refurbished teleology in German philosophy and historiography. It seems unlikely that Carlyle knew much of Hegel;
the style would not have appealed to him, and Hegel's influence
was at its height in the twenties and thirties, whereas Carlyle's
interest was focussed on the first and second phases of the
German Renaissance: Kant and Fichte, Goethe and Schiller,
Tieck and Novalis. A meeting between Carlyle and Karl Marx
would certainly provide fruitful material for an Imaginary
Conversation; but I do not think that it ever took place. The
exact extent of Carlyle's borrowing from the Germans is once
again impossible to determine with any accuracy. But it was
the general drift of their thought that mattered. As Goethe had
recovered for him the Calvinist sense of meaningfulness in the
actions of the individual, so the German philosophers gave him
back his faith in the fundamental meaningfulness of the history
of mankind. But since Carlyle was not at bottom a believer,
since he had retained the framework but thrown out the
substance of Calvinism, he must locate an alternative sense of
revelation to illuminate the path of mankind across the awful
abysses that were opening up on every side. Hence, the
doctrine of Heroes and Hero-worship. The list, as is well known,
contains some surprises. There is the Hero as Divinity (Odin);
the Hero as Prophet (Mahomet); the Hero as Poet (Dante,
Shakespeare); the Hero as Priest (Luther, Knox); the Hero as
Man of Letters (Dr Johnson, Rousseau, and Burns) and finally
—and most significantly—the Hero as King (Cromwell,
Frederick, Napoleon).

The original lectures in the spring of 1840 were received with
a mixture of tumult and delight. They were one of the sensations of the season. Bishops sat calmly at his feet while Carlyle
declared Mahomet to be a greater Hero than Jesus Christ. A
sarcasm at the expense of Bentham brought John Stuart Mill to
his feet to utter a resounding 'No!' It is as easy to ridicule this
spectacle as to point to the dangers inherent in the cult of the
Hero. But that the Victorians took his doctrines seriously enough is
evident from some remarks of Leslie Stephen half a century later:

The fact is that the hero has contributed some permanent

element to the thoughts and lives of mankind, that he has
revealed some enduring truth, that he has created some
permanent symbol of our highest feelings, or wrought some
organic change in the very structure of society. . . . The hero
may be confounded with the sham . . . but they differ for all
that and the true man recognises the difference as the religious man knows the hypocrite from the saint . . . The test
can really only be applied by one who loves the truth.

The presence of some of these heroes requires no explanation.
Dante and Shakespeare could not very well be left out; Burns
and Knox must have been Heroes to Carlyle from his Annandale
childhood. But it is the presence in their company of the 'Hero
as King' that has done Carlyle most damage, especially since
he was to spend most of the rest of his life labouring over the
speeches of Cromwell and the heroic struggles of Frederick the
Great (did they influence the initial English enthusiasm for
the Prussians in 1870? I think they did). Yet, the real difficulty,
of course, is epistemological—in effect religious. We may 'love
the truth': but how do we *know* whether any particular man is
to be regarded as a Hero or a sham? The answer to this is no
doubt that we must judge a man by the fruits of his actions.
But this requires the existence in the mazes of history of a
hidden entelechy working for the Good, for the eye of mortal
man is too easily deceived.

It is essential to Carlyle's whole doctrine of Heroes and
history, then, that a divine presence should be active in history,
and that we should have faith in its ultimate purposes and
goodness, however distressful or obscure in the short term.
But this once granted—and many of his audience would
certainly have granted it—his vision of history becomes a
great deal less alarming, and is indeed not so far from that of
Hegel, or indeed from that of orthodox Christianity. The Hero
as King, even as Conqueror, his hands necessarily stained with
blood? Well, there have been many such men, and one can
neither deny that they have changed the world nor, if one is an
orthodox Christian, that God permits them to do so. To 'deny
the world' in that sense is not open to Christian, Jew or Moslem.

He must accept, in faith, that there *is* a divine purpose behind such things—or fall into Manicheeism. Thus Carlyle, in 'Past and Present':

> Deep in the heart of the noble man it lies forever legible, that, as an Invisible Just God made him, so will and must God's Justice and this only, were it never so invisible, ultimately prosper in all controversies and enterprises and battles whatsoever. . . . Blessed divine Influence, how it ennobles even the battlefield and, in place of a Chacaw Massacre, makes it a Field of Honour.

Fichte's teleology is not dissimilar, and Carlyle may well have been influenced by it:

> Nothing really good is lost in the stream of Time: how long soever it may lie defamed, misunderstood and disregarded, the day at length arrives when it throws off its disguises and comes forth into light.

This is the underlying faith that both Fichte and Carlyle demand. But those who have argued that Carlyle would have been an admirer of Hitler or Mussolini are surely refuted by the thunderbolts he casts indifferently at the pirates Howell Davies and Napoleon:

> Howell Davies dyes the West Indian Seas with blood, piles his decks with plunder. . . . But he gains no lasting victory, lasting victory is not possible for him. Not, had he fleets larger than the combined British Navy all united with him bucaniering. . . . Your Napoleon is flung out, at last, to St Helena; the latter end of him sternly compensating the beginning. The bucanier strikes down a man, a hundred, or a million men; but what profits it? he has one enemy never to be struck down; nay, two enemies, Mankind and the Maker of Men. . . . It is not the bucanier, it is the Hero only that can gain victory, that can do more than *seem* to succeed.

But, of course, all must depend on belief in this ultimately benign entelechy. And what if we lack it? What if we disagree with Carlyle's peremptory judgments, as many today would certainly disagree with this?

> Puritanism was a genuine thing, for nature has adopted it and it has grown and grows. I say sometimes, that everything goes by wager and battle in this world; that *strength* well understood, is the measure of all worth. Give a thing time: if it can succeed it is a right thing.

Such passages have given rise to the notion that Carlyle believed, with our 20th century totalitarians, that 'Might is Right'. Let Leslie Stephen be our arbiter on this point:

> Now in one sense Carlyle's doctrine is the very reverse of this. His theory is the opposite one, that right makes might. He admires Cromwell . . . expressly on the grounds that Cromwell is the perfect embodiment of the puritan principle, and that the essence of puritanism was to 'see God's own law' made good in this world. . . . The cardinal virtue from which all others might be inferred is not benevolence, but veracity, respect for facts and hatred of sham.

I think Leslie Stephen is right: Carlyle did claim to believe that *in the long run* God is not mocked, and that Right will make Might. But all depends on belief, on belief in Carlyle's 'religion', and we have seen that Nietzsche, for one, held him to be 'an English Atheist who made it a point of honour not to be so'. Leslie Stephen, the great Agnostic, saw this clearly:

> By what signs, then, other than the ultimate test of success, can we discern the just from the unjust? That, of course, is the vital point which must decide upon the character of Carlyle's morality; and it is one which, in my opinion, he cannot be said to have answered distinctly. . . . That is right, one may say briefly, which will 'work'. The sham is hollow, and must be crushed in the tug and wrestle of the warring world. The reality survives and gathers strength. Veracity, in equivalent phrase, is the condition of vitality. Truth endures; the lie perishes.

Carlyle declared that the most important thing about a man was his religion. This test was presumably one he would have been willing to submit to himself. We are therefore justified, I think, in submitting his own historical work, which he clearly saw as an extension, a working-out of his earlier philosophico-religious speculations, to this test of veracity. By mid-century, the scene was much changed. 'Source-criticism' was coming into its own; George Eliot had translated David Friedrich Strauss' epoch-making *Leben Jesu*; and historiography itself was turning from the biographical—a mode where Carlyle was at his strongest—towards the Dry-as-Dust, Niebuhrian approach he detested. But the test of 'veracity' had already been applied, in the very year of Carlyle's lectures on 'Heroes and Hero-worship', to his first major historical work, 'The French Revolution'. A deadly and persistent critic was Herman Merivale* in the *Edinburgh Review*. We find him writing in July 1840:

> Mr. Carlyle has attained his success . . . in some measure through his method of taking his colours and perspectives invariably from contemporary narratives analysed by himself, and never at secondhand. The advantage which such a process gives, in point of fire and force, may be easily conjectured: whether it is equally advantageous for the purposes of truth, admits of some doubt . . .

Indeed. For when Merivale speaks of Carlyle taking 'his colours and perspectives from contemporary narratives', he is not implying that Carlyle is using such sources as Niebuhr

---

* Herman Merivale (1806–1874) was the son of John Herman Merivale (1779–1844) and the grandson of a certain Ann Katencamp, daughter of a German merchant settled in Exeter: hence no doubt the unusual 'Herman' Christian names of her son and grandson. His father was a considerable scholar and translator in his own right. When past middle-age he learned German and, shortly before his death, published 'The Minor Poems of Schiller'. The younger Merivale, Carlyle's critic here, had a brilliant career at Harrow and he was taken to see Coleridge at Highgate. He entered Oriel in 1823, and was elected to the Apostles on his migration to Trinity, Cambridge, in 1825. He became Professor of Political Economy in 1837 at Oxford, where his lectures on the Colonies led to his appointment as Under-Secretary of State and, in 1848, to his succeeding Sir James Stephen—Leslie Stephen's father—as Permanent Under-Secretary.

and Ranke were teaching the 19th century to use them. 'His account of the Bastille affair', he continues,

> abstracted as it is from the pages of Besanval, Dusaulx, Fauchet, and we know not how many pamphleteers and newswriters more, is full of warlike clamour and riotous hubbub, and just about as like the real event as the sieges in 'Ivanhoe' or 'Old Mortality'. After reading it through, the student will be quite as much puzzled as at the beginning, to know who took the Bastille, and why it surrendered; for the eloquent narrator has all but missed the one military point of the story, namely, that after several hours of ineffectual shouting and musket-firing on the part of the mob, the arrival of a piece or two of cannon belonging to the *Garde Française* decided the event. And what unparalleled bathos, when, after page upon page of 'fire-deluge', 'fire-Maelstrom', and fustian enough to furnish out a German ode on the Battle of Leipzig or Borodino, the list of casualties is summed up at eighty-three besiegers and *one* of the besieged!

Then there is Carlyle's description of the battle of Valmy, another 'historical turning-point', since it marked the final entrenchment of the forces of Revolution and the spiritless collapse of the forces of Counter-Revolution (this was the battle at which Goethe was present with the Duke and his miniature army). Merivale first quotes Carlyle's description in 'The French Revolution':

> Through the woods, volleying War reverberates, like huge gong-music or Moloch's kettle-drum, borne by the echo, swoln torrents boil angrily round the foot of the rocks, floating pale carcasses of men. In vain! Islettes village, with its church and steeple, rises intact in the mountain pass, between the embosoming heights: your forced marchings and climbings have become forced slidings and tumblings back. From the hill-tops thou seest nothing but dumb crags, and endless wet moaning woods. . . . Four days! Days of a rain as of Noah, without fire, without food!

Strong stuff; but under Merivale's sniping fire the balloon is efficiently deflated:

> Alas! That picturesque history should be brought to the vulgar tests of geography and meteorology. The 'mountains' and the 'torrents' of the Argonne are altogether as fabulous as the Noachan deluge with which he has vexed the invaders. The Prussian retreat had not even the excuse of bad weather . . . September, 1792, was what it usually is in that part of Europe—one of the finest portions of the year. No rain fell (except on one day, the eighth) from the first to the twentieth, the date of the affair at Valmy. Then there were three or four showery days; and again, fine weather till the end of the month.

If Carlyle's historiography cannot stand up to such withering fire, it is perhaps not surprising that his fame as a Prophet should have been in decline long before his death in 1881. He founded no school, left no followers (unless one includes Ruskin and Morris, which would be legitimate). The truth is, the rise and fall of Carlyle's reputation had something inevitable and symbolic about it. For it mirrored the attempt of the 19th century to put the infidelities of its predecessor to rout; but the new century did not itself possess any longer the faith that moves mountains. What it lacked, in the final account, was precisely 'veracity'. We can still sympathise with the man, his sufferings, and his truly heroic labours. But we cannot be blind to the fact that his labours did not bear fruit. Max Beerbohm wrote his epitaph; and in a mocking vein that would perhaps have hurt Carlyle most of all. But he was speaking the truth:

> Here's Carlyle shrieking 'Woe on woe',
> (The first edition, this, he wailed in);
> I once believed in him—but Oh—
> The many things I've tried and failed in!

Coleridge and the Coleridgeans

CHAPTER ONE

Joy and Dejection

I have argued that Carlyle left behind him no school, that his labours, heroic as they were, did not bear fruit—either in a good or an evil sense. He was neither the proto-fascist he has been painted, nor the founder or reviver of a 'religion'. It is for this reason that I have treated of him first since, though Coleridge's junior by nearly a quarter of a century, it was the apparently ineffectual Coleridge whose influence grew, through Maurice and Kingsley, Thirlwall and Sterling and Julius Hare, Thomas and Matthew Arnold, until his apotheosis at the hands of Dr Leavis, Herbert Read, T. S. Eliot, and a dozen modern literary critics of the first rank. It is always worth putting the question of any much-criticised subject: what would the subject himself have made of it? With Coleridge, who knew himself so well and was very able—as Carlyle was not—to point to what he knew to be good and what he knew to be unsatisfactory in his life and work, we can be fairly certain what he would have thought of the twentieth century's estimate of him. He would have thought that by stressing almost exclusively the poet and literary critic, it had largely misunderstood the nature of his endeavours. No doubt he would have admitted that his philosophy was never satisfactorily codified, and that his attempt to compose a *magnum opus* which should unite its views on philosophy and poetry and religion with his no less strongly held views on society was a failure. But he would have thought those critics shallow who toss aside his philosophy and his theological speculation as extraneous to the 'real' Coleridge, whom they see first and foremost as a Man of Letters. The *magnum opus* may never have been written, but there can be no doubt whatever that Coleridge looked to its realisation as the chief goal of his life. The relevant question is whether the *magnum opus* did not get written because of Coleridge's personal weaknesses, or because his thinking was lacking in fundamental logical consistency.

This must always be the main factor determining the attitude of the Coleridge-critic to his subject: are we to take Coleridge at his own valuation, or are we permitted to take a section of him and isolate it from the rest of his thinking which has come down to us, however fragmentarily, in his few books, his voluminous Table Talk, and his newly-published Notebooks and Letters? Further, we have to ask ourselves the question put above: was it weakness, or was it inconsistency? It is best, I think, to declare one's colours on both these issues at the start. I think it not only plausible, but mandatory that we take Coleridge at his own valuation; that we see him as a whole, as he wished to be seen, and do not permit ourselves to take to heart that portion of him that appeals to us, and discard those portions of his admittedly complex mind which were important to him, and may not happen to be important to us. The second question is the more difficult to answer: partly because it demands a subjective judgment, and partly because the question is intensely difficult to answer in that we only possess (and, to a large extent, for the first time in this generation) fragments of the *magnum opus* that was always about to be, and never was to be.

My own view is that, while future researchers will find ever increasing consistency in the fundamental direction of Coleridge's thought, his failure to complete the *magnum opus* of which he so often talked is largely, though by no means wholly, personal. Yet, at this point, it is necessary to add the rider that the two judgments are not completely separable. Coleridge's character was certainly, in the Victorian sense, 'unmanly'; and we know that the much-advertised weaknesses of character had to do with his addiction to opium. But it is also true that Coleridge's thought was to some extent unsystematic of its very nature. Like Carlyle, he was groping for a philosophy that would reconcile old certainties with modern doubt; and there were few to aid and guide him. One could say that, philosophically, his talent for analysis was not matched by an equal talent for synthesis. But in this, after all, he is not unlike Pascal, or his own contemporary Blake: it may well be that what he had to say could only be said in the style that came most naturally to him—that is, fragmentarily and aphoristically. As he was to put it himself in the last year of his life:

> Hooker wished to live to finish his 'Ecclesiastical Polity': so I own I wish life and strength had been spared me to complete my Philosophy. For, as God hears me, the originating, continuing, and sustaining wish and design in my heart were to exalt the glory of His name; and, which is the same thing in other words, to promote the improvement of mankind. But *visum aliter Deo*, and His will be done.

The twin dangers in Coleridge-criticism are apparent. It is easy to dismember him, and deny him any true consistency as a thinker. But it is no less tempting to pick such plums out of his pudding as are to one's liking, and to provide the systematic exposition of his 'philosophy' which he was unable to provide himself. It is between this Scylla and Charybdis, then, that the Coleridge-critic must set his face to sail. He must not exaggerate the 'confusions' of his thinking, which may be rather dialectical contradictions when examined in a broader framework; and he must not construct a system for Coleridge that would amount to little more than an arbitrary imposition of the critic's own predilections on the now vast mass of material available. I start, then, from the assumption that there exists both development and coherence in Coleridge's thinking; but that it does Coleridge's thinking a disservice to attempt to over-systematise it.

What was the mainspring of that thinking? We have it in that utterance made in the year of his death: the chief end of man is to glorify God. But he equates this, as we have seen, with 'the improvement of mankind'—which is Benthamite language. And, unlike Carlyle, he is able to justify literature as a means of glorifying God. But if the intention is on the whole much the same as Carlyle's—to restore those things that he felt the 18th century had lost—the approach is altogether different. And we shall see that it is in Coleridge's way of going about things, unsatisfactory as it has always seemed to many, that his true strength—and his superiority to Carlyle as a Prophet—can be shown to lie.

Though it is true in general that the early Coleridge anticipates the mature Coleridge who 'sat on the brow of Highgate Hill', the very earliest phases of his development are of great importance. Thus he was in extreme youth, like Hölderlin and Hegel, an enthusiast for the French Revolution. As Professor Basil Willey points out in his 'Nineteenth Century Studies', the first influences on him came from Priestley, Thelwall, and Godwin:

> Following Godwin's lead, he teaches at this time that vice is the effect of error, and the product of circumstances—amongst which must be numbered monarchy and 'that leprous stain, nobility'. But better times are coming: France will deliver us: 'France! whose crimes and miseries posterity will impute to us. France! To whom posterity will impute their virtues and happiness.'

But he had soon abandoned the revolutionary cause; and from remarks in later life we know that his hatred of France remained intimately linked with his hatred of Jacobinism. Indeed, it is reasonable to assume that for him, as for so many 19th-century Englishmen, the reverse side of philosophic Francophobia was philosophic sympathy and attraction towards the formerly unknown world of Germany. Thus Coleridge can say, as late as 1818:

> I detest Jacobinism; and as to the French, Jacobins or Royalists, even as I love what is virtuous, *hate* I them.

But that he had drunk deep of Godwin and Rousseau at the age of twenty-four is evident from a letter written shortly before settling with his family at Nether Stowey:

> My children should be bred up from earliest infancy in the simplicity of peasants, their food, dress, and habits completely rustic.

Yet it is clear also from the same letter that the break with revolutionism is near:

126

I have snapped my squeaking baby-trumpet of sedition, and have hung up its fragments in a chamber of Penitences.

We know that it was in those years at Nether Stowey, near his childhood parsonage home in the West Country, that he produced the greater part of the poetry by which he is remembered. This was the period of the 'Lyrical Ballads', of 'The Ancient Mariner' and 'Kubla Khan'. That he helped Wordsworth to express his thinking about poetry philosophically in the first preface to the 'Lyrical Ballads' seems undeniable (though Wordsworth permitted himself in the second edition to remove Coleridge's name altogether, excluding 'Christabel' while retaining 'The Ancient Mariner'). But it is not always appreciated how much of the poetry he wrote in those years is directly concerned with the political and religious situation of the England of that time. And it does not need to be stressed that he saw the condition of England as in some sense his own condition too. In 'Fears in Solitude' (April, 1798), written 'during the alarm of an invasion', he mourns from the relative happiness of Nether Stowey the state of the country at large:

> The humble man, who, in his youthful years,
> Knew just so much of folly, as had made
> His early manhood more securely wise!
> Here he might lie on fern or withered heath . . .

> And he, with many feelings, many thoughts,
> Made up a meditative joy, and found
> Religious meanings in the forms of Nature! . . .

> We have offended, Oh! My countrymen!
> We have offended very grievously,
> And been most tyrannous . . .

How has England offended? In the first place because, though no longer blowing his 'squeaking baby-trumpet of sedition', Coleridge is none the less trenchant—as he remained to the end of his life—in his indignation at the misuse of political power:

> Meanwhile, at home,
> All individual dignity and power

Engulfed in Courts, Committees, Institutions,
Associations and Societies,
A vain, speech-mouthing, speech-reporting Guild,
One Benefit-Club for mutual flattery,
We have drunk up . . .

But, significantly, the political criticism quickly turns into self-criticism, and acquires in the process a religious tinge:

We have been too long
Dupes of a deep delusion! Some, belike,
Groaning with restless enmity, expect
All change from change of constituted power;
As if a Government had been a robe,
On which our vice and wretchedness were tagged
Like fancy-points and fringes, with the robe
Pulled off at pleasure. Fondly these attach
A radical causation to a few
Poor drudges of chastising Providence,
Who borrow all their hues and qualities
From our own folly and rank wickedness,
Which gave them birth and nursed them.

We ourselves, then, are the authors of our wretched condition. What must we do to be saved? There is no doubt in Coleridge's mind that, underlying the political and social condition of the country, there is a much more frightening failure, not so much to preach, but to practise true religion:

The sweet words
Of Christian promise, words that even yet
Might stem destruction, were they wisely preached,
Are muttered o'er by men, whose tones proclaim
How flat and wearisome they feel their trade:
Rank scoffers some, but most too indolent
To deem them falsehoods or to know their truth . . .

The rich, the poor, the old man and the young;
All, all make up one scheme of perjury,
That faith doth reel; the very name of God

Sounds like a juggler's charm; and, bold with joy,
Forth from his dark and lonely hiding-place,
(Portentous sight!) the owlet Atheism,
Sailing on obscene wings athwart the noon,
Drops his blue-fringed lids, and holds them close,
And hooting at the glorious sun in heaven,
Cries out, 'Where is it?'

The conflict between 'the sweet words of Christian promise'
and the realities of ecclesiastical practice, which are in truth
the breeding ground of 'the owlet Atheism', is the root of the
matter. It is here that we have offended. But, for all Coleridge's patriotism, and his sense that the threat to his beloved
country is due to her own sinfulness, there exists here a theological problem of which he was soon to become aware: how can
a man or a nation be said to 'sin' against a merely Spinozistic
'God in nature'?

O native Britain! O my Mother Isle!
How shouldst thou prove aught else but dear and holy
To me, who from thy lakes and mountain-hills,
Thy clouds, thy quiet dales, thy rocks and seas,
Have drunk in all my intellectual life,
All sweet sensations, all ennobling thoughts,
All adoration of the God in nature,
All lovely and all honourable things,
Whatever makes this mortal spirit feel
The joy and greatness of its future being?

His countrymen's problem has become a personal problem
for Coleridge. And it is at this point that we begin to appreciate
the nature of Coleridge's 'crisis', through which Carlyle was so
insistent that any serious religious person must pass before he
can arrive at 'the firm lands of faith' (and which Carlyle maintained, of course, that Coleridge never achieved). The classical
exposition of this state of mind—admittedly, not unlike
Teufelsdröckh's—is to be found in what is perhaps the last
great poem Coleridge was destined to write:

There was a time when, though my path was rough,
This joy within me dallied with distress,

And all misfortunes were but as the stuff
    Whence Fancy made me dreams of happiness:
For hope grew round me, like the twining vine,
And fruits, and foliage, not my own, seemed mine.
But now afflictions bow me down to earth:
Nor care I that they rob me of my mirth;
        But oh! each visitation
Suspends what nature gave me at my birth,
    My shaping spirit of Imagination.
For not to think of what I needs must feel,
    But to be still and patient, all I can;
And haply by abstruse research to steal
    From my own nature all the natural man—
    This was my sole resource, my only plan:
Till that which suits a part infects the whole,
And now is almost grown the habit of my soul.

'Dejection: an Ode' was originally written to Sara Hutchinson, Wordsworth's sister-in-law, with whom he had fallen in
love; and we have, of course, to remember that Coleridge's
marriage to Southey's sister-in-law was exceedingly unhappy.
But the deeper significance of 'Dejection: an Ode' is that it
marks Coleridge's loss of faith, not only in his own talents, but
in a Wordsworthian (or, for that matter, a Goethean) 'God in
nature'. Earlier he had written of nature—and we have seen
how Carlyle would have treated such a passage—in 'This Lime-
tree Bower' as

                   A living thing
Which acts upon the mind, and with such Hues
As Cloath th'Almighty Spirit, when he makes
Spirits perceive his presence.

But now this 'Living Garment of God', by which Carlyle
set such store, was no longer enough. Pantheism or Spinozism
would not do any more; and it is the simple truth to say that
they would not do any more because they could not do anything for Coleridge. Like Carlyle, he needed a God; but he

needed, what John Sterling pointed out was lacking in Carlyle's scheme of things, a *personal* God:

> O Sara! we receive but what we give,
> And in *our* life alone does Nature live.
> Our's is her Wedding Garment, our's her shroud—
> And would we aught behold of higher Worth
> Than that inanimate cold World allowed
> To the poor loveless ever-anxious Crowd,
> Ah! from the Soul itself must issue forth
> A light, a Glory, and a luminous Cloud
> > Enveloping the Earth!
> And from the Soul itself must there be sent
> A sweet and potent Voice of its own Birth,
> Of all sweet Sounds the Life and Element.

The new, subjective note points to the intensely personal nature of Coleridge's crisis. He had to find his way back to religion and, given what Coleridge was, it had to be a religion approached upon an intellectually acceptable route—even if that route should lead, as perhaps it did, to the final loss of his poetic faculties. It is at this point that Kant enters the picture.

CHAPTER TWO

Germany

We have examined Carlyle's knowledge of Germany and concluded, not only that it was slighter and more confused than is often supposed, but that it had far less to do with Carlyle's 'conversion' than Carlyle made believe. Is it possible that we shall arrive at the same conclusion about Coleridge's 'Germanism'? I think the answer must run: yes, but with a difference. Neither had the breadth of knowledge that one would, on the face of it, expect. Of both it would be true to say, with Professor Schirmer, that they went to German literature and philosophy for what it could give them, rather than in any very objective spirit. There is no reason why we should quarrel with that. They were not professional *Germanisten*; and it is doubtful, after all, whether at this period of intense activity in German philosophy and literature and music any *German* could have summarised all that was going on without that benefit of hindsight which we enjoy. Still, quite naturally, the assumption is often made that they knew more of the country and its ways, of its life and literature, than in fact they did. Closely linked with this assumption—indeed, almost flowing from it—is the charge that both (but especially Coleridge) borrowed from the work of the German Masters to the point of plagiarism. We shall look into this matter in a moment. But first we must discover what it was that led Coleridge to take up the study of German, and to spend several months in the country in 1798–99.

We must remember, of course, that Coleridge was already extremely widely read in philosophy—ancient, medieval, and modern—long before he took up the study of German. We know that he had been reading Leibniz at Nether Stowey (the shocked librarian had taken him to be asking for 'live nits'). And it was probably the lure of the as yet untranslated Kant that first seriously attracted him to learn German and study the new philosophy. It will be best if we postpone a fuller discussion of Coleridge and Kant, central though it is to Coleridge's 'conversion', to the following chapter. Let us merely note its centrality, and imagine with what surprise Coleridge must have listened on his arrival in Germany to Klopstock's diatribe against the *Kantianer*:

> I dined at Mr. Klopstock's. . . . I asked him what he thought of Kant. He said that his reputation was much on the decline in Germany, that for his own part he was not surprised to find it so, as the works of Kant were to him utterly incomprehensible—that he had often been pestered by the Kantians, but was rarely in the practice of arguing with them . . . He spoke of Wolf as the first metaphysician they had in Germany. Wolf had followers; but they could hardly be called a sect, and luckily till the appearance of Kant, about fifteen years ago, Germany had not been pestered by any sect of philosophers whatever. . . . The Germans were now coming to their senses again. . . . He seemed pleased to hear, that as yet Kant's doctrines had not met with many admirers in England—did not doubt but that we had too much wisdom to be duped by a writer who set at defiance the common sense and common understandings of men (1798).

No doubt Coleridge made allowance for Klopstock's advanced age, and appreciated that he had had his mind formed long before the new philosophy began to spread from the centre of infection in Königsberg. But then Wordsworth's and Coleridge's first meeting with the 'Father of German Poetry' was altogether a somewhat confused affair—Wordsworth attempting to speak to the old man in French, and Coleridge in Latin. There had been, as we have seen, numerous translations of Klopstock's 'Messiah' into English over the previous half-century; and no doubt Wordsworth and Coleridge would have been aware of them. We also know that they were for the most part extremely bad; and Klopstock was not slow to express his indignation. Coleridge offered to render some of the Odes into English, and the old man was duly grateful: 'I wish you would do so', Coleridge reports Klopstock as saying in English, 'and *revenge* me of your countrymen'. But the meeting cannot be called a success, though it is perhaps worth recording as the first encounter between major English and German writers in modern times. And it is perhaps significant that it resembled so many future encounters in that it was little more than a conversation of the deaf. Milton was held by Klopstock in high esteem—had he not himself been hailed by his fellow-countrymen as 'the German Milton'? Coleridge seems to have been properly deferential; but he confided his private opinion to paper: 'A very *German* Milton, I should say'.

Coleridge, then, approached Germany in no spirit of *schwärmerei*. Earlier, in his revolutionary period, he had shown signs of Enthusiasm. In the winter of 1794 he had written to Southey, his fellow-Pantisocrat, after reading Schiller's 'Robbers':

> My God, Southey, who is this Schiller, this convulsor of the heart. . . . I tremble like an aspen leaf. . . . Why have we ever called Milton sublime?

This was the period of his poem 'To the Author of The Robbers':

> Schiller! that hour I would have wished to die,
> If thro' the shuddering midnight I had sent
> From the dark dungeon of the Tower time-rent
> That fearful voice, a famished Father's cry—
> Lest in some after moment aught more mean
> Might stamp me mortal! A triumphant shout
> Black Horror screamed, and all her goblin rout
> Diminished shrunk from the more withering scene!
> Ah! Bard tremendous in sublimity!
> Could I behold thee in thy loftier mood
> Wandering at eve with finely-frenzied eye
> Beneath some vast old tempest-swinging wood!
> Awhile with mute awe gazing I would brood:
> Then weep aloud in a wild ecstasy!

That the influence of the *Sturm und Drang* writers ran strong in that period is again confirmed by the 'German' plays of both Wordsworth and Coleridge: Wordsworth's 'The Borderers' in 1795, and Coleridge's 'Osorio' in 1797 (the play was performed in 1811, with Byron's encouragement, and ran well). Southey, too, was at this time planning to write a play about 'Banditti'. Certainly, Schiller continued to preoccupy Coleridge for many years. Yet it is difficult to know what to make of a comment such as this:

> Although Wordsworth and Goethe are not much alike, to be sure, upon the whole; yet they both have this peculiarity of utter non-sympathy with the subjects of their poetry. They were always, both of them, spectators *ab extra*—feeling *for*, but never *with*, their characters. Schiller is a thousand times more *hearty* than Goethe.

The comparison between Wordsworth and Goethe rings true: it is not far perhaps from what Schiller meant when he spoke of Goethe's genius as 'naïve'. But in what sense is Schiller more 'hearty'? It may be that Coleridge has Schiller's *Sturm und Drang* origins in mind; or it may be that he sensed that Schiller was, like himself, essentially the more introspective, cerebral, *sentimentalisch* of the two. That Coleridge did not quite appreciate how far Schiller had moved away from his origins is suggested by this remark, made in 1805, the year of Schiller's death:

> Schiller, disgusted with Kotzebuisms, deserts from Shakespeare! What! Cannot we condemn a counterfeit and yet remain admirers of the original? . . . And now the French stage is to be re-introduced. O Germany! Why this endless rage for novelty? Why this endless looking out of thyself?

Certainly, Kotzebue had become for Coleridge, quite as much as for the writers of the *Anti-Jacobin*, an obvious butt:

> Kotzebue is the German Beaumont and Fletcher, without their poetic powers and without their *vis comica*.

I fear that we are confronted at this point, not for the first or last time, with a good deal of confusion about the value, and even the nature, of the writings of leading Germans of the day.

When, for example, Coleridge is recorded in his 'Table Talk' as declaring

> Schiller has the material Sublime; to produce an effect, he sets you a whole town on fire, and throws infants with their mothers into the flames, or locks up a father in an old tower. But Shakespeare drops a handkerchief, and the same or greater effects follow.

He has evidently the Schiller of 'The Robbers' in mind, and the point he makes against the *Stürmer und Dränger* is of course apposite. But then, in putting down Schiller by forcing the comparison with Shakespeare, he is only expressing what every Anglo-Saxon is bound to feel. Hence, the famous jibe about the 'fly in a glue bottle':

> Schiller's blank verse is bad. He moves in it as a fly in a glue bottle. His thoughts have their connection and variety it is true, but there is no sufficiently corresponding movement in the verse. How different from Shakespeare's endless rhythms! . . . There is a nimiety, a too-muchness in all Germans. It is the national fault. Lessing had the best notion of blank verse . . .

The remark about the 'nimiety' in all Germans is certainly acute and memorable (what it has to do with Schiller is less clear): it was indeed to become in later times the 'national fault' *par excellence*. But did Lessing really have 'the best notion of blank verse'? Lessing was always a figure to whom Coleridge was drawn: but Lessing's blank verse would not have passed the Shakespeare-test either. There is only one German writer of the period who would, and that was Goethe. Yet it is precisely Goethe whom Coleridge found most difficult to admire among the worthies of the German Renaissance:

> The young men in Germany and England who admire Lord Byron prefer Goethe to Schiller; but you may depend upon it, Goethe does not, nor ever will, command the common mind of the people of Germany as Schiller does . . . Schiller took his true and only rightful stand in the grand historical

drama—the 'Wallenstein' . . . After this point it was, that Goethe and other writers injured by their theories the steadiness and originality of Schiller's mind; and in every one of his works after the 'Wallenstein' you may perceive the fluctuations of his taste and principles of composition . . . (Table Talk).

Coleridge had, of course, himself translated part of the 'Wallenstein' trilogy, and was certainly not at fault in pointing to its high excellence. But his judgment that Goethe 'and other writers' had in some way damaged the work of Schiller's last years is not one that will stand. Curiously, for so self-comprehending a man, Coleridge never seems to have detected the close parallel between his own relationship with Wordsworth and that which grew up between Goethe and Schiller. And, not appreciating its nature, he does not seem to have realised that it was as fruitful to Schiller as had been his own early relationship with Wordsworth. He realised that the excellence of Goethe lies in his lyric poetry, his poetic drama, and in *Wilhelm Meister*. But he persists in placing Lessing above Goethe and Schiller:

> In his ballads and lighter lyrics Goethe is most excellent. It is impossible to praise him too highly in this respect. I like the *Wilhelm Meister*, the best of his prose works. But neither Schiller's nor Goethe's prose style approaches to Lessing's, whose writings, for *manner* are absolutely perfect.

It is fairly clear that Coleridge exhibited a strong resistance to Goethe (though whether this lack of appreciation is better than Carlyle's apotheosis-cum-distortion is a delicate point). The following fragment of late Table Talk gives us, perhaps, a hint why Coleridge failed to appreciate the greatest genius of the age. Goethe was not only the last man you could build a 'religion' on, he was a complete pagan:

> I was once pressed to translate the 'Faust'; and I so far entertained the proposal as to read the work through with great attention, and to revive in my mind my own former plan of Michael Scott. . . . I debated with myself whether it

became my moral character to render into English a work much of which I thought vulgar, licentious, and blasphemous. I need not tell you that I never put pen to paper as a translator of *Faust*.

Coleridge's objection to Goethe, then, is that he is an 'immoralist'. Yet this attitude is strange, even unworthy, in a poet and critic of Coleridge's stature, who seems to have been perfectly aware of the charm of Goethe's lyric poetry and would scarcely have applied these crude strictures to other writers of equal importance. One can only conclude that Goethe represented a blind spot for Coleridge; and that the judgment constitutes something of a lapse. For it is plainly not true that Coleridge was insensitive to the virtues of German as a literary language. On the contrary, he was very much alive to its possibilities, if in a slightly bizarre way:

O for the power to persuade all the writers of Great Britain to adopt the *ver* and *zer* of the German! Why not verboil, zerboil; verrend, zerrend? I should like the words *verflossen*, *zerflossen*, to be naturalised:

> And as I look
> Now feels my soul creative throes,
> And now all joy, all sense *zerflows*.

I do not know, whether I am in earnest or in sport while I recommend this *ver* and *zer* . . .

He felt that German offered the poet permutations that other languages could not offer; though he is no less quick to point to the weaknesses:

It is in variety of termination that the German surpasses the other modern languages as to sound; for, as to position, nature seems to have dropped an acid into the language when a-forming which curdled the vowels and made all the consonants flow together.

Again, according to Coleridge,

German is inferior to English in modifications of expression of the affections, but superior to it in modifications of expression of all objects of the senses.

In fact, Coleridge was very fond of making such distinctions among the many languages he knew, which makes his dismissal of Goethe the more remarkable (although French is here the victim of his moralising):

The language in which Shakespeare wrote cannot be left out of consideration. It will not be disputed, that one language may possess advantages which another does not enjoy; and we may state with confidence that English excels all other languages in the number of its practical words. . . . Of the German it may be said that . . . it is incomparable in its metaphysical and psychological force. In another respect it nearly rivals the Greek—I mean in its capability of composition—of forming compound words. . . . Italian is the sweetest and softest language; Spanish the most majestic. . . . French is perhaps the most perspicuous and pointed language in the world, and therefore best fitted for conversation, for the expression of light and airy passion. . . . It appears as if it were all surface and had no substratum and it consequently most dangerously tampers with morals, without positively offending decency (1811).

It is evident, then, that though Coleridge knew how to value German, he was by no means an unquestioning Germanophil. And some of his criticisms of the Germans are harsher than anything one would have heard from Carlyle. There is this 'nimiety' in their national character. And of a certain Harnemann he remarks,

I don't believe in all that Harnemann says; but he is a fine fellow, and like most Germans, is not altogether wrong, and like them also, is never altogether right.

But contemporaries noted Coleridge's interest in things German, and we have it from one who should have known, Henry Crabb Robinson, that 'Coleridge's mind is much more German than English . . .' By this, I think Crabb Robinson means to say no more than that Coleridge's mind was of a strongly metaphysical cast; but many were soon to blame the tortuosities of his prose style on 'German influence'. (Coleridge is very much an exception among poets in that when he turned to prose he lost much of that felicity of expression which was still present in his Table Talk, as it had been in his youthful verse.) It was probably inevitable that when he started to express his new 'metaphysical' ideas about literature and the arts, or about philosophy and religion, he should be accused of plagiarism. Professor Schirmer, for example, argues that Coleridge must have borrowed many of his ideas on aesthetics from August Wilhelm Schlegel, though he allows that many of the so-called 'plagiarisms' *could* be simply correspondences:

> There seems no doubt that Coleridge had worked out most of his ideas about Shakespeare before his Shakespeare lectures of 1811. But the correspondences with A. W. Schlegel's Vienna lectures led to charges of plagiarism. He adopts Schlegel's distinction between ancient and modern literature, his comparisons with sculpture and painting and a large number of details, often word for word.

This is heavily fought-over territory, and it is improbable that final pronouncement will ever be made.* For Coleridge was certainly in the habit—as was Carlyle—of picking up fragments of knowledge and using them in an often unsystematic way, in the course of his writings, lectures, or Table Talk (but Coleridge's 'borrowings', of course, are in no way *limited* to German). The first to raise the charge of plagiarism was his friend-and-enemy, Hazlitt, in the *Edinburgh Review*. Coleridge's reply was to quote a comment of Hazlitt's against him, in the hope of convicting him out of his own mouth. There is no doubt, I think, that most of his intimate friends would have defended him in precisely this way:

> Hazlitt has thought proper to assert that Schlegel and the German critics *first* taught Englishmen to admire their own great countryman intelligently; and secondly, long before

* For a recent example, the reader should look at—but not submit to—Norman Fruman's 'Coleridge: the damaged Archangel' (1972).

Schlegel had given at Vienna the lectures on Shakespeare which he afterwards published, I had given eighteen lectures on the same subject *substantially* the same, proceeding from the same, the *very* same point of view, and deducing the same conclusions. . . . Even in detail the coincidence of Schlegel with my lectures was so extraordinary that all at a later period who heard the same words concluded borrowing on my part from Schlegel. . . . Mr. Hazlitt himself replied to an assertion of my plagiarism of Schlegel in these words: 'That is a lie; for I myself heard the very same character of Hamlet from Coleridge before he went to Germany and when he had neither read nor could read a page of German.' Now Hazlitt was on a visit to my cottage at Nether Stowey, Somerset, in the summer of the year 1798 in the SEPTEMBER of which I first was out of sight of the shores of Great Britain. Recorded by me, S. T. Coleridge, January the 7th, 1819, Highgate.

The same charge was, inevitably, to be raised in regard to Schelling and Fichte and Kant; and the assumption was clearly that a man with such 'a German mind', an anti-empiric and anti-utilitarian, must somehow be guilty of theft. The best answer to this is to be found in the evidence of his friends, and in this much earlier statement of Coleridge's—long before the Schlegel-Schelling affair—ending with a majestic reproof to his detractors in the final line:

In the Preface of my metaphysical works, I should say: 'Once for all, read Kant, Fichte, etc., and then you will trace, or if you are on the hunt, track me.' Why, then, not acknowledge your obligations step by step? Because I could not do so in a multitude of glaring resemblances without a lie, for they had been mine, formed and full-formed, before I ever heard of these writers. . . . I fear not him for a critic who can confound a fellow-thinker with a compiler (1804).

CHAPTER THREE

Coleridge and Kant

Most of Coleridge's later themes, then, are implicit in the poetry of the years before he made his expedition to Germany at the age of twenty-six. Thus he speaks in 'Fears in Solitude' in the spring of that year of 'the sweet words of Christian promise', and makes it clear that it is the condition into which the Church has fallen that renders these words ineffective, both for himself and for his countrymen. But we noted too that, whereas 'the owlet Atheism' is seen rather as a national peril in 'Fears in Solitude', four years later in 'Dejection: an Ode', the crisis has become very personal:

> There was a time when, though my path was rough,
>   This joy within me dallied with distress,
> And all misfortunes were but as the stuff
>   Whence Fancy made me dreams of happiness:
> For hope grew round me, like the twining vine,
> And fruits, and foliage, not my own, seemed mine.
> But now afflictions bow me down to earth:
> Nor care I that they rob me of my mirth;
>   But oh! each visitation
> Suspends what nature gave me at my birth,
>   My shaping spirit of Imagination.

This cry of distress is clearly open to several possible interpretations. By now, Coleridge was fully aware that his marriage had broken down. He was almost certainly hopelessly addicted to opium. He knew that his poetic powers were failing. He could not live by his pen, and was dependent on the charity of the Wedgwoods. Reasons enough for dejection, taken singly or together, one might say. But there seems to be a more fundamental cause for his dejection, a cause to be found in the lives of so many of the great Victorians. This was, of course, the crisis that Teufelsdröckh-Carlyle underwent. But there are certainly parallels at all times and in all ages. D. H. Lawrence was to write at the end of his life:

> The universe is dead for us, and how is it to come alive again? 'Knowledge' has killed the sun, making it a ball of gas with spots. . . . How, out of all this, are we to get back the grand orbs of the soul's heavens, that fill us with unspeakable joy? . . . The world of reason and science . . . this is the dry and sterile little world the abstracted mind inhabits . . . . The two ways of knowing for man are knowing in terms of apartness which is mental, rational, scientific, and knowing, in terms of togetherness, which is religious and poetic ('Apropos of Lady Chatterley's Lover', 1930).

The resemblance in tone and feeling to Coleridge is surely remarkable. But there is a classical description of the same mental condition in Coleridge's own time, which shows— almost comically—the 'sterility' that can inhabit the abstract mind. John Stuart Mill describes, in his 'Autobiography', how he has been listening to Weber's 'Oberon' and deriving much pleasure from it. But then a terrible doubt comes over him:

> It is very characteristic both of my then state and of the general tone of my mind at this period of my life that I was seriously tormented by the thought of the exhaustibility of musical combinations.

Mill says that he is one of the very few Englishmen of his time who grew up on a strictly non-religious diet, devised by his father, and that he could not cease to be a Christian because he had never been one. Yet, clearly, something had been lacking in the diet which James Mill had devised. What was lacking, evidently, was what Coleridge would have called Imagination; and it is this that his son finds in Wordsworth:

> What made Wordsworth's poems a medicine for my state of mind, was that they expressed, not mere outward beauty, but states of feeling and of thought coloured by feeling under

the excitement of beauty. They seemed to be the very culture of the feelings, which I was in quest of. . . . From them I seemed to learn what would be the perennial sources of happiness, when all the greater evils of life shall have been removed. And I felt myself at once better and happier as I came under their influence.

Now Coleridge himself had shared this very experience, though it was more truly of a religious nature than the psychological 'conversion' that Mill underwent. As Professor Willey put it in his 'Coleridge' (1972):

> The subject of the poetic Imagination, as Coleridge regards it, is by no means remote from his religious preoccupation: on the contrary, it is the centre part of it. With Coleridge, as we well know, no main study or topic was remote from the others or the whole, and to establish the autonomy and validity of imaginative experience was an important step in establishing the same for religious experience. And so we must take his encounter with Wordsworth's poetry as a stage in his religious progress. There was, he felt immediately, something new here . . . which had been absent from poetry since the time of Milton. What was it? It was the something he afterwards called Imagination, but in 1796 it presented itself as

> The union of deep feeling with profound thought; the fine balance of truth in observing, with the imaginative faculty in modifying the objects observed and above all the original gift of spreading the tone, the *atmosphere*, and with it the depth and height of the ideal world around forms, incidents and situations, of which, for common view, custom had bedimmed all the lustre, had dried up the sparkle and the dewdrops.

We have seen that there never was a time when Coleridge abjured religion as such; he was, if any man, *anima naturaliter Christiana*. Yet, though the son of a clergyman, his early opinions were not orthodox; he had become a Unitarian and, in common with most Dissenters, inclined to the Left in politics. It is significant, as Professor Willey points out, that the religious crisis in Coleridge's life should take on an aesthetic form. It is the 'shaping spirit of Imagination' that he had lost. This means, as we know, that he was aware that his poetic powers were failing. But it also means much more: that he has lost his belief in Nature as a surrogate for God. Teufelsdröckh, we remember, had cried, 'Nature! Why do I not call thee God?' But this pantheism or Spinozism, while it might satisfy Carlyle or Wordsworth or Mill, could never have satisfied Coleridge. He needed, like his disciple John Sterling, a *personal* God. Such a God was not to be found in Nature or in such books as Paley's 'Evidences'. He was, in any case, aware that Kant had destroyed the traditional 'proofs' of the truth of Christianity, indeed of any kind of theism. If proof of the existence of God was to be had, it must be looked for in the human heart. As Coleridge puts it in the 'Dejection Ode':

> Ah! From the Soul itself must issue forth
> A Light, a Glory, and a luminous Cloud
> Enveloping the earth!

It is not so much God who is dead, then, but Nature. Thus Coleridge distinguishes between *Natura naturata* and *Natura naturans*. The former is the dead, sterile world of the scientist of which Lawrence speaks—or for that matter, of the mere nature-fancier. When Coleridge looked now at the mountain magnificence of the Lake District, this is what he saw: the 'inanimate cold World' of the Ode. But, Coleridge argues, there is another mode of perceiving nature, which can bring it back to life. This is *Natura naturans*. Can we prove that it exists? Scientifically speaking, no. But he argues that to a truly awakened sensibility this is what nature *feels* like:

> If the artist copies the mere nature, the *natura naturata*, what idle rivalry! . . . Believe me, you must answer the essence, the *natura naturans*, which presupposes a bond between nature in the higher sense and the soul of man.

Or, as Coleridge puts it in the 'Dejection Ode' to Sara Hutchinson:

> O Sara! We receive but what we give,
> And in *our* life alone does Nature live.

True, this is Nature perceived through the eye of faith, and faith may not be granted to all. But Coleridge found support for his distinction in Kant's famous distinction between the merely phenomenal world—the *natura naturata*—and the transcendent, noumenal world of the *Ding an sich*. Yet, in the last resort, as Coleridge was only too ready to acknowledge, his new insight had its roots in his feelings:

> I feel strongly, and I think strongly; but I seldom feel without thinking, or think without feeling. . . . My philosophical opinions are blended with, or deduced from, my feelings: and this, I think, peculiarises my style of Writing.

But what Coleridge most valued in Kant was that he had set the human mind—*Vernunft* (reason) as against *Verstand* (understanding)—free from the shackles, as he saw them, of the tradition of Locke, Hartley, Priestley, and Godwin. The mind in perception is not passive, not a mere 'looker-on': it 'half-creates' what it perceives. The mind imposes its own forms or categories on the world, and we can only approach the world under these forms or categories. At this stage in Coleridge's progress, then, the 'primary Imagination' is evidently very nearly synonymous with Kant's *Vernunft*. Kant himself would not perhaps have gone so far; but we cannot say that Coleridge has misunderstood Kant, as Carlyle was to do. In the *Biographia Literaria*, the identification of aesthetic with religious perception —the problem that had vexed him ten years earlier—is thus resolved:

> The IMAGINATION then, I consider either as primary, or secondary. The primary IMAGINATION I hold to be the living Power and prime Agent of all human Perception, and as a repetition in the finite mind of the eternal act of creation in the infinite I AM.

146

From Kant, then, Coleridge has learnt four things: the nature of the perceiving mind; the distinction between Reason and Understanding; the transcendent, unknowable nature of the *Ding an sich*; and, perhaps most important, the centrality of Conscience, which we *know* as an existential reality. The hinge of this new philosophy, of course, is the link that it provides between the rationally unknowable *Ding an sich* and the knowable, indeed 'imperative', demands of Conscience. From this moment on the *Ding an sich* ceases to be wholly unknowable, for it can be known through the 'categorical imperative' of the moral law within us, which indeed we cannot *escape* knowing. Further, the *Ding an sich*, being unknowable to the mere Understanding, renders any kind of confusion of God with Nature, any kind of pantheism, untenable. Lessing, Coleridge's admiration for whom we have recorded, had declared 'There is no other philosophy than the philosophy of Spinoza.' Coleridge, too, had been fascinated by Spinoza; and Goethe often proclaimed himself Spinoza's disciple. This attachment had to be broken if Coleridge was to break with his earlier beliefs and discover a road back to Christianity. It seemed clear to Coleridge that Spinozism, or any kind of pantheism, must lead to atheism. For if God is everywhere, He is also nowhere in particular; and where He is All in All, He is not transcendent. But neither can this God of abstract Law be seen as personal or loving; and if He is the author of all things, He is as much the author of evil as of good. Again, in a world where all is rigidly fixed and determined, God is all and the individual is nothing. On this scheme of things we cannot but end up by discovering personality in neither God nor Man.

The philosophy of Spinoza may be admired for its ethics and its logical perfection; but Coleridge felt that its logic led away from Christianity, not towards it. To Coleridge, in his thirties, such philosophy had come to seem little preferable to materialism, since it must lead to atheism in the end. Kant, then, had freed him from his earlier errors. But the road towards orthodoxy vitally required the link between the world of the *Ding an sich* and the individual human conscience. Coleridge did not, of course, make Carlyle's mistake and simply identify the *Ding an sich* with God; but he knew the link to be vital. As Professor Willey puts it:

> Coleridge came to lean his whole weight upon this doctrine, and to build religious faith firmly on a moral foundation. According to Kant, Conscience—the category 'ought'—commands us to obey always and only the law we have ourselves evolved, the law of practical reason: that we must act always by maxims which are *universally* applicable. What are the postulates necessary to validate this 'categorical imperative'? They are God, freedom, immortality: God, the source and sanction of the moral law; freedom, since without it there can be no moral choice or responsibility; immortality, to right the wrongs and imbalances of this imperfect world. These ideas are not rationally demonstrable, but they are 'regulative' ideas, ideas which must be postulated—taken as real—to make sense of our moral experience. Conscience, therefore, and not 'reasoning' bids us accept as real those ideas without which it would itself have no meaning and no authority.

The chief appeal—but at the same time perhaps the great weakness—of this doctrine to Coleridge was not only that it gave him back a transcendent God in whom he could rationally believe, and a belief in freedom, but that it was a road back to Christianity along the *moral* highway. The weakness, of course, lay in Coleridge's psychology: his friends would have agreed that there was no more certain way to ensure that Coleridge would *not* do something than to persuade him he *ought* to do it. Yet that is no doubt why it appealed to him: he *ought* to ought, certainly, and if he did not he could always say with Paul, 'For the good that I would, I do not; but the evil which I would not, that I do,' and confess himself a sinner before God. It is, of course, true that the category 'ought' was often the last portion of the Christian faith to be retained by Victorian 'honest doubters'—and even passionately defended. F. W. H. Myers describes a memorable walk he took in Cambridge with George Eliot, which can hardly fail to ring faintly comic in modern ears. But there is no doubt that it is both authentic and typical:

I remember how, at Cambridge, I walked with her once in

the Fellows' Garden at Trinity, on an evening of rainy May; and she, stirred somewhat beyond her wont, and taking as her text the three words which have been used so often as the inspiring trumpet calls of men—the words *God, Immortality, Duty*—pronounced, with a terrible earnestness, how inconceivable was the *first*, how unbelievable the *second*, and yet how peremptory and absolute the *third*.

This could be Goethean in its emphasis, or Wordsworthian: but it never could have been Coleridgean. And in later years this became his main charge against Kant: that he had created a God, transcendent no doubt, but commanding rather than loving or forgiving. The quality of mercy was not in Him; and there was no quality that Coleridge needed so desperately. Kant's philosophy was thus a step on the road back to Christianity, but a step only. As he remarked to his friend J. H. Green in December, 1817:

Although I reverenced Kant as the only philosopher for thinking men, I rejected his moral teaching as Stoical and loveless.

CHAPTER FOUR

The Synthesis

Two things should now be clear: Coleridge, unlike Carlyle, *had* understood Kant; but he had come to a point where his innermost *feelings* compelled him to part company with him. Kant, in Coleridge's view, had helped him to cross the first hurdle: he had put the materialists and empiricists to rout. But he had not satisfied Coleridge's deep personal need for redemption from his own sins, and from what he felt to be the 'fact' of Original Sin. He would certainly not have responded to Carlyle's 'religion' with any warmth. Carlyle had merely arrived, despite heroic efforts, at a Hebraic-Calvinistic conception of a transcendent, wrathful and demanding God. Coleridge had said that

> The generation of the modern, worldly Dissenter was thus: Presbyterian, Arian, Socinian, and last, Unitarian.

He would certainly have seen in Carlyle a similar generation. There was no place in Carlyle's 'religion' for Christ except as a Divine Hero, which would have looked to Coleridge very much like modern Arianism or Socinianism; and he would probably not have been surprised that Carlyle should place Mahomet above Jesus Christ as a Divine Hero. What we can see now is that Coleridge was one of the first in England to understand where 'liberal theology' would lead: by demoting Jesus to the status of a Hero or Exemplar, the new theology would tear the very heart out of Christianity.

It is perhaps significant that whereas Carlyle never showed much interest in the Church as a historical and religious phenomenon, Coleridge was obsessed with it. No doubt this can be partially explained by their very different backgrounds. But in Coleridge's case there is more to it than that. One reaction to the rising tide of Utilitarianism and 'liberal theology'—of which Dr Pusey had brought back evil tidings to Oriel from his long stay in Germany in the 1820s—was that of the Oxford Movement. The Tractarians saw, logically enough, that one irrefutable reply to the onrush of the 'Higher Criticism', fed from German sources, was to pin their colours to the Church. The Bible, after all, was historically the creation of the Church, not vice-versa. Like the Church, therefore, being both a divine and a human creation, it could err. Granted that this was the true status of the Bible—which the Evangelicals could naturally never grant—the Higher Criticism might do its worst and nothing of the essence of the truth need be lost. Coleridge would certainly have agreed with this analysis, though he would have demurred at the authoritarianism implicit in Tractarianism, and still more in Romanism. Indeed, his dislike of Roman Catholicism—degenerate Catholicism, he would have said—was remarkably strong:

> The two characteristics which I have most observed in Roman Catholic mummery processions, baptisms, etc., are first, the immense *noise* and jingle-jingle as if to frighten away the demon common sense; and, secondly, the unmoved, stupid, uninterested faces of the conjurors. . . . Is not the very nature of superstition in general, as being utterly sensuous, *cold* except where it is *sensual*? Hence the older form of idolatry, as displayed in the Greek mythology, was in some sense even preferable to the Popish. . . . In the pagan it burnt with a bright flame, in the Popish it consumes the soul with a smothered fire that stinks in darkness and smoulders like a gun that burns but is incapable of light.

A cynic might perhaps observe that, in his religious polemics, Coleridge was only living up to one of the oldest of Christian traditions: turning his guns on his fellow-Christians, rather than on the enemy. Coleridge would not have seen it in that light at all. He would have argued that truth resides in no single action of the Church, but in the conflict between factions, since there is always some element of truth on both sides. In other hands such an attitude would—and did—lead to a sloppy, eclectic 'liberalism'. But Coleridge is better classified as a Broad Churchman than as a Latitudinarian: he is of the company of F. D. Maurice, not of David Friedrich Strauss. His method is often sharply polemical; but a dialectical approach (and surely that is the best name for it) is bound to be polemical to some degree. As Coleridge says:

> It is a dull and obtuse mind, that must divide in order to distinguish; but it is a still worse, that distinguishes in order to divide. In the former, we may contemplate the source of superstition and idolatry; in the latter, of schism, heresy and a seditious and sectarian spirit (Table Talk).

A man of Coleridge's mind was therefore bound to be obsessed with heresy. For what is heresy?

> My system, if I may venture to give it so fine a name, is the only attempt I know to reduce all knowledges into harmony. It opposes no other system but shows what was true in each and how that which was true in particular, in each of them became error, *because* it was only half the truth (Table Talk).

Coleridge's anti-Romanism is not anti-Catholicism, therefore; it is the Romans who are the sectarians:

> The present adherents of the Church of Rome are not, in my judgment, Catholics. We are the Catholics. We can prove that we hold the doctrines of the primitive Church for the first three hundred years. The Council of Trent made the Papists what they are.

Heresy, then, is a half-truth: that is what is wrong with it. But it follows that the half or quarter-truth that is contained in a heresy not only may, but *should*, be ferreted out and brought to the light of day. Thus Coleridge, even in his polemics, is not a doctrinaire: he is a Broad Churchman, who sees the Church of England as both Protestant *and* Catholic. As he pointed out, there were not many of like mind among the English Christians of his day:

> How much the devotional spirit of the Church has suffered by that necessary evil the Reformation, and the sects that have sprung up subsequently to it! All our modern prayers

seem tongue-tied. We appear to be thinking more of avoiding an heretical expression or thought than of opening our souls to God. We do not pray with that entire, unsuspecting, unfearing, child-like profusion of feeling, which so beautifully shines forth in Jeremy Taylor and Lancelot Andrewes and the writings of some of the older and better saints of the Romish Church, particularly of that remarkable woman St. Theresa.

The Reformation 'a necessary evil'! Carlyle would have risen, like John Stuart Mill, and delivered at this point a thundering 'No!' Coleridge can be very rude about the Puritans at times:

The Puritans adopted an absolute Bibliolatry. They would not put on a corn-plaster without scraping a text over it.

But for Luther, at least, he has the deepest admiration:

Luther is, in parts, the most evangelical writer I know, after the Apostles and Apostolic men.

Coleridge's criticism of the Reformation, then, turns out to be very similar to his criticism of post-Tridentine Catholicism:

The Reformation in the sixteenth century narrowed Reform. As soon as men began to call themselves names, all hope of further amendment was lost.

What we have called 'Broad Church', then, Coleridge would probably have called 'Catholic'; and it is not surprising that Newman should have regarded him as one of the forerunners of the Oxford Movement. What Coleridge hated in the Christian world of early 19th-century England was not only the hollowness of contemporary belief and worship, as compared with the golden age of Hooker, Taylor, and Andrewes, but the prevailing spirit of sectarianism:

I have known and still know, many Dissenters, who profess to have a zeal for Christianity; and I daresay they have. But I have known very few Dissenters indeed, whose hatred of the Church of England was not a much more active principle of action with them than their love for Christianity. The

Wesleyans, in uncorrupted parts of the country, are nearly the only exceptions. There never was an age since the days of the Apostles, in which the catholic spirit of religion was so dead and put aside for love of sects and parties as at present.

It is typical of his dialectical mode of thinking, on the other hand, that he flayed the Latitudinarians and the Romanists with equal zeal:

> The errors of the Sacramentaries, on the one hand and of the Romanists on the other are equally great. The first have volatilised the Eucharist into a metaphor; the last have condensed it into an idol.

We have noted already the stress Coleridge laid on *feeling*, though feeling must always be in accord with reason. It is therefore not surprising that John Donne was also among his heroes:

> O! Compare this manhood of our Church divinity with the feeble dotage of the Paleyan school, the 'natural' theology, or watchmaking scheme, that knows nothing of the maker but what can be proved out of the watch, the unknown nominative case of the verb impersonal *fit—et natura est*: the 'it', in short, in 'it rains', 'it snows', 'it is cold', and the like.

Does this bring us nearer to a definition of Coleridge's 'religion'? I think it does. His 'feel' for the vagaries of the Christian tradition is extremely subtle. He admits, for example, what few of us care to admit, that

> We are none of us tolerant in what concerns us deeply and entirely.

Nor, he implies, *ought* we to be so. Late in life he declares (1830):

> If an inscription be put upon my tomb, it may be that I was an enthusiastic lover of the Church; and as enthusiastic a hater of those who have betrayed it, be they who they may.

He would probably have agreed with Mill's jibe in the 'Autobiography':

> The people of England like old things. . . . And, therefore, on condition of not making too much noise about religion, or

taking it too much in earnest, the Church was supported even by philosophers, as a 'bulwark against fanaticism'. . . . The clergy of the establishment thought they had a good bargain on these terms, and kept its conditions very faithfully.

But would he, one wonders, have assented to Mill's assessment of himself and his 'school'?

It was natural that a philosophy which anathematised all that had been going on in Europe from Constantine to Luther, or even to Voltaire, should be succeeded by another . . . an impassioned vindicator of what was good in the past. This is the easy merit of all Tory and Royalist writers. But the peculiarity of the Germano-Coleridgean school, is, that they saw beyond the immediate controversy to the fundamental principles involved in all such controversies. . . . A philosophy of society, in the only form it was yet possible, that of a philosophy of history. Not a defence of particular religious or ethical doctrines, but a contribution, the largest yet made by any class of thinkers, towards the philosophy of human culture (1840).

Certainly, Mill is right to sense that Coleridge was not a 'conservative' in the usual religious—or social—meaning of the word. But, equally, Coleridge would not have cared for Mill's loose talk about 'fundamental principles' or 'a contribution . . . towards the philosophy of human culture'. This is the language rather of Hegel or of Comte. He overlooks the extraordinarily *personal* nature of Coleridge's desire to return to the Christian faith of his childhood:

Socinianism, moonlight; Methodism, a stove. Oh for some sun to unite heat and light! (1799).

Being interpreted, this does not mean that Coleridge, as a Romantic, was in any way romantic about moonshine. Quite the opposite. The moon is a dead, inert object which gains its brightness from the energy of the sun: the moon is *natura naturata*. And Methodism? Methodism, he readily agrees, has still sufficient vitality to give out energy: but heat, rather than light. 'Oh for some sun to unite heat and light!' By temperament, he was in many ways closer to Methodism (English

Lutheran Evangelicalism, as it might be called, since Wesley was 'converted' by Moravian Brethren) than he was to Unitarianism. As Coleridge said, 'It gives me pleasure to believe' (just as it gave Carlyle pain, which was what he seemed to enjoy). But the essence of Methodism was, of course, the *redemption* of sinful man through the atoning blood-sacrifice of the Saviour. A stove? Yes, by this Coleridge means that the Wesleyans had their heart in the right place—in utter, contrite submission to their Saviour. Their *feelings*, according to the Coleridgean view of things, ought not to be disputed. Their Christianity, or their sect of Christianity, was as alive as any in England. But what Coleridge had required was a Sun—which we may, I think, take to stand for Christian orthodoxy. The trouble was that just as the Unitarians did not *feel*, so the Methodists did not *think*.

Theologically, one could say that Coleridge was caught between an extreme Incarnationalism and an extreme Transcendentalism; and, unlike Carlyle, his mind could not be satisfied with the latter, if the former was not provided for too. He had travelled, with his mind, as far as Kant could take him; and perhaps a little further:

> For a very long time, indeed, I could not reconcile personality with infinity; and my head was with Spinoza, though my whole heart remained with Paul and John. Yet there had dawned upon me, even before I had met with the 'Critique of Pure Reason' a certain guiding light. . . . I became convinced, that religion, as both the corner-stone and key-stone of morality, must have a *moral* origin; so far at least, that the evidence of its doctrines could not, like the truths of abstract science, be wholly independent of the will. It were therefore to be expected that its *fundamental* truth would be such as *might* be denied; though only by the fool, and even by the fool from the madness of the *heart* alone!

But 'historical' Christianity remained always something of a stumbling-block. In February, 1805, he had written:

> Wavering in the necessary passage from Unitarianism (which as I have often said is the religion of a man, whose Reason

would make him an Atheist, but whose Heart and Common Sense will not permit him to be so) thro' Spinozism into Plato and St. John. . . . It burst upon me at once as an awful Truth: No Christ, no God!

Kant had helped him to *feel* the 'God of Nature' once again; and he felt that he had now rediscovered the Incarnation— God in Man—from his own experience. But he had done so, he must have realised, along a highly abstract route, and *not* primarily through his feelings. As Professor Willey puts it:

In the Journal he is to be seen working his way round to Trinitarian views. . . . Partly along the metaphysical route— as when he refers to the terms used by the 'Platonic Fathers': 'God, Logos and Wisdom in place of Father, Son and Holy Spirit . . .'. Miss Coburn is quite right to say, 'It will be seen that Coleridge's return to orthodox Christianity was made by a metaphysical rather than by an historical approach.' Yet we must always remember to ask what it was that drove him to return to it at all—and the answer must be, a deepening humility and sense of his own insufficiency . . .

Was this 'synthesis' finally satisfactory to Coleridge's intellect and feeling? It is not perhaps a question that one can presume to answer. But Professor Willey, for one, clearly doubts that Coleridge can be said to have found his way back to orthodoxy, though that was certainly his wish:

Coleridge never satisfactorily fitted redemption into his scheme. . . . Thus he can say that conscience commands the belief in God. . . . But does it equally prescribe belief in Election, Atonement, the Trinity? Does it involve belief in the Redemption of Mankind by Jesus Christ—specifically by his death upon the Cross? This is the heart of the conflict between Socinianism and Orthodoxy, between Coleridge young and Coleridge old. My own feeling is that he was never quite so fully reconciled as he tried to be to historical Christianity.

I would agree with Professor Willey in concluding that Coleridge probably never made the Kierkegaardian 'leap of faith' which he wished to make. Still, in the nature of things, we can never be sure. Coleridge is perhaps best seen as the English Pascal, who could apprehend intelligently and feelingly every mode of disbelief, and yet have sewn up in his jacket the famous confession that he believed in

> *Dieu d'Abraham, Dieu d'Isaac, Dieu de Jacob,*
> *non des philosophes et des savants.*

What else does Coleridge mean when he says:

> If 'God exists' were a statement of the same order as 'twice two are four', it would have no religious value; nobody could deny it. But a religious affirmation is a statement of faith, not a fact; and its religious value consists precisely in its committing the believer to a certain kind of living.

CHAPTER FIVE

The Germano-Coleridgeans

In the previous chapter I have attempted to give an outline of Coleridge's 'synthesis'. But is it claiming too much for Coleridge to claim that he ever achieved a synthesis? After all, though he himself often talked of his 'system', we know that the *magnum opus* was never to get itself written. And to one modern Anglican theologian, at least, he cannot for all his efforts be regarded as a theologian or a philosopher in the sense that his admirer F. D. Maurice can:

> He was not a philosopher or theologian in any professional or academic sense. He is best regarded as a seer who was always trying to cast his perceptions into the moulds of philosophic thought which he could never fully master . . . ('Leaders of the Church of England', David Edwards, 1971).

Yet Dr Edwards, in denying that Coleridge fully mastered the metaphysical concepts in which he dealt, is not denying the validity of his perceptions. And his perceptions were legion. We have concentrated chiefly on those that concern the central interests of his life, philosophy, and religion. But others are no less remarkable, putting him rather in the company of Blake than of Schleiermacher. Is there not, for example, a startling and Blake-like (or Goya-like) anticipation of depth-analysis in a fragment of Table Talk such as this?

> Madness is not simply a bodily disease. It is the sleep of the spirit with certain conditions of wakefulness: that is to say, lucid intervals. During this sleep, or recession of the spirit, the lower or bestial states of life rise up into action and prominence.

Yet Blake is never accused of having 'failed' to systematise his perception: he did not try, any more than his German contemporary Novalis tried (again, a man with many similarities to Coleridge). Perhaps the best definition of Coleridge's method, and of his influence on many of the best minds of the century, is that given by Matthew Arnold:

But that which will stand of Coleridge is this: the stimulus of his continual effort—not a moral effort, for he had no morals, but of his continual instinctive effort, crowned often with rich success, to get at and lay bare the real truth of the matter in hand, whether that matter were literary, or philosophical, or political, or religious; and this in a country where at that moment such an effort was almost unknown. . . . Coleridge's great usefulness lay in his supplying in England, for many years and under critical circumstances, by the spectacle of this effort of his, a stimulus to all minds capable of profiting by it. . . . His action will still be felt as long as the need for it continues.

But, of course, it is precisely this protean fertility of Coleridge's mind that makes it all but impossible to give a coherent account of the history of his influence. As he put it himself:

I have laid too many eggs in the hot sands of the wilderness, the world, with ostrich carelessness and ostrich oblivion. The greater part indeed have been trod underfoot, and are forgotten, but yet no small number have crept forth into life, some to furnish feathers for the caps of others and still more to plume the shafts in the quivers of my enemies.

It is this degree of self-knowledge, I think, that chiefly distinguishes Coleridge from Carlyle, who seems to have been singularly lacking in the quality. At times, of course, Carlyle was capable of remarkable insights into the characters of other men; it is probably his chief strength as a historian. But in spite (or perhaps because?) of the similarity of their *general* influence in the Victorian age, Carlyle certainly showed little understanding of Coleridge. In a famous passage from 'John Sterling' Carlyle describes how

Coleridge sat on the brow of Highgate Hill, in those years, looking down on London and its smoke-tumult, like a sage escaped from the inanity of life's battle; attracting towards him the thoughts of innumerable brave souls still engaged there. His express contributions to poetry, philosophy, or any specific province of human literature or enlightenment, had been small and sadly intermittent; but he had, especially among young and inquiring men, a higher than literary, a kind of prophetic or magician character. He was thought to hold, he alone in England, the key of German and other Transcendentalisms. . . . A sublime man; who, alone in those dark days, had saved his crown of spiritual manhood; escaping from the black materialisms, and revolutionary deluges, with 'God, Freedom, Immortality' still his: a king of men.

Still, Carlyle's physical characterisation of Coleridge is certainly unflattering:

He hung loosely on his limbs, with knees bent, and stooping attitude; in walking, he rather shuffled than decisively stept; and a lady once remarked, he never could fix which side of the garden walk would suit him best, but continually shifted, in corkscrew fashion, and kept trying both.

This is permissible fun, perhaps, at Coleridge's expense: it does indeed describe his life-style with painful accuracy. But, on reflection, the 'Highgate Hill' passage seems particularly contradictory. Carlyle, after all, is writing the life of his friend (and Coleridge's friend), John Sterling. Yet Sterling, of course, had all the defects that Carlyle ridicules in Coleridge, and his 'express contributions' to any genre—except, ironically, to that of Carlyle-criticism—had been infinitely less than Coleridge's. Carlyle must have known this; yet this must imply that the flattering 'a king of men' passage is either insincere or the product of a confused, or possibly jealous, mind. Yet there is no doubt that Coleridge did 'lack impact', in Victorian days and since, and that he found extreme difficulty in putting himself over or, as our jargon has it, in 'communicating'. If Carlyle put himself over with such apparent success—and we have seen that he did—it was because he employed a different instrument.

The choice between Coleridge and Carlyle is the choice between the corkscrew and the sledgehammer.

Yet the general tendency of the teachings of both Carlyle and Coleridge (though much of Coleridge is better known to us than it was to his contemporaries) worked in the same direction. Indeed, it can be seen from the pattern of their friendships that, if neither had much use for the other, their disciples—and those of Dr Arnold—saw rather what united than what divided them. Thus Sterling was most certainly a disciple of both men, and Sterling appears to have played a major role in fusing the two groups of disciples. He had met F. D. Maurice in the company of the Apostles at Cambridge. The famous Society had been founded by Thirlwall, later Bishop of St David's, and in Sterling's time included Tennyson, Hallam, Monckton Milnes, and Trench. Herman Merivale (Carlyle's later critic) describes its purpose in words very different, though not less arrogant, than those that were later to come from Keynes and Strachey:

> We began to think that we had a mission to enlighten the world upon things intellectual and spiritual. . . . Coleridge and Wordsworth were our principal divinities and Hare and Thirlwall were regarded as their prophets.

Of those mentioned above, two were to become Poets Laureate (Wordsworth and Tennyson); one Archbishop of Dublin (Richard Chevenix-Trench); one a Bishop (Thirlwall); another an Archdeacon (Julius Hare); and one, Frederick Denison Maurice, according to modern opinion possibly the most original of Victorian theologians. No mean achievement, one might say. And they were linked in many ways, not only by sympathy but—somewhat in the Bloomsbury fashion—by ties of marriage. Julius Hare married Maurice's sister; and Maurice first married Sterling's sister-in-law, Anne Martin, whom he had met at Hare's, and secondly, after her death, Georgiana, daughter of Francis Hare-Naylor, half-brother of Julius Hare. And there were further links: Froude was friendly with Charles Kingsley, Maurice's ally in the Christian Socialist movement, and was to marry Mrs Kingsley's sister, whom he had met at his house. And the Arnolds, in their fashion, come into the story too. It was Clough, Matthew Arnold's 'Thyrsis', who introduced Froude to Emerson, and later to Carlyle, with results that are well known. The elder Arnold, unlike Carlyle, did not dismiss Coleridge as 'unmanly'. Far from it:

> His mind is at once rich and vigorous, and comprehensive and critical; while the ethos is so pure all the while (Letter to Mr Justice Coleridge, September 25th, 1839).

To complete the tribe, we discover that Froude was also friendly with the Coleridge family. In 1844, he had visited the Lakes with George Butler and Hartley Coleridge (Dr Arnold had built a house there, Fox How, on a plot chosen for him by Wordsworth). And we find that in 1847 Froude preached the sermon—this was before he had lost faith in Christianity, and found it again in Carlyle—at the funeral of the Reverend George May Coleridge, the nephew of the man who had 'sat on the brow of Highgate Hill'.

These intricacies are not, I think, irrelevant. As with Bloomsbury, they are very much part of the story, and they help to account for the rapid spread of 'Germano-Coleridgean' ideas in Victorian England. But these men are chiefly important because they held certain interests and doctrines in common: indeed, they might well have been dubbed by Sydney Smith (who invented the term 'Clapham Sect' for Wilberforce and his Evangelicals) 'the Highgate Sect'. What did they have in common? Two things, certainly: most of them were in one way or another concerned with things German; and they were all concerned, not only with the state of the Church of England, but with the social condition of England. To take their 'Germanism' first. It is, of course, clear that this came to them largely through Coleridge and Carlyle, and also through Dr Arnold, who must have been one of the few scholars and churchmen of his day to have read Niebuhr in the original (he was not translated by Sarah Austin until the forties).

Both Julius Hare and Connop Thirlwall were active in the fields of translation and exegesis. Hare had travelled with his parents to Weimar in 1804 and thus made his first acquaintance

with German literature at the age of nine. He visited the
Wartburg and there, as he liked to say in later life, 'first learned
to throw inkstands at the Devil'. As an undergraduate, he was
one of the few who would have known German at that time,
and in 1820 published a translation of Fouqué's 'Sintram' (later,
in 1847, he was to translate Goethe and Schiller into English
hexameters). But it was with his great friend Thirlwall that he
began a translation of Niebuhr's 'History of Rome' (1828–32),
which came in for violent attack as a 'sceptical' work. Hare
returned to the charge with a 'Vindication of Niebuhr', the
first among many such 'Vindications' (of Luther, Bunsen, and
Coleridge) which, he said, he must one day collect in a volume
to be entitled 'Vindissiae Harianiae, or The Hare with Many
Friends'. (The villagers at Herstmonceux declared that 'he be
no winter Parson': implying, no doubt, that the Hare, with his
lengthy sermons, was inclined to keep them too long at their
devotions during inclement weather.) Thirlwall had likewise
taken up the study of German and in 1824 translated two
'Tales' by Tieck. Shortly after, he began—significantly, in
view of the many parallels with Coleridge's thinking—a translation of Schleiermacher's 'Gospel of St Luke'. It was published
anonymously, but revealed his very considerable knowledge of
German theology at that period. (Ironically, it was the arch-
sceptic, Lord Melbourne, who had read his translation of
Schleiermacher, who obtained the See of St David's for him in
1840. Melbourne had, apparently, attempted to get him
Norwich three years earlier but, taking his duties remarkably
seriously as a dispenser of ecclesiastical patronage, had first
consulted the Archbishop of Canterbury, since he was anxious
that no Bishop appointed by *him* should bear the taint of
heterodoxy. A strange new light, certainly, on Victoria's
beloved 'Lord M'!)

But the point at which the three streams of thought converge
—the Carlylean, the Coleridgean, and the Arnoldian—is,
perhaps surprisingly, their social concern. This is not, of course,
to be divorced from their religious outlook: it flowed directly
from it. There is here a clear line of division from the Evangelicals, of whom Wilberforce and Lord Shaftesbury were perhaps

the most eminent, who practised 'Philanthropy'. Coleridge
showed the same marked distaste for this activity as Carlyle:

> I have never known a trader in philanthropy who was not
> wrong in heart somewhere or other. Individuals so distin-
> guished are usually unhappy in their family relations—men
> not benovolent or beneficent to individuals, but almost
> hostile to them, yet lavishing money and labour and time on
> the race, the abstract nation . . .

The reason for this attitude, as I have suggested in the case oᵢ
Carlyle, is that both saw the Benthamite philosophy as hypo-
critical: at best a palliative; at worst (almost literally) an
attempt on the part of the rich to steal their way into the
kingdom of Heaven. But for Dr Arnold and for Coleridge—
though not for the Puritan Carlyle—the Church *was* the nation
in its spiritual aspect. The Church had a care for the nation,
which it had grossly neglected; and this neglect had contributed
to the sectarianism and secularism of the age. Coleridge remarked at the time of the Reform Bill agitation:

> What between the sectarians and the political economists,
> the English are de-nationalised. England I see as a country
> but what could reintegrate us again? Must it be another
> threat of foreign invasion?

Yet this hostility to Reform did not turn Coleridge into a
reactionary, as it had Wordsworth and Southey. Dr Arnold, of
course, was a notorious Liberal in politics and, as the Tractarians saw it, in religion. But we have Mill's word for it that
Coleridge was never a 'Tory', never a mere reactionary:

> We do not pretend to have given any sufficient account of
> Coleridge; but we have proved to some, not previously
> aware of it, that there is something both in him and in the
> school to which he belongs, not unworthy of their better
> knowledge. We may have done something to show that a
> Tory philosopher cannot be wholly a Tory, but must often
> be a better Liberal than Liberals themselves; while he is the
> natural means of rescuing from oblivion truths which Tories

have forgotten and which the prevailing schools of Liberalism never knew (1840).

This is put, surely, with great perception and subtlety. And Mill is able to articulate Coleridge's, Carlyle's, and the two Arnolds' basic point of view—though from his own Utilitarian standpoint—with no less subtlety:

> Certain essential requisites of civil society the French philosophers of the eighteenth century unfortunately overlooked. They found them already undermined by the vices of the men and of the institutions that were set up as their guardians and bulwarks. If innovators, in their theories, disregarded the elementary principles of the social union, Conservatives, in their practice, had set the first example. . . . They threw away the shell without preserving the kernel; and attempting to new-model society without the binding forces which hold society together, met with such success as might have been anticipated (1840).

Is Coleridge, then, like Carlyle and like Disraeli's Young England, better defined as a kind of Tory populist? Certainly he was no Liberal of the Manchester School:

> And what have I got for all this? What for my first daring to blow the trumpet of sound philosophy against the Lancastrian faction?

At first sight, the notion certainly seems implausible: can we legitimately identify a stream of thought which includes not only Coleridge and Carlyle, but Disraeli and Ruskin, F. D. Maurice and John Stuart Mill, Tom Hughes, Charles Kingsley and William Morris, Thomas and Matthew Arnold? Certainly, Coleridge saw the Church—the spiritual nation—as the natural protector of the poor (as did Dr Arnold, devoting his time to good works for the 'operatives' of Rugby out of school hours):

> The fatal error into which the peculiar character of the English reformation threw our church has borne bitter fruit ever since—I mean that of its clinging to court and state, instead of cultivating the people. The Church ought to be a

mediator between the people and the government, between the poor and the rich. As it is, I fear the Church has let the hearts of the common people be stolen from it. . . . For a long time past the Church of England seems to me to have been blighted with prudence, as it is called. I wish with all my heart we had a little zealous imprudence (Table Talk).

Again, like Carlyle, he despised 'gentility', while admitting with true Coleridgean frankness that he was not one to despise the good things of life:

I love warm rooms, comfortable fires, and food, books, natural scenery, music, etc.; but I do not care what binding the Books have, whether they are dusty or clean—and I *dislike* fine furniture, handsome clothes, and all the ordinary symbols and appendages of artificial superiority—or what is called, *Gentility*.

One arrives, then, at a rather different estimate of this stream of thinking, to which Coleridge and the Germano-Coleridgeans are central, than perhaps one had expected. The dialectical approach was fruitfully—and much more systematically—perceived and developed by F. D. Maurice. Dr David Edwards writes of Maurice's first major work, 'The Kingdom of Christ':

He held to the Coleridgean maxim that men are mostly right in what they affirm and wrong in what they deny. So he maintained that each of the main divisions in Christendom and each of the parties in the Church of England, and indeed each secular philosophy and movement too, stood at bottom for a true principle or at least a valid quest: their mistake was to assert their own truth exclusively against others. This has become almost a commonplace today in ecumenical circles, but it was not at all a popular view in the nineteenth century.

As we know, this led Maurice and Kingsley, and Tom Hughes of 'Tom Brown' fame, to reply to the challenge of Chartism with Christian Socialism, later to be taken up by Bishop Gore and others in a stream of thinking that affected, certainly,

Masterman of 'The Condition of England', before the First World War (he also wrote a biography of Maurice), and perhaps reached its apogee in the elevation of William Temple to the See of St Augustine. Do we arrive, then, at the view that Coleridge was among the founding fathers of English socialism? It is less paradoxical than it may sound. There is an almost Marxian ring, surely, about this fragment of Table Talk:

> I think this country is now suffering grievously under an excessive cumulation of capital, which, having no field for profitable operation, is in a state of fierce civil war with itself.

The anger is unmistakable, and here Coleridge is surely very close to the Carlyle of 'Past and Present':

> It is not uncommon for a hundred thousand *operatives* (mark this word, for *words* in this sense are *things*) to be out of employment at once in the cotton industry, and, thrown upon parochial relief to be dependent upon hard-hearted task-masters for food. The Malthusian doctrine would indeed afford a certain means of relief, if this were not a twofold question. If, when you say to a man—'You have no claim upon me: you have your allotted part to perform in the world, so have I. In a state of nature indeed, had I food, I should offer you a share from sympathy, from humanity; but in this advanced and artificial state of society, I cannot afford you relief; you must starve. You came into this world when it could not sustain you.'

What, asks Carlyle rhetorically, would the man be likely to reply? What *could* he reply other than

> 'You disclaim all connection with me; I have no claims upon you? I can then have no duties towards you, and this pistol shall put me in possession of all your wealth . . .' It is this accursed practice of ever considering *only* what seems *expedient* for the occasion, disjoined from all principle or enlarged systems of action, of never listening to the true and unerring impulses of our better nature which has

led colder-hearted men to the study of political economy, which has turned our Parliament into a real Committee of Public Safety. In it is all power vested: and in a few years we shall either be governed by an aristocracy or, what is still more likely, by a contemptible democratical oligarchy of glib economists, compared to which the worst form of aristocracy would be a blessing.

Again, we may call in Mill as adjudicator, for Mill himself became not only an economist, but a declared socialist in his later years. Mill, despite his 'conversion' through Wordsworth, never pretended to be a Christian. Nevertheless, one doubts whether Coleridge would have disagreed with much in Mill's estimate of him in his 1840 essay:

And the State fails in one of its highest obligations. . . unless, to the full extent of its power, it takes means of providing that the manner in which the land is held . . . shall be the most favourable possible for making the best use of the land: for drawing the greatest benefit of its productive resources, for securing the happiest existence to those employed on it. We believe that these opinions will become, in no very long period, universal throughout Europe and we gratefully bear testimony to the fact, that the first among us who has given the sanction of philosophy to so great a reform in the popular and current notions is a Conservative philosopher.

A Family Quarrel

CHAPTER ONE

Albert the Good

There are two evident, embarrassing, incontrovertible facts about the English people: that they were once Germans themselves, and that they have been ruled for the past two and a half centuries by Kings and Queens of almost exclusively German origin. It is, for reasons that need no elaboration, not fashionable today to speak of 'race', though the Victorians (as Lionel Trilling remarks in his study of Matthew Arnold) had no such inhibitions. Today, of course, every schoolboy knows that 'Aryan' or 'Indo-Germanic' are adjectives which properly apply to a language-grouping, not to a 'race'; and since Adolf Hitler, the term 'cephalic index' is unlikely to crop up in a political discussion—though, again, I am not sure that other, non-German 19th-century Nationalists would have been wary of such physical descriptions of 'race'. Clearly, we have here got by the tail a word which has done—and may still do— great harm in the world. Equally, we are in need of a replacement. For we know quite well what we mean when we speak of Frenchmen and Italians, or Dutchmen and Spaniards. And we are aware that in speaking of them we are speaking of something more than language: the Latin American is not a Spaniard, but he speaks Spanish or Portuguese—he is 'Iberian'. Perhaps the best word available to us is the (to the English ear) unsatisfactory 'culture'. 'Culture' is hardly more precise in practice than the discarded 'race'. The East and West Germans, the Austrians and the German-Swiss—do they belong to the same 'culture'? Unquestionably, they do. To the same 'race', then? Our grandfathers would have said so without hesitation. Indeed, they would probably have agreed, with German-influenced Victorian historians like Freeman and J. R. Green, that the freedom-loving, democratic 'instincts' of English and other Nordic peoples—does not Iceland boast the oldest

Parliament in Europe, Switzerland the second oldest?—were the expression of these fortunate peoples' Teutonic blood. Words are slippery things at the best of times: it is well to remember that they can be killers.

We lack, then, a word to remind us of the undeniable fact that the origin of the English language, and doubtless of much else in our mental, moral, and physical characteristics, is to be traced back to the way of life of a number of closely related 'tribes'—*Stämme* is the German word, and the more exact one— who lived in Roman times between Jutland and the Lower Rhine: the Jutes, the Frisians, the Saxons, and the Angles. These peoples form the basis of the English, and a large part of the Scottish, 'nation'. Nor, thinking in mid-Victorian terms, should we forget that our great-grandfathers saw the British Isles as receiving a further—and highly beneficent—Nordic infusion at the hands of the Norsemen, from Wexford to Shetland, from the Outer Hebrides to the onerous Danelaw of the South-East. And it did not end there. It was through the Frenchified Norsemen of Normandy that the English were brought back into the mainstream of cultural, spiritual and political life of Europe. And here we can with much greater confidence speak of a definable 'culture' that was to permeate almost every quarter of the British Isles. Yet, when the facts are stated, and when due allowance has been made for the particular weight the Victorians gave them, we are in a quandary. For what weight do they bear for us? Today, we are not likely to be persuaded that it was the possession of Teutonic blood that conferred on us an unquenchable thirst for freedom. Nor does the Germanic basis of our language mean that our literature or our style of thinking, bear much relation to those of the Germans. There are parallels, of course; but no more than those with the cultures of France and Italy—to which we owe far more than we owe to Germany. The Victorians were not wrong on their facts; but the way they interpreted those facts is hardly the way we should let them be interpreted to ourselves.

Yet this is perhaps to leave out something that, again, meant far more to the Victorians than it is likely to do to us. There is

one great cultural debt—or curse, as you will—that we indis-
putably owe to the people of Germany: the heritage of Luther.
What England and Germany (especially North Germany)
had in common after the wars of religion of the 16th and 17th
centuries was Protestantism—and the Defence of Protestantism.
We too easily forget that until the 18th century the Protestant
North-West of Europe was distinctly on the defensive against
the great Catholic powers of Austria, France, and Spain. True,
Sweden enjoyed a brief glorious age as a major power in
European affairs. Holland had inherited much of Italy's
commercial strength. But Prussia, despite the great Frederick,
England's much-toasted Ally (his head is still to be seen on
many English inn-signs), was a 'great power' only by the skin of
her teeth, as the defeat of Jena was to show. And England, one
might add, was a great power largely by virtue of her geo-
graphy, and thus her Navy. The bonds and the fears, then,
were real enough. The Counter-Reformation had won back
much of the territory lost to Luther. And it was, of course, these
fears that account for the presence on the English throne of a
Protestant Scotsman, James VI and I, Dutch William III, and
later a long series of Hanoverian, Protestant Georges, whose
claim to the throne derived from the marriage of a daughter of
Protestant James I to a German Protestant Prince of the
Palatinate. It was Protestantism, then, that knit Nordic
Europe together; and, in particular, brought the House of
Hanover (the medieval Guelphs) to the throne of Great
Britain.

It was Protestantism, and the constant threat of Jacobite
regression in Scotland and Ireland, that brought a Saxon king
to rule again over what had once been a Saxon kingdom. This
was a political-religious issue; not, in any sense, a 'racial' one.
Legend had it at one time that Cabinet Government had grown
out of the new King's inability to speak English; and out of his
courtiers' inability to comprehend German. It is quite true that
George I spoke little English. But, like most German Princes of
his day, George I spoke good French, and it was rather his
courtiers' inability to transact business in that language that
made for difficulties. Legend has it, likewise, that the Hanover-

ians were unpopular with their subjects because they were *German*. Through the prism of two world wars it is easy to think so. But this is certainly not Mr Roger Fulford's opinion, and few know the period better than he. There is little evidence that the Georges were liked or disliked because they were *Germans* (indeed I have argued that until the early 19th century the average Englishman had little concept of 'the Germans' at all). By Jacobites the Georges were regarded, naturally, as alien intruders: but for dynastic and religious reasons. And it is not true, in fact, that 'the Georges' were at all times unpopular with their new subjects. The history of the Georges, despite their imputed unpopularity, is not very different from the history of their predecessors and, indeed, their successors. Looking back, it might seem that the British were natural-born Royalists: we possess, and take pride in possessing, the senior and one of the most enlightened Royal Families in Europe. But that is not quite all. For the truth, of course, is that the Englishman likes to keep a King (or a Queen) in his place: the English were the first, after all, to sever a King's head when he misjudged their temper.

The truth is rather that English Royalty has enjoyed bouts of popularity and unpopularity according to the rational, or irrational, shifts of popular mood. The Georges were not always unpopular, any more than the Stuarts before them. George II was the last English King to lead his troops in battle; another, his grandson George III, enjoyed spells of great public enthusiasm, and also of profound unpopularity, between his accession in 1760 and his final lapse into madness before Napoleon's defeat. George IV fell into disrepute; yet he had been called the First Gentleman in Europe, and his open profligacy need not in itself have been a cause of Royal unpopularity. That Queen Caroline, his wife, should have been the object of a vociferous cult in England reflected perhaps more the Englishman's liking for taking his Sovereign down a peg than any deep-founded morality.

It was not an age when Kings were expected to behave like Saints. The Hanoverians were on the whole a cheerful, hearty, rumbustious lot—a social set with many of the characteristics of idle, but strong-blooded minor German Royalty. They got into scrapes, and tended to lack ingenuity in getting out of them. They had sadly little in the way of natural dignity. But the English found it the easier to forgive the occasional tumble provided Monarchy did not concern itself too closely with their affairs. The morals of the Monarch were not so different from the morals of society as a whole, especially in its upper reaches: the English were not yet Victorians. Yet there was in this, certainly, a latent contradiction. A Constitutional Monarch should keep his fingers from the levers of power. Yet it is difficult for a purely decorative Monarch to command respect: indeed, men like John Wilkes might ask why, if real power lay with Parliament and the Cabinet, have a Monarch at all? This contradiction underlay, I think, the most prolonged bout of unpopularity the Royal Family has ever had to endure: that from 1810 to Victoria's accession in 1837. The Monarchy had lost both the affection and the respect of the nation. They were simply not seen to be earning their keep. It was Albert and Victoria's triumph that they won back the affection and respect her feckless uncles had thrown away.

How was this achieved? The credit for this remarkable change of fortune is most often given to Albert, and in parti-cular to his stern Coburg education at the hands of King Leopold of the Belgians (his and Victoria's uncle), and of his servant, the ubiquitous, high-minded Baron Stockmar. The argument runs like this: after the Congress of Vienna, there had been a general restoration of the *ancien régime* throughout Europe. Yet the Bourbons, and not only the Bourbons, had learnt nothing and forgotten nothing. Sooner or later there would be a second round of Revolution, and the restored Monarchs would find themselves on their travels again. Plainly, therefore, Monarchy must change its ways. It must become Constitutional, must take account of the rise of a new class, the educated *bourgeoisie*; it must keep up with the *Zeit-geist*, with the new technologies and philosophies. Religion must be upheld; but so must freedom of thought. Monarchy must again be respected, but not by way of ostentation and extravagance. It must be upheld by force of example, moral example, such as a well-intentioned paterfamilias might hope to exert. This, or something like it, is what was being instilled into both Albert and Victoria in their strangely complementary, very lonely childhoods. This was the Great Plan of Leopold and Stockmar. And what more desirable, to crown the good work, than that the two little cousins should be united as the instruments of this new Coburg-style monarchy in Great Britain, the most powerful and progressive nation in Europe, under Uncle Leopold's watchful eye?

The story of the love-marriage of Albert and Victoria has often been told. It was indeed a love match—a rare thing among royalty in that or any age—and there is no doubt that it delighted the mass of the British people, though rather less so, as we shall see, the traditional ruling class. But before we look at why this was so, it may be worth considering the Coburg Plan and its implications more closely. (Albert himself, though not Victoria, was never happier than when drawing up a Plan: a very German trait, which was triumphant in the case of the Great Exhibition, but disastrous in the case of the Plan drawn up for the education of his eldest son, later Edward VII.) There is no doubt that Albert was a passionate believer in the Coburg Plan, and that he educated Victoria in its virtues—to the degree that even Dearest Albert could educate Victoria to work to any plan at all. Victoria was a hard worker, but she had not learned to be a systematic one. There is likewise no doubt that Albert's busy rationalisation of the ways of the English court achieved a high degree of success. He uncovered, for example, a strange anomaly at Windsor, according to which one Court functionary was responsible for cleaning the outside of the windows, whereas the inside of the windows fell into the province of another. Unfortunately, these rival authorities never troubled to co-ordinate their activities: as a result the Queen's windows were permanently dirty. Albert, the rationalist, soon put paid to that. There was a regulation by which a candle, once lit, might never be used again. Evidently, somebody was doing very well out of that, and the practice was abolished. There was the regular hogshead of wine set aside for the men in the Guard Room: it was discovered that there had been no men in the Guard Room since George III's time. And very soon the new broom made itself felt elsewhere. The Queen, though determined, found the paper-work of government heavy going. At first, Albert was shown only the odd State Paper: Victoria was jealous of her rights. But Albert was so keen and so clever; his explanations were always so knowledgeable and so clear—almost as good as Lord M's had been in the first days of her reign. It does not surprise us to hear that within a couple of years Albert was sitting in on Her Majesty's meetings with her ministers; or that Creevey, the diarist, should be hinting—when Albert was still in his mid-twenties—that he was 'to all intents and purposes, King of England'.

Does this mean that the Plan had failed, or succeeded? Certainly, there is a paradox at work here. Why, for example, did Disraeli opine in later years—and Disraeli's admiration for Albert was genuine—that, had Albert lived, 'he would have given England the benefits of absolute government'? The paradox at the heart of the Plan is evident in Disraeli's ironic, but not disrespectful, comment. For what did Stockmar—ever flitting between the Courts of Coburg, Brussels, and Windsor—really understand by 'Constitutional Monarchy' of the Coburg variety? According to Lytton Strachey, it was the opinion of Stockmar that the very lowest claim of the Royal Prerogative must include 'a right on the part of the King to be the permanent President of his Ministerial Council'. The Sovereign ought to be 'in the position of a permanent Premier, who takes rank above the temporary head of the Cabinet, and in matters of discipline exercises supreme authority'. 'The judicious exercise of this right,' wrote the Baron, 'which certainly requires a master-mind, would not only be the best guarantee for Constitutional Monarchy, but would raise it to a height of power, stability and symmetry, which has never yet been attained.' Clearly, there was a certain discrepancy here between what the English meant by Constitutional Monarchy and what Leopold and Stockmar thought, or hoped, they meant. Had no one told them of what had happened in 1649, or in 1688, or for that matter in the days of George III? For the full Coburg Plan would indeed have involved giving England 'the benefits of absolute government'. And it would have required 'a mastermind'. And herein lies Albert's tragedy, and to some extent that of his daughter and of his grandson, the Kaiser.

For Albert had been set an impossible task. He was to preside over the regeneration of the English people, as Dr Arnold saw himself presiding over the regeneration of the English ruling classes. Yet he lacked the means to do so; and had he possessed the means he would have made himself far more unpopular in England than any of the Hanoverians. The last thing the English wanted was to be 'improved'. For one thing, they did not consider they were in need of it. Yet, to 'improve' his adopted people was the task Leopold and Stockmar had set him. At first glance, this may seem strange: were not the forties and fifties the great Age of Improvement in England—from the Reform Bill, the Factory Acts, the Oxford Movement, to the Repeal of the Corn Laws and the Railway Mania of the mid-forties? Certainly, they were. And Albert might well appear to be the man appointed to comprehend and urge forward the *Zeitgeist* as, with the Great Exhibition, he did. He was in every way a product of his generation in Germany: the generation of Young Germany and Heine, whose ideals were a strange mixture of High Romanticism, Liberal politics, and a utilitarian faith in the good influence of Science and Progress on the character of men and nations. He had been educated at Brussels and Bonn universities, both citadels of Liberalism. (Berlin had been rejected by Leopold and Stockmar as likely to make the youth 'formal and priggish', as well as illiberal.) He had written a thesis at nineteen on 'The Mode of Thinking of the Germans'; and there was no discontinuity between the 'good' pupil he had been at home and at University and the 'good' Consort he intended to be in the country of his adoption. That he was an unashamed German patriot, even Nationalist, is not inconsistent with this. Young Germany, like its counterparts all over Europe, *was* Nationalist; but Nationalism and Liberalism were seen to go hand in hand. Prince Albert was not to live to see the era of German unification; but the likelihood is that, even under Bismarck, he would have approved of

it. It was—or so it seemed to his generation—the reactionary
Princes of Germany with their selfish particularism (especially
Austria) who wished to frustrate the noble goal of German
brotherhood and unity. Albert, then, would have seen no
contradiction between his ardent pro-Prussianism, his tireless
efforts to 'improve' the British and his duty to see that Britannia
continued to rule the waves.

Many of his most cherished ideals Albert was to see realised:
in particular, of course, that great monument to Science and
Improvement (and, more doubtfully, to Art), the Great Exhibition of 1851. He had progressive ideas, too, on Education and
Army Reform; and in both fields—much to the consternation
of the Cambridge Professors and the Generals—he managed to
get his way. But the tragedy of Albert, at which I have hinted.
was that to carry out the full Coburg Plan he would have had
to occupy a position of political power to which no British
Parliament or Cabinet would have dreamed of consenting:
'King, to all intents and purposes.' And yet, at bottom, a cipher.
Almost certainly there was prejudice against him as a German.
What was it in his *Deutschtum* that struck contemporaries
unfavourably? He had nothing of the bumbling, cheerful
raffishness of the Georges. He would not, like Victoria's
predecessor, the 'Sailor King' William IV, frustrated at the
refusal of the government to let him go to sea because of his
rank, have hoisted his Lord High Admiral's pennant and
merrily sailed out a squadron into the Channel—leaving their
Lordships at the Admiralty ignorant of its location and aghast
at such Royal insubordination. True, the Government was
compelled to relieve him of his post: but it had been a glorious
eighteen months, and William was forced to retire to bed,
overcome by the excitement of it all. But did the English love
him less for such an escapade? Not at all. The English love a
Character; and a Royal Character is almost too good to be true.
How different from Albert! For Albert had something—and
this is an index also of how much Germany herself had changed
since the 18th century—that appealed to the English mentality
very little. Albert was all too like Matthew Arnold's 'new
German' in 'Friendship's Garland': didactic, self-righteous, a

zealot for progress, and a bigot for improvement. The man was a regular pedagogue. Added to which was the ever-present assumption in both cases that the New Germany had rather more than her fair share of these good things and Great Britain rather less.

It is arguable, perhaps, that these unfortunate traits could, and should, have been mitigated in Albert's case by what were universally acknowledged to be his 'exquisite manners'. But the English idea of good manners is something that can baffle the foreigner alarmingly. The Germans readily acknowledge that the English have good manners; but they hold at the same time that the English are 'stiff' (*steif*). Yet this, of course, is precisely what the English are liable to say of the Germans, particularly of the North Germans, and particularly of well-meaning, pedagogical men of Albert's type. The German view of the English, then, is to a large extent a projection of their own behaviour, and of their own concept of good manners. That this misunderstanding did Albert harm in circles where it mattered is apparent from the comments of those who knew him best. Lord M. was against Germans altogether, though they appeared to be a necessity of nature whenever the question of a Royal Marriage cropped up:

> Lord M. did his best to put her against the race. For one thing, Germans *smoked*, a crime which both he and the Duchess agreed in putting down. . . . For another thing, Germans didn't wash their faces (Longford: 'Victoria R.I.').

But then Lord M. was by now against most things, especially if they involved Improvement. Yet the real trouble lay, as Albert soon realised, with the Aristocracy:

> It was not easy for the aristocracy to embrace this new scheme of things. The Georgian Princes and their contemporary peers had always felt a certain right to define the morality of their class. They resented the intrusion of this new order—this incursion of early hours and strait-laced rules. When the Sabbatarians protested against Albert's games of chess on Sunday, he immediately eschewed all such

182

extravagances and went to bed earlier than ever. Nor did the nobility admire the more *bourgeois* beauty of Albert, whose stiffness and self-conscious care of his behaviour did not fit in with their idea of good breeding (Bolitho: 'Albert the Good').

That was it. Strachey writes that the trouble was that at bottom the Prince seemed 'un-English':

Though in the eyes of Victoria he was the mirror of manly beauty, her subjects, whose eyes were of a less teutonic cast, did not agree with her. To them—and particularly to the high-born ladies and gentlemen who naturally saw him most —what was immediately and distressingly striking in Albert's face and figure and whole demeanour was his un-English look. His features were regular, no doubt, but there was something smooth and smug about them: he was tall, but he was clumsily put together and he walked with a slight slouch. Really, they thought, this youth was more like some kind of foreign tenor than anything else ('Queen Victoria').

One piece of news startled the knights of the shires, but it did not outweigh those deficiencies which Albert could do so little to remedy, and which he may well not have been aware of (the Queen, certainly, was wholly blind to them). As Anson, first Melbourne's and later Albert's secretary, writes:

The aristocracy begins to think a little more highly of Albert's capacity for Government which, in the minds of English people, is still associated with the knack of catching balls, jumping ditches and pulling live foxes to pieces.

What had happened? In November, 1843, Albert had

hunted with the Belvoir and everybody was delighted with his performance. The Queen announced to Leopold that Albert's riding so boldly had 'made such a sensation that it had been written of all over the country, and they made much more of it than if he had done some great act! . . . Intellectual merit and artistic prowess were pretty enough as affectations for Professors and women. But such attributes had never been looked upon as part of the paraphernalia of the English gentleman (Bolitho).

In the early years, as I have said, the love match was highly popular among the common people, as the huge number of Staffordshire pottery figures from that period bears witness. But the English people had, perhaps understandably, an evil reputation among European monarchs. George I had regarded them as 'shifty folk'. The sudden revulsion against Albert as a supposed 'pro-Russian' before the Crimean crisis (quite without foundation, it should be said) might seem to bear this out. A popular broadsheet appeared:

Last Monday night, all in a fright,
Al out of bed did tumble.
The German lad was raving mad,
How he did groan and grumble!

He cried to Vic, 'I've cut my stick,
To Petersburg go right slap,'
When Vic, 'tis said, jumped out of bed,
And whopped him with her nightcap.

You jolly Turk, now go to work,
And show the Bear your power.
'Tis rumoured over Britain's isle
That A—'s in the tower.

And, in fact, a small crowd gathered outside the tower to watch the Prince (some said the Queen too) hauled in through Traitor's Gate. But these things had happened in Hanoverian times too; the mood of the London mob was notoriously volatile. Nor is 'German lad' to be taken as of itself pejorative. What the incident proves is that English royalty could, and did, very easily attract unpopularity in circles high and low if they were suspected of taking too active a hand in political affairs, especially foreign affairs. At any such suspicion an Englishman's temper was easily aroused.

184

What did Albert think of *his* adopted country? Thirteen years after his death, *The Spectator* wrote:

> His English contemporaries suspected—and they were perfectly right—that the Prince never liked them. They recognised all his virtues, but they saw that the man who served them so well had—apart from his own family—left his heart with his own people.

For one thing, there was that reputation the English had for low morality:

> One reason why the Prince kept himself to himself was that he had absorbed—and allowed himself to betray—the disapproval of the British aristocracy which at that time was current on the continent, especially in Germany. . . . A friend of Greville's, returning from Germany in the 1840s, told him that the Germans believed 'the state of society in England and the character of its aristocracy was to the last degree profligate and unprincipled' (Fulford: 'Dearest Child').

This was, undeniably, not so far from the truth in the age of Melbourne and Palmerston. But it was also an anachronism. 'Victorianism' was not, of course, the creation of Victoria. It was the coming-together of a number of strands in English life: for, contradictory as they might seem, the Evangelicalism of a Lord Shaftesbury, the High Church principles of a Gladstone, the Philosophic Radicalism of the Liberal wing of the Whigs, had in common a powerful ethical impulse. It was this that Albert and Victoria served to focus. But these new impulses were embodied in the rising middle classes, and not in the old aristocracy. Melbourne and Palmerston belonged essentially to the old order, the age of her Wicked Uncles. The struggle with Palmerston seemed never-ending: he seemed to embody all that was most unregenerate in the English race, and his obvious public popularity only made matters more unbearable. Albert grieved. There were, of course, always the Highlanders.

> Here he rested, growing nearer to the sturdy highlanders, so much more like his own people than the English, if only

for the hills and the trees and the more dramatic landscapes, which were so full of memories of his own land. He was happier in Scotland. The Englishman does not belong to his earth as the Scotsman does. The passionate attachments of Sir Walter Scott have never stirred the Englishman's heart (Bolitho).

No, indeed! That was the nub of the trouble. The English were to be admired for their progressive energy, their liberal outlook, their stupendous material achievements. But in matters of the heart, of the *Gemüt*! Alas, how could one hope to make oneself understood in a language which lacks an equivalent for that word? No, the English character was decisively lacking there. He wrote to his brother:

Sentimentality is a plant that cannot grow in England. . . . An Englishman, when he finds he is being sentimental, becomes frightened at the thought as at having a dangerous illness and he shoots himself. . . . I think the plant is smothered by reading so many newspapers.

He worked harder than ever, turning himself back to the world of politics and newspapers and despatch-boxes to conceal his private melancholy. At length, despairing of the apparently impassable barriers separating the 'sentimental', *gemütlich* Germans from the in other ways so admirable English, he returned once more to the Coburg Plan. That at least must be carried through, if possible, before his strength failed him— though he was only thirty-five. Germany would one day be united, he felt sure, despite the disappointments and follies of the great assembly that had gathered in the Frankfurt *Pauls-kirche* back in '48. And how could that unity be achieved now except through Prussia? He was not thinking of Blood and Iron. But a Royal marriage might help to steer Prussia, and thus the new Germany, on to a Liberal course. There was at hand the Princess Royal, so like himself in character and out-look: she should be the instrument to carry through the Coburg Plan to completion. She should marry Frederick, the son of King William—later Kaiser William I—and Europe might then profit from the 'joint headmastership' of two Coburg-ruled houses. His work would then be done; 'I do not', as he told Victoria, 'cling to life as you do.'

One day the young Prince would rule Prussia. Married to the Princess Royal he would save Europe from both Russian reaction and French licence. This was Prince Albert's dream. The Crimean War made the marriage urgent: though France was now England's ally, Prince Albert put no trust in Napoleon III, and Prussia's obstinate neutrality was a grave shock to his hopes of a Europe under the joint head-mastership of Germany and England (Longford).

CHAPTER TWO

From Windsor to Potsdam

'The joint headmastership of Europe'—how German, but also how Arnoldian a sentiment! Yet it was not to be. True, Protestant Europe was now dominant. Power had shifted from the Catholic South of Europe to the rapidly industrialising North-West. But it is doubtful if the headship of any institution is best run in harness; and we can date the beginnings of Anglo-German political estrangement almost from Albert's death, though one may doubt whether he could have altered things materially had he lived. There were two factors which emerged to frustrate the Great Plan, neither of which Albert could have foreseen: the appearance of Bismarck on the scene in the year following his death, and the circumstance that Frederick only came to the throne, himself a dying man, when his father, William I, died in his nineties. Had Frederick lived, or succeeded to the throne in the seventies—which seemed likely to be the natural course of events—history might well have taken a different course. Or would it? There would have been a titanic struggle between the Bismarckian Conservatives and National Liberals and the new Liberal *Kaiser* and *Kaiserin* and their entourage. It can be argued that a Liberal Reich would not have surrounded itself with enemies of its own making—a process known to Germans of a later generation as *Einkreisung*, i.e. something for which, typically, foreigners were responsible, not they themselves—and that therefore war would not have broken out in 1914. Ironically, it can also be argued that a liberalised, and therefore better integrated, Germany under Frederick would have stood a better chance of winning that war than the socially divisive Reich which he inherited from his father.

But Frederick would first have had to win his war with Bismarck. And from the evidence of the famous correspondence between Queen Victoria and her daughter, the Princess Royal, Frederick does not emerge as a likely winner. Within six months of her father's death, Vicky is fulminating against 'that bad man B.'—with her father's principles, but her mother's vehemence:

> . . . Bismarck is such a wicked man that he does not care how many fibs he tells to serve his own purposes. And this is the man who is to govern this country. I assure you it makes my hair stand on end. I only hope some means may be found to avert such a calamity (July, 1862).

For, to break the deadlock over the estimates for the Army, King William had called in Bismarck and given him over-riding authority:

> If the government does anything unconstitutional Fritz will protest. He will give a written declaration that he does not pass any opinion on the present course of affairs . . . but that he will not be a party to any unconstitutional step; the King might think it necessary and advisable but it was in Fritz's eyes dangerous and he could not on his conscience acquiesce to it. . . . I think Fritz cannot do better than this and I certainly do not think he is justified to do or think anything more (May 19th, 1863).

But Fritz was far too much of a Prussian to disobey paternal authority; and the gesture he decided to make—a public speech in Danzig—only confirmed the impression that, for all the fine qualities he shared with Albert, he was at bottom a man 'willing to wound, but afraid to strike':

> I did all I could to induce Fritz that he should once express his sentiments openly and disclaim having any part in the last measures of the government. He did so accordingly in very mild and measured terms. . . . To this the King answered Fritz a furious letter, treating him quite like a little child; telling him instantly to retract in the newspapers the words he had spoken . . . charging him with disobedience, etc. . . . Fritz and I sat up till one last night writing the answer . . .

in which Fritz says he is almost broken-hearted at causing his father so much pain but that he could not retract the words . . . that he had always hoped the King's government would not act in a way which should force him to put himself in direct opposition to the King; but now it had come to that, and he would stand by his opinions. . . . As he felt that his presence must be disagreeable to the King, he begged him to name a place, or allow us to select one, where he could live in perfect retirement and not mix in politics.

The incident aroused the anger of the Court Party and Vicky poured out her indignation to Victoria:

Thank God I was born in England, where people are not slaves, and too good to allow themselves to be treated as such. . . . I hope our nation here will soon prove that we come of the same forefathers, and strive for their own lawful independence, to which they have been too long callous.

It is fair to say, then, that Frederick's battle was lost before it was fought: he was not the man to stand up to Bismarck. But there is a curiously ambivalent note in this latest outburst, a feeling that 'we come of the same forefathers', and yet also a dawning realisation that Germany was *not* England; and it is this ambivalence that was to become so marked in the character of her son, 'the Kaiser'. Of course, it needs to be stressed that the ideal Germany she had in mind was very much that of her father, so typical a product of the liberal principles of the generation that had failed in 1848. Again, we can recognise in the confidence that freedom is the birthright of the Teutonic peoples the very principles that were being taught by Freeman and Green at this time—and Vicky was something of a culture-vulture, taking both the *Edinburgh Quarterly* and the *Review*. But the Germany to which she now came 'as an Englishwoman' —though she had precious little English blood in her veins— was no longer her mother's 'dear little Germany' of a generation before. This new generation had been converted by Bismarck to the view that unification could only be achieved by 'blood and iron'. We have seen how little her father had really known the English: much the same is true of Vicky in regard to Germany, and perhaps of her son William too. For all their gifts—and the three had much more in common than is usually allowed—none had that streak of earthy commonsense so evident in Victoria. (Informed by an ecclesiastic, after Albert's death, that she must now regard Christ as her husband, she snorted, 'Now *that* is what I call *twaddle!*') Albert, Vicky, and William: each in their way had a great deal of the German idealist in their psychic make-up; they plumped for theory where Victoria would have plumped for fact and, in William's case, this degenerated to the point where he came to live largely in a world of illusion—a condition that, in the opinion of one doctor, bordered on a hysterical retreat from reality.

Of Vicky's ambivalence between Prussia and England there is plentiful evidence:

> I cannot get accustomed to live out of England, I wish to change everything and make everything English (they say); they cannot help seeing that I am full of good-will towards them and that *je ne demande pas rien* than to be friends with them.

(The reader may notice a curious fact: the Princess's English, like her father's and indeed like William's, was never to be quite idiomatic.) Yet, at the time of the Dano-Prussian war—although her brother Bertie had just married a Danish Princess, the future Queen Alexandra—her indignation could be turned as easily against the country of her birth:

> The most absurd, unjust and rude attacks in *The Times* and in Parliament upon us can only increase the irritation or rather more contempt which is expressed in no measured terms here and generally felt for England's position on the Danish question. . . . The continued meddling and inter- fering of England in other people's affairs has become so ridiculous abroad that it almost ceases to annoy. . . . The highly pathetic, philanthropic and virtuous tone in which all the attacks against Prussia are made has something intensely ludicrous about it. The English would not like, if they were

engaged in a war, to be dictated to in a pompous style how they were to conduct it.

Not, of course, that Vicky was above the occasional spot of meddling and interfering herself.

Her dislike of the Prussian Royal family was all too apparent, and Vicky was never the soul of discretion—another characteristic she seems to have passed on to her son. Thus to her mother:

> I trust my children may grow up like my Fritz, like Papa, like you and as unlike the rest of the Prussian Royal family as possible; then they can be good patriots and useful to their country—call it Prussia or call it Germany (August 17th, 1867).

During Bismarck's second war—against Austria—she reveals her ambivalence in all its nakedness:

> You know how I consider the war a mistake caused by the uncontrolled power of an unprincipled man . . . But I assure you that if the rest of Europe did but know the details of this war . . . the Prussian people would stand high in the eyes of everyone, I feel that I am now every bit as proud of being a Prussian as I am of being an Englishwoman—and that is saying a great deal—as you know what a John Bull I am and how enthusiastic about my home. I must say the Prussians are a superior race as regards intelligence and humanity, education and kind-heartedness, and therefore I hate the people all the more, the people who by their ill-government and mismanagement rob the nation of the sympathies it ought to have . . . (July 16th, 1866).

She thought, like her father, that the Germans were morally and intellectually the 'superior' race (though she did not have to say so). Thus, in a comment on the great controversy about Bishop Colenso which had all England by the ears in 1863, she has no doubt that Germany is the 'farther advanced' country. And this is what Germans of the age thought and said, and some Englishmen too: had not George Eliot spent laborious days and nights twenty years before translating the far more radical *Leben Jesu* of Strauss?

> Doctor Colenso occupies me very much . . . Sooner or later a dogma so preposterous as the Protestant church still holds, will be abandoned by all classes—as they are already now in Germany—by all the thinking and intelligent men. Science and learning are slowly preparing the ground for a new reformation. In the searching light of truth all errors will appear so absurd that people will be ashamed to hold to them. We are farther advanced in Germany than in England. Is it a wonder that there should be so many dissenters? All this is less felt in England, as the national character is perhaps not so 'thinking'—at any rate not so speculative—and because our lower and middle classes here are much more educated.

It may come as a shock to some that the supposedly pious 'Victorianism' of the age was not shared either by the Queen (*'twaddle!'*), or her Consort, or by Vicky or the rest of the Royal family. This suggests, among other things, that Strachey was mistaken in directing so much of his fire in 'Eminent Victorians' at the Victorians' *religious* hypocrisy. The Royal family held strong ethical views, but in matters of religious belief they were much closer to the Mills and Stephens of the age.

But the crucial period from which the decline in Anglo-German relations must be dated—the watershed, in a sense, of our present study—is the Franco-Prussian war of 1870–71. The exchanges between Mother and Daughter reflect the changing mood of both peoples with remarkable exactitude. Queen Victoria was, naturally, a pro-German. She could write, thinking of Dearest Albert:

> I miss dear, dear Coburg! It was full of all precious recollections—in fact I felt it like the home of my childhood . . . the dear German language, all of which I feel necessary to my very existence. Do you all cherish it, and do so when I am gone—promise me, all of you? Tell Bertie how pleased I am to hear he loves our precious Coburg.

On September 13th, 1870, after Sedan, she wrote:

> In England I can assure you the feeling is far more German than French and far the greater part of the Press is in your favour. All reflective people are. The *Pall Mall* has excellent articles . . .*

This time her daughter was unashamedly patriotic: this was the war that would achieve German unity, hopefully under a liberalised Prussia; and in the years to come she and Fritz would have a central role to play. On August 16th, she had written to her mother:

> Matters seem as if they will take a turn—and most likely a very bad one for the Emperor. His system, alas, one of corruption supported by corrupt men . . . seems to be crumbling and tumbling to pieces and Paris, which is a Sodom and Gomorrah, is in an attitude of frantic excitement, rage and disappointment. . . . I think the most incurable hater of the Prussians would be converted into an admirer if he saw and heard all we do. . . . It is owing to their moral qualities that they are so invincible—as the French have the same advantages in all purely military things.

By the turn of the year, however, with the siege-guns deployed around Paris, the Queen felt bound to point out that 'the English are very fond of Paris', and soon sensed—a good example of her practical political acumen—that English opinion was shifting against the Germans. On November 30th, she had already written:

> The feeling against foreign marriages has long been very strong here, especially if the Princes are poor or if they were of a nature to bring us in political collision one with another. A second Prussian alliance would have been very unpopular

---

* Little did her Majesty know that the 'excellent articles' were the work of Friedrich Engels, who had been introduced to the Editor by Marx. The Crown Princess, incidentally, had read *Das Kapital* when it appeared the previous year, and sent a private spy to London to beard the sage in his den. The spy was impressed, but commented, 'he is not the man who is going to make the revolution'. It is curious to reflect that European Royalty and European Revolutionaries had at least one point in common: German was their *lingua franca*

here—for while admiring and loving dear Fritz and admiring the wonderful organisation of the Prussian army—their bravery, endurance, discipline, all—the English do not like the Prussians, and instead of its bringing the two nations together, it would have the contrary effect.

By December 28th, the Queen is definitely in a state:

I hear they have begun to bombard Paris! If only it would soon end. To my despair the feeling is becoming more and more bitter here against the Prussians . . .

By the spring of 1871 the pro-Prussian feelings of the year before had quite vanished. Now, Mother and Daughter write to one another more in sorrow than in anger. Thus, Vicky:

One thing I own torments me much; it is the feeling of animosity between our two countries: it is so dangerous and productive of much harm . . . Prussia has gained no popularity for itself since some time on account of the King's illiberal government, but the feeling against us now in England is most unjust. Now dear Papa is no longer here I live in continual dread that the bonds which united our two countries for their mutual good may be in time quite severed.

The Princess had a prophetic eye. But she felt no less torn apart than her mother over the water, who wrote to her:

How difficult my path is!—distrusted and suspected on account of my relationships and feelings. To see the enmity growing up between the two nations—which I am bound to say began first in Prussia, and was most unjust and was fomented and encouraged by Bismarck—is a great sorrow and anxiety to me—and I cannot separate myself or allow myself to be separated from my own people. For it is alas! the people, who from being very German up to three months ago are now very French! I tell you this with a heavy heart but it is the fact.

CHAPTER THREE

The New Germany

On the political plane, then, it can be said with some confidence
that the transfer of popular affection from Germany to France
may be dated from the few months separating the triumph of
Sedan to the opening months of 1871—the period when a new
Kaiser—William I, King of Prussia—was chosen by acclama-
tion by the assembled Princes of Germany in the Hall of
Mirrors at Versailles. The 'Second Reich', in other words, can
be said to have been born, not only to the disapprobation of
the defeated French, but also to that of their powerful neighbour
across the Channel. But then a clash of some kind between
Germany, the *parvenu* Empire, and the Empire of Great
Britain, was perhaps inevitable. Whether *war* was ultimately
inevitable is a question which can never be finally answered;
but it is clear that rivalry in the colonial field, in trade, and
probably ultimately in naval strength was unavoidable, given
the preconceptions of that time (from what we know now
there is no reason to think that the two states could not have
lived together to their mutual benefit without thought of war,
or colonies, or naval rivalry). Since the huge growth in Germany's power formed the background to William II's development (whom we shall henceforth call 'the Kaiser'), and to that
of the Reich he was to rule for thirty years, the facts deserve
closer examination.

As early as 1833, the Secretary to the Committee of the Privy
Council for Trade described the *Zollverein* as 'an alliance
conceived in a spirit of hostility to British industry and British
commerce'—almost as pernicious, in other words, as Napoleon's
Continental System a generation earlier. In 1841, the Foreign
Secretary had been warned about 'the extent and perfection
that has for some years been progressing in the manufactures
of Germany'. Nevertheless, as we have seen, the general trend

of opinion in England was still Germanophil. For both countries, France was still the traditional enemy—the Prussians (as
they liked to imagine) had arrived just in time to save Welling-
ton's bacon at Waterloo. (He is supposed to have declaimed,
Ach, es wäre Nacht, und die Preussen kämen! Did he really say it?
Certainly, every German schoolboy was taught so.) In 1847
Palmerston commented: 'Both England and Germany are
threatened by the same danger, an attack from Russia or from
France separately, or . . . united. England and Germany have
mutually a direct interest in assisting each other to become rich,
united and strong.' 'Fear of France,' remarks Michael Balfour
in his 'The Kaiser and his Times'

> the fact that Prussia was not strong enough to be a menace,
> had ethnic and dynastic ties, all combined to produce in
> mid-Victorian Britain a general predisposition in favour of
> things German.

This was true in many fields, but especially in the field of
learning.

In 1844, Jowett met Erdmann, Hegel's chief disciple, at
Dresden, and thereafter began the introduction of Hegelian
philosophy at Oxford where by the seventies it was to achieve
a dominating position. Germanophilia lasted into the opening
weeks of the Franco-Prussian war, but began to change into
doubt when Germany was seen to emerge as the strongest
military power in the world.

But Germany could not have achieved this position without,
on the one hand, the unique genius of Bismarck and, on the
other, the rapid industrialisation of what a generation before
had been still a largely agrarian country (W. W. Rostow puts
the British 'take-off' period as between 1783 and 1802 and
the German as between 1850 and 1870, suggesting—though
his figures have been challenged—that Germany had already
reached in 1840 a level of production relative to 1914 which
Britain had reached in 1829). A time-gap of some thirty years,
then, still existed at the period of the Franco-Prussian war
between the relative strengths of Britain and Germany. But

now there is a striking spurt in the German figures which put Germany well ahead of Britain in certain vital sectors between 1871 and 1914. Let us look at the balance-sheet as it would have appeared in 1871:

	BRITAIN	GERMANY
Population	32,000,000	41,000,000
Area	120,000 sq miles	208,000 sq miles
Army (1872)	197,000	407,000
Proportion of national income devoted to defence	2·38%	2·6%

The 'menacing' aspect of these figures lies, of course, in the greater resources in land and men, less in the slightly higher budget devoted to armaments. From all other points of view Britain is still far in advance (though from a strictly German point of view the naval discrepancy might also be made to appear 'menacing': namely Britain's 60,000 men to Germany's 6,500).

In other words, the British had little to fear in 1871. The German Army was, of course, much stronger, but was scarcely a threat to an island which enjoyed a tenfold naval superiority. Still it was the potential that mattered; and it did not escape notice in England that the Germans were catching up fast, and might soon overtake Britain in the most modern fields of industrial activity: chemicals, steel, electrical goods. Thus, the comparative figures for *c.* 1871 and *c.* 1914 bear a very different aspect:

	BRITAIN	GERMANY
Population		
1871	32,000,000	41,000,000
1913	46,000,000	67,000,000

(a twenty million, instead of a ten million lead, due to a rapid population increase not dissimilar to that which Britain enjoyed during a similar phase of industrialisation).

	BRITAIN	GERMANY
Railways		
1850	10,000 miles	6,000 miles
1910	38,000 miles	61,000 miles

(a fourfold increase in British mileage; a tenfold increase in the German: and German railways were strategically planned with great care).

	BRITAIN	GERMANY
Steel		
1880	980,000 tons	1,550,000 tons
1913	6,900,000 tons	18,600,000 tons

(a shift, roughly, from a German/British ratio of 1·5 : 1 to a ratio of 3 : 1; not only an increased ratio, but also an enormous absolute increase). In military terms the figures are still more revealing:

	BRITAIN	GERMANY
Army		
1872	197,000	407,000
1914	247,000	790,000
Navy		
1872	60,000	6,500
1914	146,000	73,000

Looked at another way, while the proportion of the population engaged in military activities was higher in Germany in 1914 (but the Germans had conscription), the proportion of National Income devoted to defence was not so unequal, even misleading: 3·26 per cent for Britain as against 2·88 per cent for Germany (but navies are more expensive, while needing less men, than armies; and Britain had her far-flung Empire). Yet it cannot escape the eye that whereas the German Army was, relative to Great Britain, over three times as strong in 1914 as in 1872, the German Navy had improved its ratio from 1 : 10

to 1 : 2 a startling transformation in which William II had notoriously taken a very active part. A 'menace' certainly existed now, if Germany had possessed powerful allies; but the Army could still not rely on the Navy to ferry it across the water and, in this sense, the menace was still unreal.

How far is the story true that Germany 'provoked' Britain by stealing her overseas markets: a thesis once believed in as heartily by Britain's commercial travellers as by British Marxists? Once again, it is evident that the menace was fundamentally unreal. Thus, while British exports declined *relatively* in these years from 38 to 27 per cent of world trade (which caused much speculation as to the 'Decline of Britain' abroad), the German total rose only 5 per cent—from 17 to 22 per cent of the total; and the volume of increase of British trade in absolute terms did not persuade the British that they were in fact a 'decaying nation'. The figures bear this out:

	BRITAIN	GERMANY
Exports		
1870	235,000,000	114,000,000
1913	525,000,000	496,000,000

A breakdown of these figures is of interest because it has considerable bearing on the political and economic thinking of Keynes, which we shall be examining in the next section (it also influenced a German Liberal like Friedrich Naumann in his conception of *Mitteleuropa*).

Where did the German exports go?

		BRITAIN	GERMANY
Western Europe	1880	85,000,000	64,000,000
	1910	136,000,000	187,000,000
Russia and Eastern Europe	1890	14,000,000	15,000,000
	1910	20,000,000	58,000,000
Colonial British markets	1913	228,000,000	21·7,000,000

There are two conclusions to be drawn from this breakdown: one (in my opinion) almost certainly wrong, and the other probably correct (and pointing to developments later in the twentieth century). Thus, German trade was increasing very fast with the countries that we would now call the Common Market (just as our *mutual* trade was steadily on the increase). The positions had been reversed: from 1·5 as against 1 in 1880 they had beaten us down to roughly 1 to 1·6. In Russia and Eastern Europe they had got us down—for evident geographical reasons—from a ratio of 1 : 1 to a ratio of 4 : 1. In the 'Empire' we remained, of course, well ahead. The ratio was 10 : 1 against the Germans, and it can easily be seen that this ratio rankled. If only we Germans had an Empire, protected by a great fleet, could we not do as well as—or better than—the British? From the perspective of the nineteen seventies this may all seem a little peculiar. In 1913 the figures certainly seemed most unfair to those with the smaller Navy and limited *Lebensraum*: a ratio of 10 : 1! Ten times as great! But whereas these figures persuaded some Germans (not Bismarck) that a world-wide territorial empire was something militarily and economically desirable, they could be read in quite another way. Economic growth had certainly *not* increased most in the British colonies, nor even in the German: the Hereros in South-West Africa had proved doughty fighters. The real increase in exports had proved to be in Europe, as the figures show—in Western Europe and in the contiguous lands of Eastern Europe—and, of course, in the Americas. But the biggest market for Germany, as both Naumann and Hitler correctly perceived, lay in the *Eastern* countries. Like Bismarck, Hitler was no colonial enthusiast and the perceptions of both men were correct. German economic interests lay, as time has shown, in peaceful trade with Europe, both East and West; and with the independent countries of North and South America. But it was not necessary to *conquer* these countries to fill German coffers. Would it be going too far to claim that a 'Common Market' should have been the true goal of German economic expansion—combined, perhaps, with a peaceful *Ostpolitik*? Little of this was visible to the victors of 1871. Yet we can see that it was in harmony with the whole history of peaceful exchange between the nations of Europe over the

period. It is not surprising that the overriding wealth of Britain
should have been attributed to the fact that she ruled a quarter
of mankind. A glance at North (or South) American development would have served to correct this illusion: that was where
most British capital was invested. But it was on Britain that the
admiring and envious eyes of Europe were focussed.

To argue that neither of the German Wars of this century
was 'necessary' in an economic sense is, I think, perfectly
plausible. The Germany of the 1970s has no colonies; yet she
is wealthier than ever before in her history (as, indeed, are we).
But, of course, the idea was very much in the air at the time—
one has only to think of Seeley's 'Expansion of England' (1883)
—although here, once again, a closer examination of Britain's
rise to economic power might have suggested that it owed
extremely little to her possession of colonial territories, and a
great deal to her profitable investments in North and South
America and, not least, in Europe itself: that is where the
returns were (and are) greatest, and not one of these areas was
a British colony (Seeley was actually very clear-sighted on this
point). But what is important is not so much what happened—
as historians know all too well—but what is thought to have
happened. Indisputably, a clash might come: none knew this
better than Bismarck with his *cauchemar de la Grande Coalition*.
While Bismarck was at the helm, the ship could be held on
course. But what is too often forgotten is that the new Imperial
ship of state was a construction of a kind so ingenious and
complex, that only its inventor could hope to master it. In lesser
hands it might be blown off course, or blown up, as indeed
proved to be the case. 'Dropping the pilot' was therefore bound
to be disastrous. Yet, sooner or later, that moment had to come.

The basic fault in the design is obvious enough in retrospect:
it required a 'master-mind' at the helm, combining great
intelligence and a forceful character with a subtle ear for
nuances. Thus it had just the same defect as the Coburg Plan.
Theoretically, the helmsman had been William, first as King
of Prussia, then as Kaiser William I of Germany. Yet, in
practice, the first Kaiser was always putty in Bismarck's hands.
But the true political weakness of the Second Reich was more

fundamental, and may not unreasonably be said to have contributed to its downfall in 1918. Bismarck had introduced
universal male suffrage in 1871: on the face of it, a most progressive thing to do (this was for the Reichstag as a whole; the
Prussian Landtag was elected by an altogether less democratic
system). But Bismarck never intended to introduce responsible
Parliamentary government. The Reichstag could not initiate
legislation, and no member of it was eligible to be a Minister—
let alone a Chancellor—of the government of his Imperial
Majesty. Still worse, the heads of the Army and Navy were
made directly responsible to the Chancellor and the Kaiser.
With Bismarck as Chancellor, all the threads could be held in
one hand, and some sort of majority found by manipulating a
Reichstag that was basically in opposition to him. Thus the
figures for Reichstag deputies give a very accurate indication of
the true state of opinion in the country during William II's
reign:

	CONSERVATIVES	NATIONAL LIBERALS	PROGRESSIVES	CENTRUM	SOCIAL DEMOCRATS
1890	93	42	93	106	35
1912	57	45	42	91	110

The two most striking points in this comparison of party
strengths, at the beginning of William's reign, and towards its
close, are the dramatic rise in the Social Democratic vote and
the rapid fall in the Conservative, agrarian vote. Bismarck's
friends, the Conservatives and the National Liberals, no longer
dominated the scene. Indeed, if Germany had adopted the
English system, an anti-William, anti-Prussian coalition
government *could* have been formed (though with difficulty)
even in 1890 (234 to 135, depending on how the Progressives
moved), and with ease in 1912: 201 to 144, without the
Progressives (roughly equivalent to the English Liberals), and
243 to 102 with Progressive assistance. On paper, in other words,
the development of a kind of Salisbury-Chamberlain coalition
could have been followed by a powerful Asquithian Lib-Lab
government in the years leading up to the First World War.

The core of such a government would have been Agrarian-Capitalist in the earlier case, and Socialist-Catholic-Liberal in the latter. Such groupings may seem strange to the English reader, but it must be remembered that the Catholic Centrum had a large working-class vote, and scores to pay off thanks to Bismarck's *Kulturkampf*. And, in fact, such groupings did take shape in the pre-war Reichstag, and later came to form the backbone (if that is the word) of the Weimar Republic. No, the Reichstag reflected the interests and movements in German society accurately enough—more accurately, it could be argued, than the British Parliament. But as no party leader could sit in the Cabinet, responsible government was impossible, and the standard of recruitment of deputies for the Reichstag correspondingly low. The Bismarckian set around William did not want any change in this situation; and did not make those concessions which one would have thought expedient, to say the least, in the event of a future war which would ultimately be won or lost, not by Junkers and Industrialists, but by the mass armies of the peoples of Europe.

CHAPTER FOUR

The Kaiser

This brief excursion into Prussian-German history is necessary if one is to appreciate the nature of the situation into which William was thrust. It is evident that only one man could have led Germany into the new age without endangering Bismarck's ingenious structure, and that man had to be the Kaiser. There was no doubt about the efficiency of the German Army; or of the new Navy—William's toy—which became so efficient a force that the British were humiliatingly outgunned at the battle of Jutland, and only narrowly escaped starvation during the ruthless submarine campaign of 1917. There was no danger of Revolution. Nor was there any doubt as to the patriotism of the German people, save for inferior breeds such as Danes, Poles, Alsace-Lorrainers, and Hanoverians (who had not forgiven the Prussian conquest of Hanover in 1865). Indeed, one can see now that it was the overweening folly of the élite that they did not take measures to bind their fundamentally loyal subjects to the new Prussian-German state, with consequences that were fatal to German morale. But William, a young man of twenty-nine at his accession, had been captured by the 'Hohenzollern tradition', and though he had much of his mother, and indeed of Albert, in his character—both Albert and William were in some ways remarkably feminine in their psychological make-up—he felt always that his first loyalty was to his grandfather, the first Kaiser, and to the dynasty. And we must remember that he had powers which neither Albert nor Vicky ever possessed.

Almost everything, then, depended on the character of the Kaiser. Indeed, it is clear that William's personal character is of altogether greater historical significance than that of Vicky or Albert. Albert passed on; England passed him by. For all his brave endeavours, England was as if he had never been. Vicky might have reigned over *Mitteleuropa*, as her mother reigned as Empress over brown and black, white and yellow. But death had cut short that old Coburg dream. Who, then, was this William who was to leave so sad an impression on history, and indeed on his contemporaries? He started well, with a special effusion of affection on the part of his grandmama:

> Accept on this day my warmest good wishes for our darling William, that beloved and promising child was adored Papa's great favourite. . . . But bring him up simply, plainly, not with that terrible Prussian pride and ambition, which grieved dear Papa so much and which he always said would stand in the way of Prussia taking that lead in Germany which he ever wished her to do! Pride and ambition are not only very wrong in themselves but they alienate affection and are in every way unworthy of really great minds and great nations (January 27th, 1865).

At first, Willy could do no wrong with his grandmama: he was affectionate, thoughtful, and quick. If there were doubts in the Queen's or in Vicky's minds, it was because of the 'bad' Hohenzollern constituent in his heredity, which might prove stronger than the 'good' Coburg influence. Thus, quite early on, Queen Victoria was writing with Imperial disapproval to Vicky:

> Why does Willy always sign himself 'William of Prussia'?— his father never did.

She sensed the insidious influence of the Hohenzollerns and 'that bad man B.', and wrote very frankly to her daughter in 1874—not that the warning was necessary—that Willy, then fifteen, was

> Straightforward and honest and kind-hearted and to a certain extent obstinate, not *conceited* but absurdly proud, as all his family are, thinking *no* family greater or *higher* than the Hohenzollerns.

Yet there were plenty to speak well of him, including some

whom one might have thought among his inveterate enemies. Thus Professor Balfour writes:

> Many people spoke of his ability to please, perhaps the most remarkable being Queen Mary. He was said to have the gift of making the person he was talking to appear at his best and of giving the impression that they commanded his exclusive attention. . . . Slow, stiff, or unduly serious people got on his nerves. A. J. Balfour said that William II and George V were the only Princes to whom he found he could talk as man to man.

But then it was early evident that, whereas in company he always found it necessary to strike a pose, in private he could be natural and charming. Tirpitz, the founder of the new German Navy, remarked that it was necessary

> to talk tête-à-tête with William since the presence of more than two parties to the conversation was easily calculated to divert his own true personal judgment by playing upon his urge to show off. . . . One of his friend Eulenburg's merits was that by observing these principles, he was able to get plans and outlooks changed. He once suggested that William's frequent success in manoeuvres was prearranged and to the Kaiser's protestations replied: 'I should be very glad to learn some day that your Majesty had been defeated.'

What was William's true psychology? He was, of course, the victim of the past, in particular of Bismarck's settlement of Germany after 1871. But that is only half the story. Churchill cruelly, perhaps, but accurately summed up what his German contemporaries were saying:

> We have a weakling on the throne. Our War Lord is a Pacifist. Is the new arrived, and late arrived Germany with all its tremendous and expanding forces to be led by a President of the Young Men's Christian Association? Was it for this that the immortal Frederick and the great Bismarck schemed and conquered?

Another experienced judge of men, Theodore Roosevelt, gave

207

a still more devastating analysis of how German affairs were in fact run:

> Down at the bottom of his heart, the Kaiser knew perfectly well that he was not an absolute sovereign. He had never had a chance to try. . . . On the contrary, when Germany made up its mind to go in a given direction, he could only stay at the head of affairs by scampering to take the lead and going in that direction. . . . But together with his underlying consciousness of the real facts of the situation went a curious make-believe to himself that each sovereign did represent his country in the sense that would have been true two or three centuries ago.

What was the source of the Kaiser's lack of confidence? Here we trespass into psychological waters which perhaps run too deep for the historian. Yet the point cannot be avoided. As if it were not enough that Nature had burdened him with his mother's ambivalence towards the values of his own family, she had played a cruel trick on his physique. The origins of the trouble are not entirely clear. But it seems likely that, in the course of a difficult birth, the English doctor sent over by Queen Victoria directed his attention first to the welfare of the mother and only later appreciated that the baby's left arm had been wrenched from its socket—hence the famous 'withered arm' of which so much was to be heard (it was doubly unfortunate, naturally, in that an *English* doctor had been in charge). But, in fact, the truth was worse than is often realised. The whole left side of the body was affected, and especially the ear. As a result, the Kaiser was never able to run, or climb, or ride as a boy. Because of the unequal development of the two sides of the body, he found difficulty in holding his head straight. A 'machine' was devised that would hold the head in position, and he was compelled to wear it several hours every day. All of this was kept secret, as far as was possible; but the effect on the boy can be imagined. Aural attacks were liable to come on suddenly in later life and made for a considerable degree of nervous irritability and—far worse for a man in his position—for those rapid changes of mind which undermined his political and personal judgment. It is clearly difficult to speculate where such matters are concerned: but the physical disabilities of the Kaiser have been, if anything, underplayed as a factor in his mental development. The situation was far more serious than people were permitted to realise.

It is easy to argue—in so far as such arguments have validity at all—that in William the Hohenzollern blood predominated over the Coburg, Hanoverian, or Saxe-Weimar. But this is to do the Hohenzollerns an injustice; and to show the Coburgs too much favour. In Anglo-Saxon lands the popular concept of the Hohenzollerns is that they were overbearing, boorish, rapacious, and given to ostentation. But when Vicky argued to her mother that it was the 'moral' qualities of the Prussian soldier that gave him his advantage (we should speak today of 'morale', no doubt) she was not so far wrong. The Prussian character is often said to be summed up in Moltke's famous phrase *mehr sein als scheinen* (Be more than you appear); and there is much truth in that. The old Kaiser William I would make a point of stopping the Imperial train for lunch at the next convenient station, and taking his meal in the station dining-room. (One can hardly imagine a Romanov or Habsburg doing that.) The virtues instilled into the Prussian child were certainly Spartan: thrift was enjoined, and the principles of simple living and high thinking were the order of the day at the—by this time universally admired—Prussian schools and universities (on which Matthew Arnold wrote a report in his official capacity). It is almost certainly true that Prussia was in the mid-Victorian period the best educated country in Europe. Were the Prussians truly 'modest'—as they certainly considered they were? This is more ambiguous ground. The Prussian Court was certainly modest to a fault, in Vicky's opinion. In Albert's eyes, and in those of many foreign and many German admirers, the Prussian was the 'good German' *par excellence*: none doubted his courage or his earnestness for truth; all admired his quiet sobriety, his capacity for hard work, his orderly ways, his simple loyalty to 'Throne and Altar'. True, since the heroic days of the Great Elector, his son and his grandson Frederick, the Hohenzollerns had produced no ruler of outstanding ability, but neither had they troubled the peace of Europe. They were indeed, until the advent of Bismarck, the 'good boys' of Europe. The Coburgs were, as we have seen, dynastically far more ambitious—if also far more able—than the House of Hohenzollern.

The advent of Bismarck, and Industrialisation: these were the factors that were to sweep away the old kingdom of Prussia and bring into being the *parvenu*, over-reaching empire of which William II was so disastrous and appropriate an exemplar. It should be observed that both events were fortuitous. Prussia had been short on political talent since the 'reform period' at the close of the Napoleonic wars: the age of Hardenberg and Stein, Wilhelm von Humboldt, Scharnhorst and Gneisenau. A Bismarck was an uncovenanted grace—or disaster. Equally, if Prussia had consisted solely of the March of Brandenburg and the sandy soils of Pomerania and East and West Prussia, she would not have become the first state in Germany to achieve 'take off', and thus snatch the leadership from Austria so easily. This advantage she owed to the fortuitous circumstance that Germany's main coal and iron deposits lay in Upper Silesia and in the Catholic, but Prussian, Rhineland, a large part of which had been wished on her at the Congress of Vienna by Castlereagh, who desired to see Prussia strongly entrenched on the borders of France. In addition Berlin itself was a powerful and growing industrial city, despite its lack of mineral resources. But in the new industrial age these were to matter less, as the rapid rise of Siemens and A.E.G. testifies. What Berlin could offer, of course, was a long tradition of discipline, hard work and high craftsmanship—in fact, the old Prussian virtues.

These then were the historical and psychological factors that went to the making of William's personality. And we have seen that the Constitution had been so constructed that, in the last resort, all rested on the shoulders of one man. The simplest answer to the riddle of William's failure is perhaps the best: the burden was too great. Symptoms of this appeared early on, and just before the First World War an observer was to note:

> He has been long in showing any development of character; the man of forty-nine has advanced little on the subaltern who came to the throne at twenty-nine.

By 1914, William had lost the respect of his own caste, as well as of the nation as a whole, and won the enmity of at least three powerful neighbours. Crown Prince Rudolf of Austria-Hungary—officially, his Ally—wrote in 1889 shortly before the sensational double-suicide at Mayerling:

> The Kaiser is likely to cause great confusion in Europe before long. He is just the man for it; energetic and capricious, he will in the course of a few years bring the Germany of the Hohenzollerns to the position it deserves.

Frederick, surprisingly perhaps, had been an excellent soldier; his son did not, in the view of contemporaries, inherit his gifts:

> There is a disturbing element of dilettantism in the army and navy. He is less of a soldier than his father and grandfather because he lacks the steadiness of view which only down to earth hard work can give. Yet he is not only convinced that he possesses such a view but that he is a born leader.

Professor Balfour comments, and puts his finger, surely on the nub of the problem:

> A Court official said to the chief of the military secretariat, 'It is extraordinary that in every department the Kaiser should have someone about him who deceives him . . .' He berated the Foreign Office for not showing dispatches to him promptly, but does not seem to have realised that sometimes, as in 1905, 1909, 1911 and 1914, the important ones were not shown to him at all . . . the Germans had then (as they retain today) a reputation for extreme efficiency. But a complex of out of date attitudes towards the Monarchy and politics had saddled them with an almost incredible state of inefficiency in a vital sector of their system.

William had, it is fair to say, two principal—perhaps inter-related—faults. He could not keep his mouth shut; and he could not make decisions. Thus a great number of his public speeches were disastrous (*Rednerische entgleisungen*, 'Speech-derailments', as they became known in Germany). He delighted to give marks and sum up the general performance of the Army after manœuvres, a habit which caused both consternation and merriment among the General Staff. He would lecture his Admirals on the best methods of ship production, and once ventured to design a warship himself, which the Admiralty had the delicate task of explaining would do almost everything but float. Nor was his advice restricted to officers of his own nation. As an honorary Admiral of the Fleet, he was prepared to give the benefit of his advice to the Board of Admiralty. Uncle Bertie, submitted to this kind of thing at a dinner, found his own solution: he fell asleep. But not all could summon up Uncle Bertie's placidity. Many of his speeches to the German people were sheer, manic bravado: a weak man covering up his weakness:

> There is only one person who is master in this Empire, and I am not going to tolerate any other.

> I am the sole master of German policy, and my country must follow me wherever I go.

> What the public says is a matter of entire indifference to me. I make decisions according to my convictions and expect my officials to reply to the mistaken ideas of my people in a suitable manner.

> I have never read the Constitution and know nothing about it.

The resemblance to certain of Adolf Hitler's utterances may strike the reader: in particular the curious mixture of (only apparent, in the Kaiser) brutal resolution and an affectation of somnambulism. But the speech that will be longest remembered as the acme of Wilhelminian egotism was delivered on the occasion of the embarkation of the German expeditionary force to help suppress the Boxer Rising:

> There has been no precedent in world history for the presumptuous action of the Chinese in disregarding national rights of a thousand years standing. . . . All heathen cultures, no matter how attractive and excellent they may seem,

collapse at the first catastrophe. Live up to Prussia's traditional steadfastness! Show yourselves Christians, happily
enduring in the face of the heathen! You are well aware that
you have to face a brave, well-armed savage foe. . . . No
pardon will be given and prisoners will not be made. Anyone
who falls into your hands falls to your sword! Just as the
Huns under their King Attila created for themselves a
thousand years ago a name which men still respect, you
should give the name of German such cause to be remembered in China that no Chinaman, whether his eyes be slit
or not, will dare to look a German in the face. . . . Open the
road for *Kultur* once and for all!

This outburst hardly requires comment. But it had at least one
memorable sequel: it was this speech that caused the Germans
of 1914–18 to be called 'Huns' in England.

'Hang the Kaiser!' went the cry in the Coupon Election of
1918; and one can see how the sentiment arose. Yet how far
does the Kaiser's guilt for the First World War in fact extend?
It is evident that the Kaiser's attention to political and foreign
affairs was never very close; and it is perhaps charitable to see
in this a mitigating factor. He was never the great War Lord,
der allerhöchste Kriegsherr, that he would have liked to have been,
and that Northcliffe's propaganda made him out to be. That
role was filled jointly by Hindenburg and Ludendorff. In the
years after 1910, and especially during the war, the Kaiser
seemed strangely resigned to many observers: resigned to the
inevitability of war, and perhaps of defeat, and resigned to his
having no real say in it either way. Yet he can hardly escape
all blame. Would war have failed to come between the Great
Powers in the second decade of the 20th century had the Kaiser
never lived? There can be no certain answer. But it is certain—
as Bismarck knew well—that once German unity was a fact, it
was *Germany* that had the greatest interest in keeping the peace of
Europe. There, as we have seen, lay the best chances for her
trade. And in her very strength there lay a new danger: how to
prevent Bismarck's *cauchemar de la Grande Coalition* from coming
true? Certainly, William's government made every mistake in

the book. Within a few months of his accession a French squadron had paid a visit to the Russian naval base at Kronstadt. Bismarck had said that Germany must always be the stronger partner in any alliance, meaning that she must always be in control. Yet he set up an alliance with Austria-Hungary, whose internal weaknesses were all too plain, and over whose polities the new Reich had no direct control. Indeed, Bismarck himself said that no Balkan issue was 'worth the bones of a single Pomeranian grenadier'.

Austria-Hungary was certainly the worst ally that the new Germany could have chosen. An alliance with France was, no doubt, out of the question. This left only Russia and England. Bismarck's general inclination, we know, would have been to go for the 'line to St Petersburg': Germany would then have had indisputable military hegemony in Europe. But England, too, was a possibility, and it is surely to be reckoned a fault in Bismarck that he underrated her, as it was a fault in his pupil that he became obsessed by her. For an English alliance—on the principle of 'if you can't beat 'em, join 'em'—would have meant a blockade of France and Russia, without the need to build a single German ship. As the First World War showed, it was quite on the cards that without Anglo-Saxon help both Russia and France might have been beaten (as, indeed, they were in effect by the end of 1917). But an alliance with England would have meant that Germany would have had to play, in some respects, the role of junior partner: Uncle England (Bertie) lording it over Nephew Germany (Willy). There is no reason, as we can see in retrospect, why such an arrangement should not have worked. After all, Holland and Sweden did not require powerful Navies to sustain their positions as important trading nations. And, indeed, it can be argued that it seems to work well enough now, where the British have near-total naval and nuclear superiority over Germany, and both sides trade not only more profitably with one another than ever, but also with the world at large.

It is here, then, that William should be held chiefly to blame. He could have tried for the English alliance—as Albert had intended and as men like Joseph Chamberlain still wished—but he could not have it unless he would agree to Britannia ruling the waves, and rest content with the senior partnership (as it were) on land. Yet this touched his ambivalence towards his mother's and grandmother's country at its sorest point. There were, of course, many other factors at work: the rapid expansion of world trade and communications, the popular enthusiasm for acquisition of colonies, the pressure of the great steel-barons of the Ruhr and the ship-owners of Hamburg—expressed vociferously through the Navy League—for a German presence on the high seas. The Navy League was very much the child of the rising Wilhelminian middle class; and it became a dogma that, without a Navy, it would be a question of *Weltmacht oder Untergang* for the new Germany, although Tirpitz was aware that there could never be any question of outbuilding Britain at sea, since Germany could not afford it.

William's personal ambivalence was thus *ein weltpolitischer Faktor* that requires to be examined. As always, he was quick to change his mind, and yet strangely constant in his long-term affections—or, more unkindly, obsessions. He said to the British ambassador soon after his accession:

My mother and I have the same characters. I have inherited hers. That good stubborn English blood which will not give way runs in both our veins.

Yet there is a story that, bleeding from a wound as a child, he had said, through his tears, 'I want to get rid of every drop of English blood in my veins!' Still, as late as 1911 he could say to Theodore Roosevelt, 'I ADORE England.' On a visit to England, where the yachting at Cowes exercised an irresistible fascination, he wrote:

I was made an Admiral of the Fleet. Fancy wearing the same uniform as St. Vincent and Nelson! It is enough to make me quite giddy.

The story that he chose to wear this uniform for a gala performance of *The Flying Dutchman* is probably a Berlin joke. But it is clear that, as Professor Balfour remarks,

At bottom his attitude to the Fleet was part of his love-hate relationship with his mother's country. He wanted a Navy because the English had one. Because it was a means of forcing the English to pay him attention, of making Germany an attractive ally.

This love-hate relationship with the apparently all-powerful British was of course typical of his generation in Germany, and particularly of the industrialists and shipping magnates who backed the Navy League. Yet his affection for England was real, indeed very personal. To his grandmama he remained, despite the occasional dressing-down, 'her adored William'. On her death-bed, he and Uncle Bertie had held the dying woman in their arms; the Kaiser, on the left side of the bed, suffering great pain for three hours, since his disability prevented him from changing sides with Uncle Bertie. It is a touching scene, and we note that this time there is nothing of the actor in William's behaviour:

> As a rule he wore uniform. . . . But he returned from his grandmother's funeral in such a state of Anglophile euphoria that for a time he adopted the English practice of wearing plain clothes and continued at intervals down to the war . . .
> He was not for nothing the great-grandnephew of a man who arrived late at the Battle of Leipzig owing to inability to decide whether he should appear in Prussian or Russian uniform, or the great-great-grandson of one who frequently dined in his crown (Balfour).

Again, on another trip to England, he stayed with a friend in the Hampshire countryside. Once more, he was in rhapsodies:

> I have at last sampled, as I had long wanted to do, all the delights and comforts of English home and country life. Comfortable affluence, excellence of culture and their elegance and friendliness. . . . I found it immensely refreshing and soothing. . . . The way these British refrain from discussing our affairs has made me ashamed. Such a matter in our Parliament would be an utter impossibility.

This outburst is surely significant. In Hampshire, as later in Doorn, he was at last able to relax. William was fundamentally a private man compelled to wear a public face. But these bouts of affability were not always returned. Sir Frederick Ponsonby minuted:

> No English gentleman would behave like the Emperor W. to his Uncle or Bismarck father and son. But we must not forget that none of them happen to be *English gentlemen*—and we must take them as we find them—pure Prussians . . . All cordiality, all real friendship in Berlin is gone forever, and the cause is the *Empress Frederick*—whose champion the P. of W. is regarded to be.

Though this judgment, current in Berlin, may be mistaken, it shows well enough the deadlock that had been reached in Anglo-German relations. Uncle Bertie had in fact always been —as was his nature—most affable to his nephew William. But the affability was bound to be resented, since it was the product of self-confidence and experience of the world that William singularly lacked.

The rest of the story, with Uncle Bertie dead, and George V on the English throne, is of diminishing historical significance. It can be argued that the decline, and brusque expulsion of William to end his life in exile in Holland, was the expression both of the self-contempt and need for a scapegoat, indeed almost the death-wish, of his caste (selfish and dishonourable and un-Prussian behaviour indeed, since it meant renouncing their vows to their Supreme War Lord, only to renew them to their true class-enemy, Adolf Hitler, in August, 1934, after the Night of the Long Knives). William lingered during the war years near Headquarters, playing his part by making patriotic speeches, but in fact succumbing to the intolerable pressure Bismarck's Constitution had imposed on him. He was soon pushed aside. Long before the guns fell silent it was evident that he had given up the struggle (had he perhaps something of Albert in him after all?):

> One night as they were sitting on the terrace someone brought out a picture and asked William if he had painted it. He identified it as the work of someone else and added, 'You

know, if I had that man's talent, I should have been a painter instead of an Emperor and I shouldn't be in such a horrifying position today.'

One is reminded vividly of the last days in the *Führerbunker*, with the broken Hitler still sketching designs for the great new capital that he would never build, at Linz. The truth, indeed, is that the picture of the Kaiser as some kind of modern Attila was an invention of Allied propaganda. As the feline Holstein chose to put it to a friend:

You will be in a much better position to see what is to be done once you have discarded the misleading saying, 'The King can do no wrong,' which was invented in a country where the King has no power.

One of the Kaiser's staff remarked that:

His bark was always worse than his bite. He said rather pathetically to one ambassador, 'I am not really a wicked man,' and puzzled another by remarking, with equal truth, '*I* am not the strong man—you must look elsewhere for him.' But the remark that goes most to the root of the matter was made to Bülow after the Chancellor had criticised him for a tactless speech: 'I know you wish me well, but *I am what I am and I cannot change.*'

As the beaten German armies flooded back into the Fatherland, the Kaiser was bundled off by night to the castle of Count Bentinck in Holland:

As the car came through the gateway in the pouring rain, he turned to his host, Count Bentinck, and said, 'Now give me a cup of real good English tea' (he got it, with Scotch scones added!) (Balfour).

He settled down, as he had often wished, to live the life of an English country gentleman at the neighbouring castle of Doorn. He allowed two of his sons—but not the Crown Prince—to be active in Nazi organisations. But the Nazis were distinctly ungenerous in return. He might not return to Germany;

although Goering, who had some Monarchist sympathies, arranged for a generous financial settlement. To the Nazis he was an embarrassment, since many of their conservative allies were Monarchists, as was a large part of the Army officer corps and, inevitably, the Navy. What he thought of later Nazi behaviour can be gathered from this remark: when he heard of the Nazi pogrom of the Jews during the *Kristallnacht* in November, 1938, he said: 'For the first time I am ashamed to be a German' (though this did not prevent him from sending a congratulatory cable to Hitler on the fall of Paris in 1940).

For fairness' sake, perhaps, the final comment should go to another German of the old school, a Bavarian Count, who remarked ironically when he heard that the House of Hanover, as if to celebrate its two hundredth birthday in England, had changed its name at the behest of the House of Harmsworth to 'Windsor':

The true Royal tradition died on that day in 1917 when, for a mere war, King George V changed his name.

The Political Consequences
of John Maynard Keynes

CHAPTER ONE

Kultur and Civilisation

To the inhabitants of Bloomsbury, as to Matthew Arnold a generation before, the world was divided between the civilised and the philistines and barbarians. The task of the former was to spread *sophrosune*, 'sweetness and light'—or *Geist*, as Arminius, 'Baron von Thunder-ten-Tronck' of 'Friendship's Garland' has it. The good baron's origins are to be found in Voltaire: 'there lived in Westphalia a young lad blessed by nature with the most agreeable manners. You could read his character in his face. He combined sound judgment with unaffected simplicity; and that, I suppose, was why he was called Candide . . .' They were the bearers of *Kultur*, the Elect against the Philistines, bound one to another by a platonic friendship's garland of their own. But between 1870 and the Cambridge cabals of around 1900, out of which Bloomsbury proper was to emerge, a subtle change of meaning had occurred. Arnold had distinguished between Barbarians (the upper classes) and Philistines (the middle classes). But to young Bloomsbury it was all one. Whereas in Matthew Arnold there is still something of the great Doctor's will to proselytise, to flog philistinism and barbarism into submission, by 1900 the worldly battle is given up for lost. None would have agreed more fervently than Lytton Strachey, Clive Bell, Leonard Woolf, and the young John Maynard Keynes, members of the 'Apostles'—founded, as we have seen, by Thirlwall and Hare, and which counted Sterling, Tennyson, and Maurice among their number. Art, Literature, Music, Philosophy, and Love in all its forms: these were 'good states of mind' to be cultivated, under that gentle prophet of *sophrosune*, G. E. Moore. It would have occurred to none of them that they had among their number one who was destined to change the course of the world's affairs in the 20th century: John Maynard Keynes. At that age all would have agreed with

223

Lytton Strachey—already almost the Lytton of 'Eminent Victorians' eighteen years later—that busybodies like Dr Arnold, Cardinal Manning, Florence Nightingale or General Gordon were fair game for ridicule.

There has been some dispute as to when 'Bloomsbury' may properly be said to have begun and, indeed, in what—to borrow Moore's famous query—*exactly* it may be said to consist. 'Philistine', as we have seen, is a borrowing from the German around 1827: it meant, essentially, the 'town' as against the 'gown'. Whether 'culture', a word never quite at home in the English language, has a similar origin I am not sure (it is just possible, since according to the O.E.D. it first entered the language in this sense in 1805, when German *Kultur* itself was being discovered). Be that as it may, the reasons for the uncomfortableness of the concept of 'culture' in English, and its different and deeper roots in the German mind, are evident enough. The English gentleman of the 18th century—over-idealised as he is in Clive Bell's 'civilisation'—had no need of the word 'culture' in the sectarian sense which it acquired at the hands of Matthew Arnold, Pater, and Bloomsbury. 'Cultured' is indeed recorded as in use in 1717, but it meant no more than 'refined', 'polished'—or, indeed, 'civilised'. Would the 18th-century gentleman, asked in what civilisation consisted, have replied, like Lytton Strachey, 'Sir, I am the civilisation for which you are fighting!' Not every notable at the Court of the *Roi Soleil* was, as Clive Bell too often seems to imply, a minor Molière, Racine or La Fontaine. But neither did there exist the need to distinguish between 'civilisation' and 'culture'.

In Germany, the story is very different. To the 19th century it would have made good sense to distinguish an advanced *Kulturvolk* from a primitive *Naturvolk*. A *Kulturvolk* meant, precisely, a 'civilised people'. But by the time Thomas Mann— not that he was original in using the terms in this way—came to write his 'Confessions of an Unpolitical Man', as his contribution to the 1914–18 war-effort (Mann was a more or less exact contemporary of the Bloomsberries), he was contrasting *echt* German *Kultur* with the trivial, materialistic *Zivilisation* of the Western Allies. In the days of Weimar, Mann was to repudiate this position and all it implied: he made his new confession of faith in *Von Deutscher Republik*. But the distinction was one that had been latent in the German mind at least since the Romantics. To the Anglo-Saxon mind it is not difficult to conceive how, under the stresses and strains of war, a nation can come to consider itself as the defender of *Kultur* against a host of enemies—except that we should have used the word 'civilisation'.

What is strange to us is that the enemy should be dubbed, not barbarism, but *Zivilisation*. This is the 'civilisation' contemptuously dismissed by Baudelaire: 'Theory of the true civilisation. It is not to be found in gas, or steam or table-turning: it consists in the diminution of the traces of original sin.' (*Mon coeur mis à nu.*) Rilke, George, and Hofmannsthal would no doubt have agreed. Civilisation, as Baudelaire rudely put it, is an *idée Belge*. In other words: Manchester and the Ruhr, the grimy ruthless new world of capitalist industrialism. In the German tradition this new world became—as for Blake, Coleridge, Carlyle, Ruskin, and William Morris—the antithesis of that unfallen world of *Natur*, and the imputed harmony of the Middle Ages. Of course, without the Ruhr there would have been no breech-loading Krupp needle guns to garner the victories of Sadowa and Sedan. By this standard Germany was in 1914 a great deal more *zivilisiert* than any of the Allies—more so than munitions-starved Britain. But it is the *mythos* that counts. A German victory must somehow cleanse Europe of the horrors of industrial capitalism and bring back a nature-delighting pre-industrial paradise, as in Faust's vision:

> *Solch ein Gewimmel möcht' ich sehen,*
> *Ein freies Volk auf freiem Felde Stehen!*

But we should remember that this beatific vision, so like Langland's vision on the Malverns of a 'Fair field full of folk', or Blake's 'Jerusalem' or Morris' 'News from Nowhere', was shared not only by *Wandervögel*, by Socialists and Romantics of all stripes—but later also by the Nazis.

It would not be wrong, then, to suggest that the civilisation that Bloomsbury so prized was more or less the opposite of that

Zivilisation disparaged by Thomas Mann, and more or less identical with his cherished *Kultur*. And one might add that the fact that the two words should have come to have directly contrary meanings in the two cultures is a fair measure of the spiritual gulf separating intellectual Germany from intellectual England on the brink of the First World War. But what was this civilisation that Bloomsbury prized, and prided itself on? The question is as complex as the nature of the Bloomsbury group itself. Did it ever exist outside the hostile, philistine imagination of the popular press, or the righteous fury of Dr Leavis? If it did, did it begin in 1912–14 (as Leonard Woolf would have it), or around 1908, or back in the sunlit days of the Kings and Trinity Apostles, when the Stracheys (Lytton and James), the Keyneses (Maynard and Geoffrey), and the Stephens (Thoby and Adrian)—and Desmond McCarthy, Forster, and Woolf—first met under the aegis of M'Taggart and Russell and G. E. Moore? Mr Michael Holroyd, who has been into these matters very thoroughly, tends to regard the 'Cambridge' period as essentially one of incubation, and would date Bloomsbury proper from the years 1908–10 when the tribe descended on London (admitting, for the first time, female companions in the persons of Virginia Stephen, soon to marry Leonard Woolf; and her sister Vanessa, soon to become Mrs Clive Bell). That the group was tightly enough knit, by kinship and marriage, not to speak of those labyrinthine homo-and-heterosexual attachments recent writers have explored, is not to be denied. (Noel Annan, in his study of Leslie Stephen, traces the origins of the sect back to the famous evangelical-reforming 'Clapham Sect'; I have suggested that there is also a strong affinity with the 'Highgate Sect'.) There *was* a Bloomsbury group, indeed a Bloomsbury Sect. And it was in the company of these men and women that the mind—not the economic side of it, which was indeed looked down upon as a trifle worldly and un-Apostolic—of John Maynard Keynes came to be formed.

Yet his economic interests (in both senses of that word) were never wholly distinguished in Keynes' mind from his political and artistic interests and, above all, from that categorical imperative of Moore's: the cultivation of the affection of one's friends. It is this quality of *uomo universale* in Keynes which, at this distance, seems to set him above—though not apart from—the Duncan Grants, the Lytton Stracheys, even the Morgan Forsters of the Sect. (Only Leonard Woolf shared, if in a more minor key, Keynes' politico-economic concerns.) And we know that this is to some extent how Keynes saw the matter himself. Keynes was the very opposite of a Sectarian; in Coleridge's definition of that term, he was a Catholic. The arts, logic, political economy, personal relations, philosophy, and the ballet: all inhabited the same world—a world whose simplest designation was 'civilisation'. As a lover of the arts, he bought his friends' paintings: in later life, he helped to found the Cambridge Arts Theatre and became the first Chairman of the Arts Council of Great Britain. As a logician, he laboured over a dissertation which, he was assured, would open the way to a fellowship at Kings. He was a distinguished book collector. He was, as all the world knows, a great balletomane—the first practitioner of the Dismal Science, surely, to choose a ballerina for a wife? As a politician, he remained a life-long Liberal. But his politico-economic influence was exerted not only through the *Nation* and later the *New Statesman*, of which he was Chairman, but—more effectively no doubt—through his contacts at the Treasury and in Washington, through a succession of famous pamphlets (of which 'The Economic Consequences of the Peace' is rightly seen as the most famous and most influential) and, of course, through his major work on 'Money, Employment, and Exchange'.

But it is worth repeating that he never saw these things in the contemporary fashion, as rigidly compartmentalised, self-sufficient activities. In Keynes' day and indeed in his father's (in his own right one of the great Cambridge worthies), there was no such subject as economics: there was only something known as Political Economy. And Keynes, I think, would have preferred the out-moded, but traditional and—I daresay he would have maintained—more appropriate designation. In his essay on Alfred Marshall* ('Essays in Biography') Keynes tells

* Incidentally, he quotes Marshall in 1868, 'when he was in his metaphysical

the charming story of how the renowned German discoverer of the Quantum Theory, Max Planck, once remarked to him that, in early life, 'he once thought of studying economics, but had found it too difficult'. As Keynes remarks, Max Planck could easily have mastered the whole corpus of mathematical economics in a few days. But that was not the point:

> The amalgam of logic and intuition and wide knowledge of the facts, most of which are not precise, which is required for economic interpretation in its highest form is, quite truly, overwhelmingly difficult for those whose gift mainly consists in the power ... to pursue to their furthest points the implications ... of comparatively simple facts which are known with a high degree of precision.

A sense of the wholeness of the world of fact and perception is here implicit which is sadly lacking in many of Keynes' successors. Though he and his Apostolic friends like Russell and Moore had rejected the Hegelianism of MacTaggart as young men, the Edwardian world they were entering still possessed a unity: a wholeness with a myriad dialectical inter-relations, but a wholeness none the less. It was an age of Principles: a magic word in Cambridge since Newton's day. In 1874 there had been Jevons' 'Principles of Science'; in 1890 there had come Marshall's 'Principles of Economics'; in Keynes' own time as an undergraduate, Moore's 'Principia Ethica', Russell and Whitehead's 'Principia Mathematica' (1903), and Keynes' father's own 'Principles of Economics' (1905). And the tradition persisted: 1924 saw I. A. Richards' 'Principles of Literary Criticism'. For many, though not for Keynes, the First World War was to shatter that unity for ever —or induce them to accept some neo-Hegelian wholeness, such as Marxism-Leninism. But Bloomsbury—perhaps because it was still Victorian at heart—still clung precariously to a wholeness that might tend towards some higher goal, not God, still

stage', going to Dresden to 'learn the language of Kant': 'Kant was my guide ... The only man I ever worshipped ... But I could get no further: beyond seemed misty, and social problems came imperiously to the front . . .' How great a distance it seems between 1868—the Hegelian Oxford of Freeman and Green— and the Cambridge of embryonic Bloomsbury around 1900!

less the Hegelian *Weltgeist*, but something that might—with all due scepticism—still be invoked as 'civilisation'.

'Civilisation!' Keynes himself (in 'Two Memoirs') defined it, with the ambience of proto-Bloomsbury very much in mind:

> We repudiated all versions of the doctrine of original sin, of there being insane and irrational springs of wickedness in most men. We were not aware that civilisation is a thin and precarious crust, erected by the will and personality of a very few, and only maintained by rules and conventions skilfully put across and guilefully preserved (September 9th, 1938).

Writing thus, in mid-life, with the gathering stormclouds very much in mind, the mature Keynes has not lost faith in 'civilisation', evidently. But if the Apostles felt able to ridicule the concept of original sin, the older Keynes is prepared to admit that there are 'insane and irrational springs of wickedness in most men', that civilisation is a 'thin and precarious crust'. (Shades of Baudelaire's 'diminution of the trace of original sin'!) Nevertheless, civilisation must be 'maintained'. And who knows but that it might fall to the 'worldly' men, the political economists to maintain it? Later, much later, when Keynes was negotiating the American Loan to Britain in 1945, the fore-runner, with wartime Lend-Lease, of the Marshall Plan of 1947, and of those other economic and military measures which ensured the survival of civilisation in Europe, thoughts not dissimilar passed through Keynes' mind. What follows is Roy Harrod's paraphrase in his 'Life'; but Keynes' thinking is rendered accurately enough:

> And now he, Keynes, had to carry the heavy responsibility of speaking for Britain on this matter, which was also in its own way one of life and death. For the condition of Britain was indeed parlous. If his negotiations were not successful, rations would have to be drastically cut; the factories would stand idle for lack of materials; there would certainly be inflation. . . . There might be violence of a kind unknown in this fair island for many generations. Its consequences could not be foreseen; many precious features of our civilisation

might be lost. There would have to be a long period of grinding poverty and mendicancy. One might think of the troubles of Germany in the early years after the first world war and the disruption in her social fabric which was their consequence. . . . He thought of the amiable life of the Sussex countryside and the labourers whom he loved. . . . He thought of the universities—with their precious modes of life, philosophy, civilised discussion; he thought of talks with Lytton by the fireside, he thought of the cultivated gentle-people all over England, living modestly, loving books and music, disseminating sweetness and light. Were they all to be ground down by harsh distress and social strife? The next few weeks mattered much . . .

CHAPTER TWO

Consequences

It may be argued that Maynard Keynes' concept of civilisation was narrow, 'Lytton by the fireside', 'gentle-people . . . disseminating sweetness and light'; but it cannot be denied that it was all of a piece. Keynes had a clear idea of the civilisation he had set out to save (surely not an ignoble one); and he fought hard to save it—indeed heroically, for it is likely that he would have lived longer than his sixty-two years had the burden of the negotiations over Lend-Lease and the American Loan not undermined his never too robust health. But civilisation for what, and for whom? Undoubtedly, there was more than a whiff of self-satisfied sectarianism in Bloomsbury's concept of civilisation; and it was this that brought the Sect into disrepute over the past two generations (though the tide is turning now). I do not see any purpose in denying the 'Sectarian' charge: it is perhaps more relevant to see how it came about. Mr Holroyd has concluded that the Bloomsberries were in fact the last of the Victorians; and it is clear—from Strachey's ambivalence towards his Eminent Victorians, and still more towards their Queen, as from Keynes' or Leonard Woolf's fundamental belief in rationality and progress—that the shadow of the Victorians lay heavy on the Bloomsberries. 'Modern art', 'modern poetry', 'modern music', as we think of them today, still lay in the future: it was not in 1900, but in 1910 that the great explosion of genius which we associate with the names of Braque and Picasso, Eliot and Joyce, Diaghilev and Stravinsky, first blazed above the horizon. These indeed were observed with delight and devotion by Bloomsbury: Roger Fry organised the great Post-Impressionist exhibition—with Leonard Woolf, newly returned from Ceylon, at one time installed at the seat of custom. But, with the exception of Morgan Forster and Virginia Woolf, it would be fair to say that the Bloomsberries were essentially middle-men, patrons and champions of the Cause, not themselves greatly creative. Those who disseminate civilisation do not themselves have to be creative: it is enough to see and cherish creativity in others. And in this they did not betray their trust.

The sentence that is likely to arrest the reader of a later generation is this: 'One might think of the troubles of Germany in the early years after the first world war and the disruption in her social fabric which was their consequence.' For we know what Keynes had in mind here; and we know that he saw far more clearly than his friends just how precarious was the crust of civilisation which he and his friends had once taken for granted. As far as is known, Keynes had no specialised knowledge of Germany, as he had, for example, of India from his time at the India Office. Nor had he any special liking for German *Kultur*. Indeed, in the context of our story, Bloomsbury represents, rather, a sharp break with the Germanophil tendencies of many of the Eminent Victorians. Bloomsbury stood for a return to the Francophil predilections of the 18th century of Voltaire and Diderot: in painting, in literature, in architecture, and not least in anti-metaphysical Rationalism. Also we find Strachey, early in life, enthusing over Dostoevsky (in French translation, though the Garnett translations were on their way). And the impact of the Russian ballet on the Bloomsberries, and Keynes in particular, is familiar enough.

True, to the young Englishman or Englishwoman of 1900 Germany had perhaps less to offer—except in music—in the field of *Kultur* than at any time since the death of Goethe. Hofmannsthal, Rilke, and George were not yet European figures; and if Wagner stood, unsurprisingly, for all they wished to reject in Victorian culture, his great antagonist, Nietzsche, must have seemed—though as thoroughgoing an anti-Victorian as themselves—to belong altogether too much in the company of those oppressive giants, their parents and grand-parents ('Kant was my guide . . . the only man I ever worshipped') had tended to revere. Yet of what writer might one assume, forgivably, Virginia Woolf to be writing in a passage such as this?:

> In reading—we find ourselves repeating the word 'soul'
> again and again. It sprinkles his pages. . . . Indeed it is the
> soul that is the chief character in this fiction. . . . It is liable
> to violent diseases and raging fevers, but still the predomin-
> ant concern. Perhaps that is why it needs so great an effort
> on the part of an English reader . . . the 'soul' is alien to
> him. It is even antipathetic. It has little sense of humour
> and no sense of comedy. It is formless. . . . It is confused,
> diffuse, tumultuous, incapable, it seems, of submitting to the
> control of logic . . . out of Shakespeare there is no more
> exciting reading. . . .

High praise, indeed—and yet how un-Bloomsbury in tone! This, surely, is the true voice of *schwärmerei*, of some early Victorian English literary lady who has discovered a culture both alien and enthralling, a culture that places *Gemüt* and *Seele*, the values of the heart, above the intricate social choreo- graphy and delicious gossip that too often are the substance of the English novel. Can Virginia Woolf be speaking of the *Kultur* of the Germans in this passage? She could have been; and, half a century earlier, she might have been. But, of course, she is not. She is speaking of Turgenev and Dostoevsky and Tolstoy and Chekhov. It is a measure of how far the understanding and appreciation of German *Kultur*, which had begun with Coleridge and Scott and de Quincey and Carlyle, had vanished from the English literary scene during the latter years of the 19th century and the opening decades of the 20th.

How grotesque, then, that the pacifists of Garsington, sowing and reaping under the protective eye of Lady Ottoline, should have been labelled 'pro-Germans' and how absurd that the same label should have become attached to that book of Keynes (no pacifist he) that might without exaggeration be described as the key to the understanding of the intellectual and political attitudes of educated Englishmen from 1919 to 1939. Can 'The Economic Consequences of the Peace' be described as pro-German? Intellectually, as we have seen, Keynes and his friends had taken little interest in German politics, literature or art before 1914, and they did not share the growing enthusiasm for the arts of Weimar during the twenties. That majority of them which took a pacifist line during the war did so on the grounds that there could be little to choose in political wickedness between the Germany and Austria-Hungary of the two Kaisers, and the repressive colonialism of the French, Dutch, Belgian and British Empires (on which subject, thanks to their Anglo-Indian connections—Woolf in Ceylon, Strachey with his famous father and uncles, Keynes at the India Office, Forster in India—they were intimately informed). In all these countries—not to speak of Turkey or Czarist Russia—Barbarism was enthroned; and in England public school Philistinism was its footstool. In addition, the Sectarian spirit of the descendants of the Clapham Sect ran strong. If there was any civilisation in England worth defending, it lay with the Elect, elegantly or angularly sprawled in Lady Ottoline's deck-chairs on the lawns of Garsington. *That* and Cambridge, at all costs, must be preserved; and if others chose (or, later, were conscripted) to defend that heritage from alien Barbarians and Philistines—well, that was their business. The business of Bloomsbury was to keep up the good talk, guard the hearth, plunging in, if necessary, the occasional poker. Rupert Brooke might be gone (he had never really belonged), but the church clock at Grantchester still stood at ten to three, and there *was* honey still for tea. Their position might well be compared with that of a Sectarian of a very different kind, Vladimir Ilyitch Ulianov waiting impatiently in Zürich, preaching 'revolutionary defeatism', soon to board the sealed train to the Finland Station.

This, needless to say, was not Maynard Keynes' concept of civilisation. And it is here, I believe, that the superiority not only of his mind—only Russell was his equal—but the superiority of his political and historical vision becomes apparent. Unlike Thomas Mann, he did not believe in any distinction between *Kultur* and *Zivilisation*. Unlike his friends, he did not believe that any particular group had a monopoly of culture;

indeed he had a healthy, almost Johnsonian respect for the worldier side of life, for the things that money can buy ('It is almost impossible,' he remarked to the young Strachey, 'to overrate the importance of money'). In Thomas Mann's terms, for all his 'culture', he thought *Zivilisation* well worth fighting for too. Without it, he saw that there would be precious little place for culture in society. Equally, he knew that without the leaven of culture there would be precious little value in maintaining *Zivilisation*: indeed, that *Zivilisation* could be but another name for technological barbarism. But civilisation— to revert to the English usage and thus, implicitly, to resolve Thomas Mann's artificial antinomy—must have a healthy material-physical, as well as an intellectual, basis. There must be gas and steam, *pace* Baudelaire, or there would be no future Baudelaires or Diaghilevs or Bloomsberries. There must be money and exchange of goods, however vulgar such operations might seem; there must be interest and there must, as he came to see a decade after his first famous pamphlet, be an end to the misery of mass unemployment. Prosaic things! But without them there would be no gentlepeople disseminating their sweetness and light, and no more talks with Lytton by the fireside.

What was to be done? On the first page of 'The Economic Consequences' Keynes sets the tone for his onslaught, and it is striking how little 'pro-German' it is:

> Moved by insane delusion and reckless self-regard, the German people overturned the foundations on which we all lived and built. But the spokesmen of the French and British peoples have run the risk of completing the ruin, which Germany began, by a Peace which, if it is carried into effect, must impair yet further, when it might have restored, the delicate, complicated organisation . . . through which alone the European peoples can employ themselves and live.

Keynes (he is writing for the layman, from whose number he would not have excluded most politicians of his day, and indeed his Cambridge friends) is anxious to impress on us the complexities and inherent instability of the civilisation of pre-1914 Europe. He is anxious that we should see it as it was: a whole, a whole easily disrupted by internal and external shocks, but yet capable of restoration. Here, for example, is Keynes' account of the place Germany (or to use his German contemporary, Friedrich Naumann's term, *Mitteleuropa*) held in the pre-1914 system:

In 1870, Germany had a population of about forty million. By 1892 this figure had risen to fifty million, and by June 30th, 1914 to about sixty-eight million. . . . From being agricultural and mainly self-supporting, Germany transformed herself into a vast and complicated industrial machine, dependent for its working on the equipoise of many factors outside Germany as well as within. . . . The German machine was like a top which to maintain its equilibrium must spin ever faster and faster; to understand the present situation, we must apprehend what an extraordinary centre of population the development of the Germanic system had enabled Central Europe to become. Before the war the population of Germany and Austria-Hungary together not only substantially exceeded that of the United States, but was about equal to the whole of that of North America. . . . In these numbers situated within a compact territory lay the military strength of the Central Powers. But these same numbers, if deprived of the means of life, remain a hardly less danger to European order. . . . Round Germany as a central support the rest of the European economic system grouped itself, and on the prosperity and enterprise of Germany the prosperity of the rest of the continent mainly depended. . . . In our own case we sent more exports to Germany than to any other country in the world except India, and we bought more from her than from any other country in the world except the United States. . . .

Keynes was English of the English; but he knew that England had never stood apart from the European *Staatensystem*, the concert of Europe, and never could. His concern for the condition of the Continent, so evident here, was therefore far from sentimental:

> But perhaps it is only in England (and America) that it is possible to be so unconscious. In continental Europe the earth heaves and no one is but aware of the rumblings. There it is not just a matter of extravagance or 'labour troubles'; but of life and death, of starvation and existence, and of the fearful convulsions of a dying civilisation.
>
> England still stands outside Europe. Europe's voiceless tremors do not reach her. Europe is apart and England is not of her flesh and body. But Europe is solid with herself. France, Germany, Italy, Austria, and Holland, Russia and Rumania and Poland, throb together, and their structure and civilisation are essentially one. . . . If the European Civil War is to end with France and Italy abusing their momentary victorious power to destroy Germany and Austria-Hungary now prostrate, they invite their own destruction also, being so deeply and inextricably inter-twined with their victims by hidden psychic and economic bonds. . . . At any rate an Englishman who took part in the Conference of Paris and was during those months a member of the Supreme Economic Council of the Allied Powers, was bound to become, for him a new experience, a *European* in his cares and outlook . . . (my italics).

Is it going too far to see in this confession—for Keynes, contrary to popular myth, was a highly passionate man—a commitment not unlike that which he took on himself during the Second World War and after—a commitment, like that of Jean Monnet, to see to it that, as far as lay within his power, there should be no Third Act to the European Tragedy?

But how had the disaster of Versailles come about in the first place? On the chief actors in the drama Keynes is devastatingly funny; and has been, predictably, rebuked for it by more sober minds among his own fraternity:

> The French had a policy. Although Clemenceau might curtly abandon the claims of a Klotz or Loucheur, or close

his eyes with an air of fatigue when French interests were no longer involved in the discussion, he knew which points were vital. . . . In so far as the main economic lines of the Treaty represented an intellectual idea, it was the idea of France and of Clemenceau. . . .

'Une certaine idée de la France!' Indeed, if the rigid posture of a later French statesman comes to mind, it is no chance. Clemenceau knew what he wanted, and he saw that it was within his power to buy off the unfortunate Signor Orlando, and to 'bamboozle' (Keynes' word) the increasingly befuddled, but still vain and ambitious President Wilson, whom Keynes regarded evidently as a priggish, provincial bore, at sea among quick-witted, worldly men of affairs.

So much for the first three actors in the drama. But there remained Lloyd George, as wily and unprincipled as Clemenceau perhaps, but a darker horse. In English folk-memory the Coupon Election—that pyrrhic victory of the wily Goat—lives on in certain famous phrases: 'Hang the Kaiser!'; 'Squeeze Germany till the pips squeak!'; 'Hard-faced men who look as if they have done well out of the war'. I am sure I am not alone in having been brought up to think of these phrases as of the Goat's own minting: for in my Asquithian-Liberal childhood it was axiomatic that the Goat could do no right. But here folk-memory nods. For Maynard Keynes and David Lloyd George were far more of a mind— as Martin Gilbert has shown in his *Roots of Appeasement*—than the Goat could allow it to appear. The Goat was fighting an election, and his trump card was that he was the man who had won the war. Yet Lloyd George was not to be counted among the professional anti-Germans: had he not gone to Germany ten years before to study the advanced social security system instituted by Bismarck? Lloyd George, the statesman, wanted a peace that would endure; a second Congress of Vienna, at the very least. But Lloyd George the politician needed to win an election; and he leant on men with ideas of a very different kind, Northcliffe and Rothermere and Beaverbrook. Observe the progression of his electioneering:

On November 24th, 1918, Lloyd George made the following speech:

> When Germany defeated France she made France pay . . . and that is the principle we should proceed upon—that Germany must pay the costs of the war *up to the limit of her capacity to do so* . . . There is no doubt as to the justice of the demand. She ought to pay, she must pay *as far as she can,* but *we are not going to allow her to pay in such a way as to wreck our industries* (my italics).

I italicise the above passages with reason: they show the Goat carefully hedging his bets. Later in the campaign he was to refer to 'Treasury officials . . . who took a different view'; (did he have Keynes and certain of his colleagues in mind?). But that was not what the ex-war leader *appeared* to be saying: he had uncorked the bottle, and now a genie was at work. Thus, on November 30th, Mr Barnes, a member of the War Cabinet where (in Keynes' words) 'He was supposed to represent Labour', shouted from the platform, 'I am for hanging the Kaiser!' On December 9th, with the Northcliffe press baying behind him, Sir Eric Geddes followed up with: 'We will get out of her all we can squeeze out of a lemon and a bit more. . . . I will squeeze her until you can hear the pips squeak.' Lloyd George, no doubt becoming aware of the trap he had fallen into, spoke (in ridicule?) of

> . . . a high City authority who has committed himself to the opinion that Germany could certainly pay 29 billion and that he for his part would not care to discredit a figure of twice that sum. The Treasury officials . . . take a different view. . . .

They did, indeed. In the latter part of the 'Economic Consequences' Keynes gives his own estimate both of what the Germans can be expected to pay and in what proportions he would like to see the reparations handed out. As he himself remarks, 'I need not impress on the reader that there is much guesswork here. . . . But I feel some confidence that the general *magnitude* is not hopelessly erroneous.'

Belgium	£500,000,000
France	£800,000,000
Great Britain	£570,000,000
Other Allies	£250,000,000
Total:	£2,120,000,000

Keynes was not a man to quantify lightly. But his final calculation of the demands made by the Treaty on Germany make the demands of the egregious Lord Cunliffe of the Bank of England (to whom Lloyd George was no doubt referring) appear more than slightly insane. Succinctly, Keynes gives his verdict on the financial provisions of the Treaty, and it is a damning one:

If she is to discharge the capital sum in thirty years from 1936, i.e. in forty-eight years from the armistice, she must pay an additional 130 billion pounds annually, making 780 billion in all (or maybe 480 billion annually). It is, in my judgment, as certain as anything can be that Germany cannot pay anything approaching this sum. Until the Treaty is altered Germany has in effect engaged herself to hand over to the Allies the whole of her surplus production in perpetuity.

As his famous sketch of Dr Melchior ('Two Memoirs') reveals, Keynes was no natural Germanophil. Yet he could respect a German Jew like Dr Melchior who preserved a dignity in defeat sadly lacking in the conduct of Ludendorff, Hindenburg, and the last of the Hohenzollerns. His complaint was rather that the Germans (though not invited, contrary to international protocol, to the Conference itself) did not speak out when at last they were given the opportunity:

A statesman representing not himself but his country may prove, without incurring excessive blame—as history often records—vindictive, perfidious and egotistic. These qualities are familiar in treaties imposed by victors. But the German delegation did not succeed in exposing in burning and prophetic words the quality which chiefly distinguishes this transaction from all its historical predecessors—its insincerity.

CHAPTER THREE

Appeasement and After

'The Economic Consequences of the Peace', though intended
as no more than a pamphlet, is as much a part of our literary
and historical heritage as 'The Conduct of the Allies' or
'Reflections on the French Revolution'. Yet its subsequent
history has provoked considerable ambivalence. Keynes wrote
it with a passion very different from that '*pa-a-assion*' with
which D. H. Lawrence cruelly tormented Bloomsbury, and
that caused him to write of Bertrand Russell:

> What ails Russell is, in matters of life and emotion, the
> inexperience of youth . . . It isn't that life has been too much
> for him, but too little (quoted by Dr F. R. Leavis in his
> essay 'Keynes, Cambridge and Lawrence').

But how wrong of the Doctor—surely—to apply glibly to
Keynes what it is hard to misapply to Strachey's 'Eminent
Victorians'! (It is interesting to note that the two books, both
epoch-making in their way, were written within a year of one
another, when their authors were thirty-seven.) To put
Keynes' pamphlet in the class I have indicated will no doubt
arouse the wrath of those who are bound to see his 'serious'
work in such monuments to industry as 'Indian Finance', 'A
Tract on Monetary Reform', 'A Treatise on Money', 'A
Treatise on Probability', and—the crowning achievement—
'A General Theory of Employment, Interest and Exchange'.
That is as it may be: to comment on these works is not my
competence, and I gladly leave the valuation of them to those
more proficient.

For it is, as the heading to this section implies, the *political*
consequences of John Maynard Keynes on which I wish to
place the emphasis (which is not to deny, despite recent
criticism, that his writings on Money and Unemployment

were as effective in shoring up 'civilisation' as his pamphlet).
But here, I repeat, there is an ambiguity which cannot be so
easily resolved, since it involves not only Maynard Keynes,
but all those whose feelings about the inter-war period are still
active, and even those for whom (like myself) they are
necessarily passive—though not the less potent for that. As a
political thinker, Keynes left an ambiguous legacy, then. As
the author of the 'Economic Consequences' he was bound to
be labelled a 'pro-German'. That he was nothing of the kind
is evident from the opening words of his pamphlet: it was by
their own recklessness that the Germans had brought such
miseries upon themselves. Keynes does not question the
orthodox view about this (though probably the majority of his
Bloomsbury friends would have done). In later years he was
often to be charged with the fathering of 'Appeasement', of
having advocated concessions to Germany that merely whetted
her appetite, of being one of those who prepared the road to
Munich.

I would ask the reader to discard from his mind for a
moment the connotations of Appeasement in the late thirties,
and consider briefly the original sense of the word. What
exactly does 'Appeasement' mean? In what sense was Keynes
an apostle of 'Appeasement'? In the sense that all diplomacy,
all negotiations require appeasement of a kind, Keynes was
most certainly an appeasing kind of man. His skill in negotia-
tion was indeed one of his highest qualities. This does not
mean that he could not be a bonny fighter. On the contrary,
he spent much of his life advocating causes, and cajoling
colleagues to support them, that were distinctly at odds with
received wisdom, whether at the Treasury or in the board-
room of the *New Statesman*. But his mind was a flexible one,
never dogmatic, never devious; and he possessed—one has
only to compare him here with Russell—a consistency and
determination of purpose that is rare in the intellectual-turned-
politician. That the speed of his mind often raced ahead where
others could not so swiftly follow is no doubt true. His arrogance,
on occasions, is undeniable: he did not suffer fools gladly.
But at no time was he a 'pure' intellectual. For all his

pragmatism and apparent flippancy (which was to irritate American financiers as much as it had once irritated Lawrence), he was a constructive visionary: a Bentham or a Bagehot, not a Carlyle or a Shaw. If he saw matters with swifter intuition than the other fellows, what he saw was more likely to be a solution than (in the manner of Apostolic Cambridge) a puzzle or a problem. In his essay on Newton he tells a story which we could well take (was it perhaps so intended?) as a self-portrait:

> There is the story of how [Newton] informed Halley of one of his most fundamental discoveries, planetary motion. 'Yes', replied Halley, 'but how do you know that? Have you proved it?' Newton was taken aback: 'Why, I've known it for years', he replied. 'If you'll give me a few days, I'll certainly find you the proof of it'—as in due course he did.

From what I have said it is clear that it would not be unreasonable to apply the neutral term 'appeaser' to the Keynes of 1919, or indeed later. I have spoken of the ambiguity of the subsequent history of Keynes' central concept. He wished to re-establish the Concert of Europe, though on a fresh territorial basis. Yet he recognised that in the half century since Bismarck's Versailles the European landscape had changed radically. Bismarck had understood and worked within the old *staatensystem*: when the fighting was done with he had carefully mended his fences with Austria, England, and, less successfully, with Russia: only France persisted in a sullen mood of *revanche*. But Bismarck well knew that the combination of his political acumen and the late arrival of the industrial revolution had put the potential hegemony of Europe into the hands of the new Reich. He feared that his successors would fail to preserve the balance, that they might try to convert a potential into an actual hegemony, which might unite the rest of Europe in enmity to the Reich and bring down the structure he had meticulously built up. These facts were of course familiar to Keynes, and we shall see how closely the solution he sketched out in 'Economic Consequences' resembles that worked out by Marshall and Monnet, Schuman and Spaak and others within five years of his death.

In sketching out this solution he was practising, I would argue, nothing more nor less than traditional diplomatic appeasement: that appeasement without which civilised life among men and nations is impossible. But it is the other consequences of Keynes' 'appeasement' to which we must now turn our attention. I need not re-tell the sorry tale of how the Western powers failed to make concessions to Germany while they were still strong, only to make them ineptly and near-suicidally when they were too weak. It is, and will always remain, a shameful tale; even if there are those, like Lord Butler, who cling to the time-worn argument that Munich 'gained us a year'. (It gained the Nazis a year too, which they proceeded to make better use of.) But it needs to be emphasised that this is no simple conflict between the goodies and the baddies. The 'men of good-will', the pacifists and the semi-pacifists, the disarmament-mongers, the Peace Pledge Union, the loyal League of Nations men, indeed the greater part of the English Left were 'Appeasers' and 'pro-German' before 1933. But they reflected a national mood. Could a former conscientious objector—Ramsay MacDonald—have become Prime Minister in, say, France, Italy, Poland, Hungary, Rumania? Plainly not: England suffered a revulsion from the War and all that had gone with it whose only analogues are to be found in the Weimar Republic, or in America. Perhaps England was suffering herself from a mood of isolationism: certainly her motives were not universally seen as high-minded. Be that as it may, it was on the 'goodies' of the Left that the impact of Keynes was strongest, and from this seeding-ground that his indignation began to spread through educated society, until it reached from All Souls to the drawing-rooms of Cliveden.

Just how deep-rooted this will to self-deception had grown ten years after the publication of Keynes' indictment may be illustrated by a comment in Garvin's *Observer* for July 20th, 1930:

> Hitler is not a man but a megaphone. He has a surprising power of making patriotic noises and shouting in perfect

sincerity the most impossible nonsense against Parliaments and Jews and the Young Plan. In himself he is a lightweight . . . Hitler is dramatic, violent and shallow. But to his garish banner he has rallied honest and earnest elements, especially among the splendid young people of the German middle-classes.

With hindsight, it is not hard to mock such a judgment, for there is hardly a statement in this (and it is not, I think, untypical) that is not self-deceiving or wilfully ignorant. Consider the wording: Hitler is capable of abusing Jews and Parliaments *in perfect sincerity*. In others, doubtless, this would be a sterling virtue: but in Hitler? Very few who have studied the by now voluminous literature would deny, I think, that the leading Nazis were *sincere*. But it is possible for a man to butcher his opponent in perfect sincerity, indeed in a torrent of self-righteousness: we do not therefore acquit him.

Or again: 'In himself he is a lightweight . . . dramatic, violent and shallow'. True, Hitler was weak on spelling, spoke with a harsh 'provincial' accent, and had not even made it to the Vienna Academy of Art. But a political 'lightweight', a 'shallow' man? No one who had studied his career even up to July, 1930, could have mistaken him for that. The 1923 Munich putsch had been a flop: but Hitler's response—his defiance of the new Republic in open court—represented a political comeback that showed powers of resilience, oratory, and political shrewdness of a very high order. Nor had the years since 1924 been wasted. As prosperity flowed back, Hitler lay low and schemed for a second chance. A party apparatus was built up, on Leninist lines, which gave the N.S.D.A.P. an organisational strength far beyond its actual numbers. And its innovations in the field of propaganda should not have failed to impress the trained correspondent. But it is the final comment that brings one up with a start: Hitler has 'rallied honest and earnest elements, especially among the splendid young people of the German middle-classes'. These words were written at a moment when droves of just such 'splendid young people' were abandoning the middle-class democratic parties and making possible the first great electoral triumph in the autumn of 1930, when the Nazis emerged as the second most powerful party in the Reichstag. What can one say? Such will to see good in blatant and palpable evil can have few parallels. But then in the heart of the English progressive, one must allow, hope springs eternal; it is axiomatic that the young are splendid, that the next generation is bound to be more liberal-minded, more honest, more earnest—in every way better than our own.

Evidently, then, the roots of Appeasement lie deep: they lie in the English penchant for wishful-thinking, they lie in English easy-goingness and tolerance, they lie in that insularity which for the greatest part of our history has been our greatest boon, but which over the past century has proved, arguably, our greatest curse. But this is to say that they lie, to a striking extent, in our virtues. We knew that the Coupon Election had been a racket, we knew that the Treaty had been in reality a *diktat*, we knew that responsibility for altering the political pattern of Central and Eastern Europe could be put at our door. When the opportunity lay open in 1919 our consciences were too calloused; when, by the light of common sense, we should have hardened our hearts, the 'splendid young men' had already long hardened theirs, and the march to war was inevitable. It is not difficult to see why 'Keynesianism'— however misunderstood—soon took possession of the conscience of the intelligentsia. What is more difficult is to explain how a concept which had originated on the Left of the political spectrum should have become common property until, at last, it was put disastrously into action by men of the traditional Right.

True, a progressive might argue, it is usually the case in England that the Left has the ideas, and that the Right carries them out. 'Dishing the Whigs', after all, is a traditional sport of the English Right. But this does not quite explain the phenomenon. Nor, I think, does the popular theory that the English Right was motivated in the thirties chiefly by fear of Communism, so that press barons like Rothermere had become pro-Germans and the cream of London Society was not ashamed to be wined and dined by the ex-champagne-salesman 'von' Ribbentrop at the German Embassy. For it is apparent from a study such as Dr A. L. Rowse's 'All Souls and Appeasement' that it was not the case that the whole establishment was pro-Appeasement. It was a quite special and somewhat esoteric—though temporarily very powerful—section of it, which Dr Rowse was able to observe at All Souls from a ringside seat. Who were these men? They shared a remarkably similar background. They were, as Dr Rowse points out, 'men of peace, no use for confronting force, guile, or wickedness'. They were mostly middle class and of nonconformist background; this made for a self-righteousness not much less potent than Bloomsbury's own. (In age they were in fact the contemporaries of the Bloomsberries.) But—far more significant—they were men, as Dr Rowse says, *without knowledge of Europe*, its history or its languages, or of diplomacy, let alone of strategy or of war' (my italics). In their intellectual insularity, therefore, they mirrored and magnified the natural insularity of the people they led.

To say that a group of men such as these had 'no knowledge of diplomacy, let alone of strategy or of war' may seem strange, since there existed among them a hard core of men who, thirty years before, had belonged to 'Milner's Kindergarten' (Lord Brand, Lord Lothian, Lionel Curtis, Geoffrey Dawson); and most of the others had served at one time or another in connection with Colonial affairs (Hoare, Halifax, Sir Reginald Coupland, Dawson again, and Lionel Curtis; even Chamberlain had begun life—unsatisfactorily—attempting to grow sisal in the Bahamas). A many-sided assembly of experience—or of prejudice—it might seem. Yet there is, as Dr Rowse points out, something missing. Keynes' chief concern in 'Economic Consequences' had been with Europe; he was only secondarily concerned with the United States, and the problems of what would now be called the Third World—then, 'the Empire'—came only a poor third. Keynes was a diplomat by nature, but not by training; and he was certainly no expert on strategy nor swayer of multitudes. (The real criticism that can be made of 'Economic Consequences' is that he did not see, as Vansittart did, that the French were primarily concerned with the *military* balance of power, and only secondarily with economic consequences of the Treaty. It is possible, while assenting to Keynes' analysis, to hold that the French were basically right in their order of priorities.) What is typical of these men to whose counsels both Baldwin and Chamberlain harkened was not that they were ivory-tower, Oxford intellectuals. They knew much of the world, but the part that they knew was not that which mattered to England in 1938; and their knowledge was essentially of the wrong kind. As Churchill cruelly said of one of them (presumably Halifax): 'Grovel, grovel, grovel! First grovel to the Indians, then grovel to the Germans, next grovel to the Americans, then it's grovel to the Russians.' 'The plain truth', Dr Rowse remarks, 'is that their deepest instinct was defeatist, their highest wisdom surrender.'

Is this an accurate summary? Up to a point, I fear that it is. But not all of us would buy the whole package. For just as it was rational for English statesmen to 'appease' Germans in the days of Weimar's promise, it was rational to 'appease' Indian nationalism in the thirties (had we not, our position during the coming war would have been correspondingly weaker). And it has been argued with some justice that by devoting so much of his time to the Indian Question in the early thirties, Churchill alienated both the Left and his own colleagues and let himself be diverted from the far greater danger looming across the North Sea. But the Baldwin-Chamberlain entourage's ignorance of European affairs is the intellectual key to the disastrous policies they initiated and the false expectations they nursed. They had moved too long in spheres where Britain's enemies could be conciliated or, to borrow Cecil Rhodes's cruder phrase, 'squared': because Britain in the long run '*had* got the ships, *had* got the men, *and* got the money too'. But the European world was not like that. And by 1938 England was more vulnerable than she had been since Trafalgar; only strength and determination could frustrate Hitler in his purposes.

There is another factor of some interest. Generation for

generation, the two leadership groups in Britain and Germany were far from equally matched. In the year of Munich (when Keynes was 54) Neville Chamberlain was 69, Halifax 57, Dawson 64, Hoare 58, Simon 65, Runciman 68, Lionel Curtis 64, Tom Jones, confidant of all and sundry, 68. By way of contrast, Hitler himself was 49, Hess 46, Ribbentrop and Goering 45, Goebbels 41, Himmler 38, Heydrich 34, and Speer 33. It will be seen that a rough average of these two leadership groups works out at about 43 for the Nazis and 63 for the Appeasers: a whole generation. The Nazis represented (as indeed they claimed) *'die Frontgeneration'*: the men who wanted another go. The English leadership represented (apart from Eden and Duff Cooper, the resigners) the generation that had waited in fear and trembling for the fatal telegram to arrive and the casualty lists to go up; who believed that any policy, however ignominious, was preferable to one that would lead to a second slaughter of the innocents. Their feelings did them honour; but the conclusions they drew led them and their country into the blackest dishonour. The story of Munich is the story of men who, in upholding what they saw as the best of British and Western civilisation, overlooked the blunt fact that Britain had always faced her greatest dangers, and drawn her truest friends, from that Europe of which they knew so little.

CHAPTER FOUR

Black and White

It is not, in general, the English tendency to see things 'in black and white'. Or so we like to think. Indeed, it is one of the things for which we like to blame the Germans, and we are apt to contrast our own grey, sensible moderation with the doctrinaire *Schwarzweissmalerei*—yes, the Germans have a word for it, and a long one—of those born and reared in foreign parts. The story of 'Appeasement and After' does not, unhappily, bear this out. Consider the following passages from a pamphlet as famous in its day as Keynes' own:

> History puts it to you plainly. The *German* is often a moral creature; the *Germans* never; and it is the Germans who count. You will always think of Germans in the plural, if you are wise (author's italics).

or this:

> I shall not attempt to deal with such virtues or vices as Germans, singular or plural, possess. These are mainly un-related to the facts from which the world has repeatedly suffered at German hands.

And what are these facts?

> It is necessary to discard once and for all what Sainte-Beuve rightly called the 'vague and lyrical' view of Germany diffused by Madame de Staël, and to keep strictly to the record—the worst ever. . . .
> German barbarism first crushed Latin civilisation at the battle of Adrianople in the year 378, and it has again crushed Latin civilisation in France today. . . .
> A fact early and universally recognised was that the Germans were not only very dirty fighters but they never kept a

pledge or treaty. Gibbon has commented on this characteristic. It is worth noting that the first German national hero to make himself a name for treachery was Hermann in the year 9. The centuries have rolled by and brought us Hermann Goering!

So it did not begin with Frederick or Bismarck or the Kaiser, as we had been taught: the Teutons were anti-Christian *avant le fait*. And, as it began, so it rolls on:

By the time they got to their famous warmonger, Frederick Barbarossa, in the twelfth century, the only bone of contention was not whether they should remain at peace, but which race should they conquer and dominate—should it be the Italians or Slavs?

And then, of course, 'the Junkers' (the source of the quotation is not given: it is, no doubt, von Treitschke):

Any picture of Prussianism would be incomplete without some reference to Frederick the Great. On the Germans' own franker showing before 1914, 'the political history of Germany from the accession of Frederick in 1740 to the present hour, had admittedly no meaning unless it be regarded as a movement towards the establishment of a world empire, with the war against England as the necessary preliminary.'

After which it is only logical for our author to conclude:

This lust of world domination has been working in them for generations. . . . I have seen the idea of the German empire emerging . . . it has had three elements to work on, all of which are well-known to those with any knowledge of German psychology. The three are Envy, Self-pity and Cruelty.

Let me tease the reader no further: the author of these *obiter dicta* is none other than the late Lord Vansittart; and the title of his pamphlet is—suitably enough—'Black Record'. To correct the balance it is, of course, necessary to add that these comments on German history and the German character were made in the hate-filled atmosphere of war-making in the autumn of 1940, just as Keynes' comments were set down in the scarcely less hate-filled atmosphere of peace-making in 1919 (though it will be allowed that Keynes kept the cooler head). But, of course, the comparison is unfair. Lord Vansittart possessed no less fine and cool a mind than Lord Keynes; and any reader of his autobiography, 'The Mist Procession', will realise that, though it reflects his long-held opinions fairly enough, 'Black Record' is the work of a man writing under great strain and well *unter seinem Niveau*. And it should be unnecessary to add that Britain has been served by few so courageous and percipient public servants in the present century. But, for all this, once the phrase 'Vansittartism' had been coined, it was to live with him for the rest of his life: to his great regret, as he confesses in 'The Mist Procession'. Vansittart and 'Vansittartism' should not, therefore, be equated. Nevertheless, 'Vansittartism' was instrumental in creating a climate different, but not entirely dissimilar from that created twenty-one years before by Keynes' 'Economic Consequences'.

For the true meaning of 'Vansittartism'—as expressed later in the war, say, in the hare-brained Morgenthau Plan to turn Germany back into a purely agrarian country—is uncomfortably clear to the latter-day reader of 'Black Record'. It is implicit, I think, in the following quotations:

> There is no horror that Germans have not committed; and the hurricane of cruelty must be succeeded by the wave of indignation. Beware therefore lest another sham reformation is staged. Take nothing for granted. Make sure for yourselves and for your chidren.
>
> This bird of prey is no sudden apparition. It is a species. Hitler is no accident, he is the natural and continuous produce of a breed which from the dawn of history has been predatory, bellicose. . . .

Very well, it is an interpretation of German History; but it is hardly one—one has only to think of the long centuries of German somnolence or, say, of the *Biedermeier* period—that a serious student of German history could accept. Looked at more closely, it is also something else:

> This urge towards world domination had become so strong that the temporary setback of 1918 would *in no circumstances*

have sufficed to stem it. After a period of disappointment and recovery, Germany ... would have had her fifth fling *in any event* (my italics).

For Churchill 1939–1945 was 'the unnecessary war'. But not for the author of 'Black Record'. Vansittart, in this black mood, will not admit of *any* circumstances in which the post-1918 treatment of Germany would have produced a different result; though he was himself, contradictorily, a fount of more or less practicable ideas, as he makes clear in 'The Mist Procession', which he was forever urging his political masters to put into practice. Yet here he is saying that Germany would have had her 'fifth fling' *in any event*. The second war, like the first, was thus not an 'unnecessary war'. In those words of which German nationalists had been so fond, the second was *Notwendigkeit*, *Weltmacht oder Niedergang*: it was Fate, Necessity, *Schicksal*. But this is a deterministic, fatalistic view of history hardly different from that to be found in von Treitschke or Spengler. (It is interesting that post-war German historians like Karl Dietrich Bracher have argued strongly that the coming to power of Adolf Hitler in January, 1933, was *not* necessity, *not Schicksal*.) It is all too clear, then, what has happened: 'Vansittartism' has taken over the assumptions of the Nazis about the German character and German history and drawn identical conclusions. *Schwarzweissmalerei*, indeed! The wheel had come full circle.

How far should we take 'Vansittartism' as expressive of the national mood, in the First War, in 'Our Finest Hour', and indeed later? Mr John Terraine has given, in his 'Impacts of War 1914–1918', a brilliant analysis of the manner in which the British people, and their political and military leaders, reacted to the utterly new kind of warfare they were compelled to wage —for the Germans, as he points out, laid down the rules of the game from the beginning. The evidence of literature—Robert Graves, Siegfried Sassoon, Wilfred Owen or Carl Zuckmayer and Erich Maria Remarque—points to a sharp contrast between the bellicosity of the non-combatant and a strangely brotherly, professional enmity between those who fought in the trenches. Mr Terraine argues convincingly, I think, from the evidence of actual letters written home from the front, that this version—like Joan Littlewood's in *Oh What a Lovely War!*—can be overdone. There were plenty of men in the trenches eager to get their bayonet into a 'Hun', a 'Fritz', or a 'Jerry': and no wonder, with memories of comrades mutilated by shrapnel, or mown down by deadly German machine-gun fire, fresh in mind. There were again, notoriously, those lanky, lounging Blooms-berries down at Lady Ottoline's doing their 'agricultural war-work', and Bertie Russell in prison. In other words, while there were few—if any—true 'pro-Germans' (contrary to popular rumour, real German sympathisers as well as intelligence agents were quickly mopped up, as they were in the Second World War), there were plenty who still saw the Germans as decent enough fellows, who must certainly be fought, but whose private attitudes might very well resemble their own. There was, indeed, an eruption of 'Vansittartism' during the Coupon Election; but that was the work, as we have seen, not so much of Lloyd George, as of his newspaper-magnate friends.

The fluctuation in the Anglo-Saxon estimate of the German character has been one of our main themes in this book. No-where is it better illustrated than in the rapid swing from the mood of the Coupon Election to the mood that brought a former conscientious objector, Ramsay MacDonald, to the Prime Ministership of Britain five years later, and in the 'appeasing' conferences: Rapallo, Locarno and the rest. Perhaps it is that the English are not good haters. Perhaps its true roots are to be found in a profound revulsion from the realities of modern land-warfare, of which Anglo-Saxons had known so little before 1914. There were, it is true, a few true pro-Germans in the Weimar period—to be distinguished from the generation of Auden, Spender, and Isherwood who were certainly fascinated (for the first time since Matthew Arnold, one might say) with the new *Kultur* of Weimar, without being necessarily 'pro-German'—and on these true pro-Germans, such as the young Rolf Gardiner, Vansittart is very shrewd:

This 'Old Heidelberg' business is partly responsible for the illusion that Germans are sentimental. That isn't the right word. 'Emotional' is nearer. Now *emotionalism* can produce tears. It can also produce savagery. It can also produce both together. After the massacre of Rotterdam Ribbentrop started snivelling, '*Wir haben dies nicht gewollt*'—we didn't want to do it. Such cant only makes the action more contemptible. . . . The Walrus wept over the oysters, but he and the Carpenter ate every one. (Vansittart's italics)

This is just, indeed profound; distinguished psychiatrists who have studied the problem, such as Dr H. V. Dicks, would agree. And if it strikes the reader that Vansittart is once again overdoing it when he concludes abruptly:

Indeed we live at opposite poles. We have not a main idea in common because . . . words have entirely different meanings in our respective tongues. Our terms and concepts, our aims and admirations, are in complete contrast, even if the labels are the same. We have no real mental relations with Germans.

he should perhaps look up a well-meant and once-famous book called 'Britain and Germany: A Frank Discussion Instigated by Members of the Younger Generation', edited by Rolf Gardiner and Heinz Rocholl, and published in the year 1928 (Williams and Norgate). It is a fascinating book for what is, I fear, a somewhat negative reason. There is plenty of goodwill on the British side. But there is no meeting of minds to be found in the book at all. Rather, a stark contrast between a blend of arrogance and self-pity on the German side, and a deal of cooing and fluttering on the British, bearing out all that Vansittart has to say on the subject in 'Black Record'.

Did the mood of the Second War vary from the mood, or moods, of the first? I do not myself think that 'Vansittartism' was uppermost in the British or American mind, either on the 'home front' or in the firing line from 1939 to 1945 (the Morgenthau Plan remained after all a 'plan', not a policy). Interestingly, the term 'Hun' almost disappeared, and the substitution of the term 'Jerry' (like 'Fritz' for 'Boche' in France) suggested a strangely mild attitude on the part of the public ('Is it one of ours?' 'No, it's Jerry's') towards an enemy capable of unparalleled ferocity. True, Britons and Americans did not suffer as did Poles or Russians. True, our casualties for the entire war (i.e. including civilians) bear no comparison to those for France, Poland or Yugoslavia, or to the British casualties of the First War. Yet the 'impact of war' had certainly come closer home: it was a case of Mum or Dad in Coventry or Mile End, not of Tommy Atkins out in Flanders, in distant Mespot or Macedonia. Arguably, this very fact bridged the—in the First War—so fatal separation between the soldier in the field and the folks back home, as well as between the bombed British in Coventry or London and the bombed Germans in the shelters of Hamburg or Berlin. The British, who had suffered in the great raids in the autumn of 1940, did not find it difficult to imagine, later on, the full impact of R.A.F. and U.S. bombing in 1943 and 1944. They knew what 'Jerry' must be suffering; there were few tears shed, but there was comprehension. And the distinction between the passive, imputedly terrorised German *Volk* and the Death's-Head-bedecked and jack-booted Nazi was fairly firmly (if not entirely accurately) fixed in the mind of the average Briton. Perhaps that was why the word Hun was no longer needed: the word Nazi sufficed.

Notoriously, it was not until after the defeat of Germany that 'Vansittartism' really came into its own. It was the discovery of the death camps at Belsen and Buchenwald that let loose a flood of Hun-hatred with which (deservedly and understandably) that of 1914 or of the Coupon Election can bear no comparison. (Indeed, if Churchill had 'done a Lloyd George' in June, 1945, it might have been his party that would have swept into the House with a majority of two-hundred-odd, not the party of Major Attlee.) There is nothing to be said about these events that could be adequate; the account is not settled yet, and perhaps never will be. But the thread of Anglo-German relations cannot be snapped even at this, its weakest point—as perhaps some would prefer. And Vansittart, indeed, was among the first to realise this. Germany, beaten, dismembered, voiceless, was still in being. It remained, spiritually and geographically, at the heart of Europe. There could be no settlement in Europe—no settlement in particular with Soviet Russia—without a solution of this fresh 'German Problem'. Abandonment of Germany, connivance at its eventual incorporation into the Soviet Empire, would have been one way out. It would have been, as Vansittart was soon to argue in 'Events and Shadows', Appeasement twice over:

> With Russia there are two ways of being on good terms, and as always appeasement is not one of them.

Yet appeasement of Soviet Russia there was; and Yalta was not to be the end of it. Once the Russians had failed to win German favour by a direct appeal to Nationalism—a course that both Vansittart, and the Russians, were confident would succeed—there had to be a strategic retreat. Perhaps the Allies could be squeezed out of Berlin by judicious pressure? But Harry Truman was no Appeaser: within a year the Berlin Airlift of 1948–9 had brought this strategy to heel. Yet it was not abandoned. In 1958 Khrushchev renewed pressure on the Allies to relinquish their rights in the city. As in the thirties, there were voices in Britain to plead for appeasement. As the flood of refugees increased during the summer of 1961—shortly after the abortive Kennedy-Khrushchev meeting in Vienna— these voices grew more strident. To Mr Macmillan, golfing at Gleneagles, it was 'all got up by the press'. On the left, Mr Richard Crossman was writing in the *New Statesman*:

> Must we really permit a mob of hysterical West Berliners to drag us to the brink of war so that we can start the negotiations under duress which we should have begun of our own accord three years ago? I believe that both President Kennedy and Mr Macmillan have long since realised that the right policy would be to accept the existence of the two Germanies and negotiate a settlement based upon it—*even if this involves overriding the protests of Bonn and West Berlin*. But they can start the negotiations over the heads of the Germans only if public opinion is alerted to the danger of drifting into war (24th August 1961) (my italics).

'Overriding the protests of Bonn and West Berlin'—echoes of Lord Runciman in Czechoslovakia! (Yet both Macmillan and

258

Crossman had good records over Munich.) And, as in the dark years *entre deux guerres*, there came the predictable echo from the Right:

> There exists a conspiracy of silence ... designed to make people forget the unpalatable name and personality of the real boss of Brussels, who is neither smooth nor pleasant nor French but a German—none other than Dr Adenauer's old and trusted crony, Professor Walter Hallstein. . . . Hallstein, frankly, sees himself as the first president of Europe. Where Hitler failed in war, Hallstein expects to succeed in peace. . . . To Adenauer and Hallstein no economic sacrifice is too great if it helps to bring about an advance towards German-controlled political domination of Europe (Willi Frischauer, *Evening Standard*, January 29th, 1962).

CHAPTER FIVE

Postscript

So both 'Munich' and 'Vansittartism' lived on, at least until the early sixties: and I doubt that we have seen the last of them. (The Spirit of Munich, as Solzhenitsyn writes in his Nobel speech, is the spirit of our civilisation in this century.) *Schwarzweissmalerei* made out not only that the Germans were once again up to no good; but that every Russian provocation should be interpreted as yet another devious plot by the Germans to regain hegemony in Europe. In his early post-war writings, and in a speech to the House of Lords, Vansittart himself still holds to the view that the Germans of 1945—and he cites some very dubious, and certainly premature, evidence to support this in 'Bones of Contention' (1945)—are again the beaten, unrepentant Huns of 1918. But only a few years later, in 'Events and Shadows' he is arguing that the 'Muscovites' have simply taken over Nazi foreign policy, and that the remedy is the same. But he goes now—and here he comes close to Keynes and to men like Spaak and Marshall, Churchill and Schuman and Jean Monnet—beyond the 'negative' postures for which he has been criticised in the past. Resistance there must be; yet it cannot now be based solely on the Franco-British ties he exalted in the years before 1939, but on a broader and more tightly organised community. For the United Nations he has little use; it will be the League of Nations all over again. He writes:

> *It would be unthinkable that Britain should stand outside Europe* . . . and bless a federation headed by France and Germany in partnership. . . . The integration of the West should be the first step forward toward an ideal which is not yet a project. . . . It is my hope that a western integration will at some later stage turn, without need of magic, into a Western Federation. If an Eastern bloc blocks the way to World Federation, let

a Western example keep it open. It has ever been the destiny
of the West to set examples, and we must continue to be true
to that destiny . . . (my italics).

'Vansittartism' is here cast aside by its originator; and it is
fascinating to compare what Vansittart is now saying, in the
post-war years, with what Maynard Keynes had written after
the first war in the 'Economic Consequences';

A Free Trade Union comprising the whole of Central,
Eastern, and south-Eastern Europe, Siberia, Turkey, and
(I should hope) *the United Kingdom*, Egypt and India might
do as much for the peace and prosperity of the world as the
League of Nations itself. Belgium, Holland, Scandinavia,
and Switzerland might be expected to adhere to it shortly.
And it would be greatly to be desired by their friends if
France and Italy also should see their way to adhesion. . . .
By the proposed Free Trade Union some part of the loss of
organisation and economic efficiency may be retrieved,
which must otherwise result from the innumerable new
political frontiers now created between needy, jealous, im-
mature, and economically incomplete nationalist States. . . .
The adherence of other states would be voluntary from the
outset. *But it is to be hoped that the United Kingdom, at any rate,
would become an original member* . . . (my italics).

Vansittart and Keynes, to many, may appear strange enough
bedfellows (though they were, in fact, near contemporaries at
Eton). Vansittart, certainly, is the archetypal Foreign Office
man. But then the Foreign Office under Vansittart and Rum-
bold, Kirkpatrick and Eden (and under Vansittart's great
mentor Eyre Crowe) had often been right, and many amateur
'experts' in foreign affairs woefully wrong. Keynes is the poli-
tician-economist, the Treasury maverick, the defender of
'civilisation' as Bloomsbury had understood it in the far-off
days before the First World War. Yet here, as I say, we see the
notorious 'Appeaser' and the famous 'Hun-baiter' at one. But
then, in the reasoning of both men, politics and economics are
of their essence interdependent. The need for political unity,
if not union, is urgent: not less urgent after 1945 than after

1918. But the urgency of economic rehabilitation in Europe is still greater. Keynes had been the moving spirit behind the Lend-Lease negotiations, and those for the American Loan of 1945. Had he lived, he would surely have played a leading role in the Marshall Aid and other post-war negotiations, and perhaps even in the negotiations for British participation in a wider Europe which Churchill had mooted (or had he?) in his Zürich speech, but which his government was never in fact to carry through. In 'Economic Consequences' Keynes had written:

> The requirements of Europe are *immediate*. . . . It will be very difficult for European production to get started again without a temporary measure of external assistance. I am therefore a supporter of an international loan in some shape or form, such as has been advocated in many quarters in France, Germany and England, and also in the United States. In whatever way the ultimate responsibility of the repayment is distributed, the burden of finding the immediate resources must inevitably fall in major part upon the United States . . . (Keynes' italics).

In 1947, Vansittart found himself echoing the man he had often damned as the arch-Appeaser:

> The redrawing of Western Germany into its normal sphere is the counter-attraction to the compulsion of another one-party Nationalism. We must provide Germany with a regulated prosperity, so ordered as not again to land her and us in war, but to give her opportunity for the joint boons of freedom and prosperity ('Events and Shadows').

Pace Messrs Crossman and Frischauer, it is precisely these 'joint boons' which Western Germany has enjoyed since the foundation of the Federal Republic.

'It is to be hoped that the United Kingdom, at any rate, would become an original member,' Keynes had written; and Vansittart, a generation later, 'It would be unthinkable that Britain should stand outside Europe . . . and bless a federation headed by France and Germany.' But thinkable it was; and much as it was to be hoped that Britain would give Europe a lead, in 1919 as in 1945, it did not happen. Why it did not, it is not the business of this book to enquire; and, since Britain's entry into the Community, it is not necessary to flog that dead horse further. Yet there is no getting away from the fact that it *was* the role and status of West Germany that dominated the long-fought battles between Gaitskellites and Bevanites and between Marketeers and Anti-Marketeers, Labour or Conservative. For Marketeers, the logic of the 'German problem' demanded a 'European' solution. For the latter, Right and Left, it was the prospect of the eventual domination of a United Europe (shades of Naumann's *Mitteleuropa*, or even of Hitler's New Order) by West Germany that was often presented as a decisive reason *against* joining. But these, to the coming generation, are likely to appear battles fought long ago, and fought with incomprehensible and almost irrational passion.

Is this to say that the 'German problem', then, is resolved? It would be a bold man who would commit himself to so sweeping a judgment. None of us is going to live 'happily ever afterwards', not in a United Europe, nor in a United World. Worldly-wise men such as Vansittart would not have thought so; and the subtler, gentler—but in reality not less worldly—mind of a John Maynard Keynes would not have demurred. What of Europe, what of Germany 'in the long run'? We know Keynes' own answer: 'In the long run, we are all dead.' Vansittart's would probably have been no different; change is the only certainty in history. What, then, can we claim? We can claim at least that Europe—though not the Third World—has known peace for almost two generations, and that such peace as Europe, especially Western Europe, has enjoyed it owes in no small measure to the wisdom of men like Keynes and Marshall, Monnet and Vansittart, Spaak and Adenauer and Brandt.

Aha! the reader will exclaim, but what of the *Germans*—can the leopard change his spots? I would not deny that the evidence I have presented in this book is ambiguous. There *is* a 'German Problem'; and perhaps there will always be. Yet it could be argued on the evidence I have presented that the Germans are rather *more* capable than other peoples of changing their spots. Certainly, 'Nazi' ideas can be traced—or read into, if you prefer—the writings of Wagner and Nietzsche, Kleist and the Romantics, as they can into the political thinking of Frederick or Bismarck or Holstein. But one thing is sure: German history is not all of a piece. The Germans that Coleridge and earlier explorers discovered were not the Germans of Young Germany in 1848, or those of 1871, or 1914, or 1933: those Germans had far to go to equal the 'Black Record' of aggressiveness of Peter's Russia, or Richelieu's France, or Philip's Spain. Indeed, they were perhaps the least aggressive, least politically ambitious people in all Europe (after all that is what later German nationalists charged them with). The Germans will not return, so much is sure, to what they were in 1800. But then, in my opinion, it would be unhealthy for Europe if they were to try to do so. There can be no Europe without Germany: and without a Europe and a Germany reasonably at ease with themselves there can, I believe, be no secure future for 'civilisation'. Why should we be interested in Germany and the Germans? For the most selfish, as well as for the most idealistic, of motives: since we cannot live without them, we must learn to live with them.

Select Bibliography

ANNAN, NOEL Leslie Stephen, 1951
ARNOLD, MATTHEW Essays in Criticism, 1865–88
— Friendship's Garland, 1871
— Higher Schools and Universities in Germany, 1882
BALFOUR, MICHAEL The Kaiser and his Times, 1964
BELL, CLIVE Civilisation, 1928
BELL, QUENTIN Bloomsbury, 1968
BOLITHO, HECTOR Albert the Good, 1932
BONDY, FRANÇOIS So Sehen sie Deutschland, 1970
BOYD, JAMES Goethe's Knowledge of English Literature, 1932
BRACHER, K. D. The German Dictatorship, 1971
BULLOCK, ALAN Hitler, A Study in Tyranny, 1952
CARLYLE, THOMAS Life of Schiller, 1825
— German Romance, 1827
— Sartor Resartus, 1834
— The French Revolution, 1839
— Heroes, Hero-worship, and the Heroic in History, 1841
— Past and Present, 1843
— Life of Sterling, 1851
— History of Frederick the Great, 1865
COLERIDGE, S. T. Biographia Literaria, 1817
— Aids to Reflection, 1825
— Table Talk, 1835
— The Letters of Samuel Taylor Coleridge (ed. Earl Griggs), 1971
DAHRENDORF, RALF Society and Democracy in Germany, 1965
EDWARDS, DAVID Leaders of the Church of England, 1971
FISCHER, FRITZ Germany's Aims in the First World War, 1961
FORSTER, E. M. Howard's End, 1910
FULFORD, ROGER Dearest Child, 1964
— Dearest Mama, 1968
— Your Dear Letter, 1971
GARDINER, ROLF Britain and Germany, 1928
GAY, PETER Weimar Culture, 1968
GILBERT, MARTIN } The Appeasers, 1963
GOTT, RICHARD

GILBERT, MARTIN The Roots of Appeasement, 1966

GRANZOW, BRIGITTE A Mirror of Nazism, 1964

GRIERSON, H. J. C. Carlyle and Hitler, 1933

GROSS, JOHN The Rise and Fall of the Man of Letters, 1969

HARROD, ROY The Life of John Maynard Keynes, 1951

HARROLD, CHARLES FREDERICK Carlyle and German Thought, 1927

HEROLD, J. CHRISTOPHER Mistress to an Age, 1959

HOLBORN, HAJO A History of Modern Germany, 1965

HOLROYD, MICHAEL Lytton Strachey, 1967

HOWARD, MICHAEL The Franco-Prussian War, 1961

KEYNES, JOHN MAYNARD The Economic Consequences of the Peace, 1919

— A Revision of the Treaty, 1922

— Two Memories, 1949

KOHN, HANS The Mind of Germany, 1960

LAQUEUR, WALTER Russia and Germany, 1965

LONGFORD, ELIZABETH Victoria R.I., 1964

MANN, THOMAS Bekenntnisse eines Unpolitischen, 1918

— Von Deutscher Republik, 1923

MILL, JOHN STUART Autobiography, 1870

MITSCHERLICH, ALEXANDER Auf dem Weg zur vaterlosen Gesellschaft, 1963

— Die Unfähigkeit zu Trauern, 1967

NAMIER, LEWIS Conflicts, 1942

— Diplomatic Prelude, 1948

— Europe in Decay, 1950

— In the Nazi Era, 1952

— Avenues of History, 1952

— Personalities and Powers, 1955

NAUMANN, FRIEDRICH Central Europe, 1916

ROBERTSON, J. G. A History of German Literature (Revised by Edna Purdie), 1968

ROBINSON, HENRY CRABB Diary, 1869

ROWSE, A. L. All Souls and Appeasement, 1961

SCHIRMER, WALTER Deutsche Einflüsse auf die Englische Literatur im Neunzehnten Jahrhundert, 1947

STAËL, MADAME DE De l'Allemagne, 1813

STEPHEN, LESLIE Hours in a Library, 1879

STOCKLEY, V. German Literature in England 1750–1830, 1929

STRACHEY, LYTTON Queen Victoria, 1921
SYKES, CHRISTOPHER Troubled Loyalty, 1968
TAYLOR, A. J. P. The Course of German History, 1945
— Bismarck: The Man and the Statesman, 1955
— The Origins of the Second World War, 1961
— English History 1914–45, 1965
TERRAINE, JOHN Impacts of War 1914–1918, 1970
VANSITTART, ROBERT Black Record, 1940
— Events and Shadows, 1945
— The Mist Procession, 1958
WATT, D. C. Britain looks to Germany, 1965
— Personalities and Policies, 1965
WHEELER-BENNETT, JOHN Hindenburg: The Wooden Titan, 1936
— The Nemesis of Power, 1953
WILLEY, BASIL Nineteenth Century Studies, 1949
— Samuel Taylor Coleridge, 1972
WOOLF, LEONARD Autobiography, 1969

Index

Adenauer, Konrad, 3, 6, 8, 259, 263
Albert, Prince Consort, 11, 62, 65, 173, 177–87, 188, 189, 191, 193, 195, 205, 209, 214, 217
Arnim, Countess von, 11
Arnim, Achim von, 42
Arnold, Matthew, 9, 73, 80, 97, 123, 160, 163, 166, 181, 209, 223, 224
Friendship's Garland, 181, 223.
Arnold, Dr Thomas, 9, 69, 112, 123, 162, 163, 165, 166, 180, 223, 224
Auden, W. H., 1, 255
Austen, Jane, 29
Austin, John, 72
Austin, Sarah, 60, 68, 72, 163

Bacon, Francis, 77, 86
Baldwin, Stanley, 249
Baudelaire, Charles, 225, 229, 235
Beddoes, Thomas Lovell, 60
Beethoven, Ludwig van, 50, 53, 78
Bell, Clive, 12, 33, 223, 224
Bentham, Jeremy, 93
Bernadotte, Jean-Baptiste, King of Sweden, 46
Bismarck, Otto von, 6, 7, 11, 12, 14, 72, 180, 188, 189, 190, 195, 197, 201, 202, 203, 204, 206, 210, 213, 214, 217, 238, 244, 252, 264
Blake, William, 80, 125, 159, 225
Bonn University, 61, 180
Borrow, George, 60, 68, 69, 70
Boswell, James, 8
Bracher, Karl Dietrich, 254
Brandt, Willy, 8, 263
Brentano, Clemens von, 42
Brooke, Rupert, 234
Brougham, Henry, 62, 63
Bucer, Martin, 19
Büchner, Georg, 10
Bülow, Bernard von, 218
Bürger, Gottfried August, 10, 29
Burke, Edmund, 86
Burns, Robert, 110, 114, 115
Byron, Lord, 8, 35, 48–9, 51, 54, 64, 135, 136

Calvin, John, 51
Campbell, Thomas, 61, 62, 63
Canning, George, 30
Carlyle, Jane, 81, 82.
Carlyle, Thomas, 8, 9, 20, 23, 55, 56–7, 58, 60, 68, 69, 70, 72, 79–120, and Goethe, 100–7, 123, 124, 125, 126, 129, 130, 132, 139, 140, 143, 145, 147, 150, 153, 156, 160–2, 163, 165, 166, 167, 168, 225, 233
Life of Schiller, 68, 87
Sartor Resartus, 84, 87, 88, 90, 93, 99
The French Revolution, 88, 118
Heroes and Hero-worship, 118
Past and Present, 108, 109, 111, 116, 168
Life of Sterling, 87, 95, 160
Frederick the Great, 108
Castlereagh, Lord, 210
Chamberlain, Joseph, 214
Chamberlain, Neville, 248, 249, 250
Chamisso, Adelbert von, 68, 69
Churchill, Winston, 207, 249, 254, 257, 260
Clemenceau, Georges, 237–8
Clough, Arthur Hugh, 163
Colenso, Bishop, 192–3
Coleridge, Samuel Taylor, 8, 20, 23, 27, 32, 55, 60, 61, 69, 70, 79, 80, 89, 90, 91, 95, 97, 98, 102, 110, 123–69, 225, 227, 233
'To the Author of The Robbers', 134
The Lime-Tree Bower, 130
Fears in Solitude, 127, 142
The Ancient Mariner, 127
Osorio, 135
Christabel, 127
Lyrical Ballads, 127
Kubla Khan, 127
Dejection: an Ode, 129–31, 142, 145, 146
Comte, Auguste, 155
Constant, Benjamin, 35, 41, 44, 48
Cowper, William, 25
Creevey, Thomas, 179
Crossman, Richard, 258, 259, 262

269

INDEX

INDEX

Voltaire, 8, 19, 20, 36, 77, 223, 232

Wackenroder, Wilhelm Heinrich, 79
Wesley, Charles, 26
Wesley, John, 26, 156
Wieland, Christoph Martin, 19, 21, 24, 35, 41, 68, 69
Wilberforce, William, 48, 163, 164
William I, Kaiser, 2, 186, 188, 189, 190, 195, 196, 202, 209
William II, Kaiser, 2, 180, 190, 191, 196, 200, 203, 204, 205–19, 238, 240, 252

Wilson, President, 238
Woolf, Leonard, 12, 223, 226, 227, 231, 234
Woolf, Virginia, 226, 231, 233
Wootton, Sir Henry, 19
Wordsworth, William, 8, 27, 32, 60, 79, 80, 89, 100, 102, 127, 133, 135, 137, 143, 145, 162, 163, 165, 169

Young, Edward, 19
Young Germany, 11, 180

Zuckmayer, Carl, 254